AF699502
WITHDRAWN

EXPERT SYSTEMS IN PUBLIC ADMINISTRATION

Evolving Practices and Norms

EXPERT SYSTEMS IN PUBLIC ADMINISTRATION

Evolving Practices and Norms

Edited by

Ignace Th. M. SNELLEN
Department of Public Administration and Informatics Law, Tilburg University
Tilburg, The Netherlands

Wim B.H.J. VAN DE DONK
Department of Public Administration and Informatics Law, Tilburg University
Tilburg, The Netherlands

Jean-Paul BAQUIAST
French Interministerial Committee on Informatisation in Public Administration
Paris, France

1989

ELSEVIER SCIENCE PUBLISHERS
AMSTERDAM • NEW YORK • OXFORD • TOKYO

ELSEVIER SCIENCE PUBLISHERS B.V.
Sara Burgerhartstraat 25
P.O. Box 211, 1000 AE Amsterdam, The Netherlands

Distributors for the United States and Canada:

ELSEVIER SCIENCE PUBLISHING COMPANY, INC.
655 Avenue of the Americas
New York, N.Y. 10010, U.S.A.

Library of Congress Cataloging-in-Publication Data

Expert systems in public administration : evolving practices and norms / edited by Ignace Th. M. Snellen, Wim B.H.J. van de Donk, Jean-Paul Baquiast.
p. cm.
Includes bibliographical references.
ISBN 0-444-88038-0
1. Public administration--Data processing--Congresses.
2. Information storage and retrieval systems--Public administration--Congresses. 3. Expert systems (Computer science)--Congresses.
I. Snellen, I. Th. M. II. Donk, Wim B. H. J. van de.
III. Baquiast, Jean-Paul.
JF1525.A8E97 1989
350'.00028'5--dc20 89-37706
CIP

JF
1525
.A8
E97
1989

ISBN: 0 444 88038 0

© ELSEVIER SCIENCE PUBLISHERS B.V., 1989

All rights reserved. No part of this publication may be reproduced, stored in a retrieval system, or transmitted, in any form or by any means, electronic, mechanical, photocopying, recording or otherwise, without the prior written permission of the publisher, Elsevier Science Publishers B.V. /Physical Sciences and Engineering Division, P.O. Box 1991, 1000 BZ Amsterdam, The Netherlands.

Special regulations for readers in the U.S.A. - This publication has been registered with the Copyright Clearance Center Inc. (CCC), Salem, Massachusetts. Information can be obtained from the CCC about conditions under which photocopies of parts of this publication may be made in the U.S.A. All other copyright questions, including photocopying outside of the U.S.A., should be referred to the copyright owner, Elsevier Science Publishers B.V., unless otherwise specified.

No responsibility is assumed by the publisher for any injury and/or damage to persons or property as a matter of products liability, negligence or otherwise, or from any use or operation of any methods, products, instructions or ideas contained in the material herein.

Printed in The Netherlands

Preface

"The adjustment of a culture to a new invention involves much more than its immediate use." Ogburn and Nimkoff made this observation in their Handbook of Sociology (1947), where they discussed advancing technology and lagging social institutions. While new inventions, especially within a competitive environment, spread in a rapid pace, cultural adjustments in terms of values, norms, expectations and beliefs generally lag behind. Although we are not used any more to consider such cultural lags as signs of social disorganization, they non-the-less deserve our serious attention. This, we believe, is especially true when such technical innovations are introduced in public administrations. The meaning of such innovations for and their impact on the political, juridical, economical and professional dimensions of public administrations have to be studied carefully.

Expert systems, or more generally, knowledge-based systems form nowadays the pinnacle of information technology. As an application of artificial intelligence they may contain implicit notions of intelligent administrative behaviour, that are rather unidimensional in their technological determination. As such, expert systems are no neutral devices, but value laden and power related instruments which are influencing the orientations in and around the administrative apparatus of government. For expert systems in a special way represent the basic characteristic of informatization: **functional rationalization**. They are expected to expand progressively - and even more successfully than the existing "traditional" information systems do - the domain in which applications of modern information technology can support and realize further administrative rationalization and modernization.

In view of the normative dimensions of public administration, mentioned above, possibly emerging cultural lags with respect to the application of expert systems in that context have to be watched carefully. In 1987 interest in the "natural" evolution of norms within public administration, which may accompany the application of those systems, and the wish to find out whether new norms might have to be developed, brought together in Leuven (Belgium) scientists of public administration and practitioners in the field. In that city the permanent study-group on "Informatization in Public Administration" of the European Group of Public Administration (EGPA) organized a conference on the introduction of expert systems in public administration.

The aim of this conference was twofold:

First, the participants wanted to exchange their experiences with expert systems, which in one way or other were developed for, introduced in, or used by public administrative authorities.

Secondly, they wanted to undertake a first and preliminary (ex-ante) evaluation of the possible promises and threats related to the introduction and use of expert systems in public administration. The "four rationalities model", developed by Snellen, which is explained in Chapter 1 of this volume, was used as guidance for the discussion about normative implications of expert systems.

Some of the participants to the conference could be brought together in the team of authors that decided to publish this volume about "evolving practices and norms" through implicit and explicit value orientations with respect to the use of expert systems in public administration. Thus the book reflects the objectives of the Louvain conference. It contains a description of some expert systems in use. It presents practical experiences as well as theoretical reflections on the normative aspects related to their application in public administration. The still immature state of development of expert systems gives the attempt to evaluate these normative aspects a preliminary status.

Structure of the book

This book consists of three parts.

Part 1 contains indications, how to approach the different normative aspects, that may be implied in expert systems, and against the background of which these systems are applied in public administration. A typology of applications of expert systems (knowledge based systems) is given and the relevant "rationalities" of public administration, that may be affected by the use of expert systems, are presented. Also an attempt is made to develop a methodology for the determination and assessment of the value-orientations, which are intrinsically or extrinsically related to expert systems in use in public administration. The last chapter of this Part approaches the subject from a different angle, by assessing the impact of the use of expert systems in public administration for the various interest groups involved.

Part 2 gives a description of expert systems that are used by public authorities in different countries of Europe. Each description is placed by its author in the context of the normative dimensions that are one way or another implied in the use of those expert systems. In this way the main purpose of this book, not only to highlight the evolving practices with respect to expert systems, but to raise also the level of consciousness as to their normativity, is realized. Chapters 4 through 8 try to assess the ways in which the juridical rationality of public administration may be influenced by the use of expert systems in the legal domain. In chapters 9 and 10 attention is paid to some distributive impacts of expert systems, bordering upon the political rationality of public administration. The possible impact of expert systems on the professional-administrative rationality of public administration is discussed in chapters 11 and 12, while the economic rationality, as affected by the application of those systems, is the main object of study in the remainder of Part 2. In this way Part 2 offers a representative overview of expert systems, used in public administration, and at the same time of the growing awareness of the importance of the normative dimensions of this use.

Part 3 of the book concentrates on existing and desirable policies with respect to the development and application of expert systems by public authorities. The development of methods for ex-ante and ex-post evaluation is advocated. Frameworks for cost-effectiveness analyses are proposed. Some directions for social-scientific research are indicated. Systematic attention to evolving practices and norms in the field of expert systems, the "message" of this book, in this way hopefully will be furthered.

Acknowledgements

The realization of this book is made possible by the help of many persons. Anne Bedel, assistant to Jean-Paul Baquiast, supported the editors very efficiently.

The hospitality of Louvain University to the Study-group on "Informatization in Public Administration" of the European Group of Public Administration (EGPA) was arranged by Marie-Anne Estas of the International Institute of Administrative Science (IIAS) in Brussels and Hugo van Hasselt, our distinguished colleague at the same university.

Furthermore we want to express our gratitude to Guus Donker and to Hans Henkes, who showed us the advanced state of the art of desk top editing.

Ignace Snellen
Wim van de Donk
Jean-Paul Baquiast

Contents

Part 3 Some policy dimensions

Part 1

Approaching normativity in expert systems

Expert Systems in Public Administration
I. Th.M. Snellen, W.B.H.J. van de Donk, J.-P. Baquiast (Eds.)
© Elsevier Science Publishers B.V. (North-Holland), 1989

Chapter 1

Knowledge-based systems in public administration: Evolving practices and norms

*Wim B.H.J. van de Donk**
*Ignace Th.M. Snellen**

Abstract

In this chapter, the questions surrounding the development and introduction of so-called knowledge systems are discussed from a point of view of the specific context of public administration. We are concerned with applications of what is already a new generation of information technology, with which as yet no extensive experience has been gained. Often the introduction of such systems takes place in a still experimental context which must show under what conditions it would be worthwhile to introduce them in public administration. This chapter commences with a general examination of these knowledge-based systems. 'Knowledge-based systems' is a collective name for various systems which, as will be shown, differ as to nature and type of the knowledge with which they work. Three kinds of systems are distinguished in this chapter: handling systems, advisory systems and expert systems. In each case a short characterization is given, as well as a description of an application as is at present encountered in public administration.

Next follows an exploration of the problems which result from the specific nature of public administration as application area of these knowledge systems.

We argue that norms for the functioning of public administration derive simultaneously from political, legal, technical-scientific and economic ratio-

* Department of Public Administration and Informatics Law, Tilburg University, P/Obox 90153, 5000 LE TILBURG, The Netherlands

nalities. We want to show that the use of knowledge systems within public administration is also subject to the norms set by these rationalities. To this end, we first of all discuss the various meanings and functions of knowledge in public administration attaching to the rationalities. We then attempt a first general exploration of the specific significance of each of the four rationalities for the development and use of knowledge-based systems in public administration.

1 Types of knowledge and knowledge based systems

Knowledge and expertise

Wherein lies the distinction between the expert and the non-expert or layman? This question may be answered in various ways. Koenemann (1986:23) points out that expertise is not absolute but relative. Expertise entails extensive knowledge of a mainly specialistic nature. The expert will certainly command encyclopaedic knowledge in a particular field. But this knowledge alone is not sufficient to mark him as an expert. The expert is distinguishable from the non-expert especially in the manner in which he makes use of this fund of specific knowledge: in other words, the way in which he reasons. The expert is able to apply the basic structure of reasoning in his own field without hesitation, without deliberation. For the expert, be he a lawyer, an economist or a physicist, the basic structure of reasoning in his own discipline is so self-evident, that it is impossible for him to violate this line of reasoning. A student, at least a very good one, may attain this level. The real expert however transcends this level by possessing internalized practical experience (heuristic knowledge, or even intuition) which in given situations enables him to apply the most plausible reasoning in order to arrive at a judgement of the situation. The logical sequence to a judgement arrived at on the basis of plausibility will then be a conclusion which, within the framework of solutions offered by proficient reasoning, presents the most likely (practical) solution.

Analysing the above, expertise may be concluded to contain the following elements:

1. encyclopaedic knowledge of facts and relationships concerning a certain field;
2. proficient reasoning as the basis of a diagnosis;
3. practical short-circuit reasoning to arrive at a diagnosis;
4. proficient reasoning as the basis for a solution;
5. practical short-circuit reasoning to arrive at a solution.

Especially elements 3 and 5 distinguish the expert from the proficient non-expert and especially from the layman.

Computerized knowledge systems

Modern knowledge systems are characterized by the fact that they are capable of storing various types of knowledge at various levels.

Some systems contain the combination 1. knowledge of facts and relationships (rules), 2. proficient lines of reasoning as the basis for a diagnosis and 4. proficient reasoning as the basis for a solution. Such knowledge systems might be termed *handling (processing) systems*.

Other systems contain the combination 1. knowledge of facts and relationships (rules), 2. proficient reasoning as basis for a diagnosis, 3. practical short-circult reasoning for a diagnosis and 4. proficient lines of reasoning as basis for a solution. Such knowledge systems may be termed *advisory systems*.

Real expert systems would contain all five elements. In addition to a knowledge of facts and knowledge which may be classified as structured (in the shape of algorithms), real expert systems contain types of knowledge which may be designated as 'informal knowledge' (Bonnet, 1987), or as 'heuristic' knowledge. This is precisely the type of knowledge which makes an expert an expert. (Clifford, Jarke and Vassiliou, 1983). Such systems are relatively scarce, certainly in public administration.

Handling systems are applicable to cases and situations of such a nature that knowledge of a limited number of facts is sufficient for it to be possible to apply a proficient line of reasoning in order to place the case or situation in a certain category, and the designation of the category is sufficient to arrive at a solution with the aid of a proficient line of reasoning.

In handling systems, the unique constellation of facts introduced for each case guides the proficient line of reasoning present in the system towards a diagnosis. The diagnosis in turn guides the proficient reasoning towards a solution, decision or therapy.

In handling systems, the facts consequently determine the outcome of this process of reasoning.

Advisory systems are applicable in cases and situations where knowledge of the facts and the available proficient lines of reasoning are insufficient for reaching a solution. It may be that uncertainty surrounds various facts or circumstances so that they must be estimated. Certain qualifications needed for a decision may be vague, thus neccessitating further assessment.

The available proficient lines of reasoning may be insufficient for instance because they only permit of estimating (causal or purposive) relationships. In such circumstances, the advisory system provides an approximation of a solution which calls for a further assessment in the light of the missing elements relative to the facts, qualification of these facts or relationships. Within government organizations they are often applied as aids to civil servants who are in possession of certain discretionary powers pertaining to the execution of a policy (the application of rules); as is the case with many so-called 'streetlevel bureaucrats' (see Snellen, 1986, 1987).

The advisory systems (also called 'consultancy systems') which are developed for welfare officers or for citizens, and are distributed on floppy disks, are often a mirror image of handling systems present in public administration. Sometimes in systems of this nature only a specific set of laws and rules is translated into computer programs. For instance, with the aid of such a program which has been put on the market by a large publishing company, the Dutch citizen can calculate - after deduction of the rebates indicated by the program - how much income tax he owes the government.

There are various characteristics which distinguish expert systems from advisory systems (Ford, 1985). Whereas advisory systems leave estimations and approximations to the user, expert systems themselves present the estimations and approximations, based on expertise, which are necessary for reaching a decision. The system shows the user why a certain line of reasoning has been followed and certain choices have been made. Furthermore, an expert system can build up expertise by registration of the cases and solutions which have been treated with the aid of the expert system itself.

Expert systems are thus advisory systems which contain a special form of knowledge that can be used in ill-defined situations to reach an optimum solution or decision.

2 Knowledge-based systems in public administration

The analysis in the foregoing pages of various sorts of knowledge led to a description of three types of knowledge systems which, with the aid of modern information technology, have since the early eighties been developed by and for various sections of public administration.

Developments in the area of information technology, both as regards hardware and software, make it increasingly possible to automate various official roles and functions by means of these knowledge systems. (Inbar, 1979; Glastonbury, 1985) Increasingly too nowadays they are applied in public administration as aids to or even as substitutes for experts and decision-makers in research and diagnosis, interpretation, the solution of problems and monitoring. They are also used as tutors (Course-ware, see Bonnet, 1987:208). As was already mentioned above, internal and external dissemination of knowledge also takes place by means of on-line accessible knowledge systems or by means of advisory programs brought out on floppy disks by non-profit or commercial establishments.

All three of the knowledge systems mentioned are to be found in public administration. Only here and there however, and often as yet with only an experimental character, are applications of real 'expert systems' to be found. Moreover, even in these cases there has often been an integration ('embedding'; cf. Kwee & De Witte, 1987:47; Kwee, 1988; Van Dijck et al., 1987) of an expert system and a handling system in order to arrive at an 'intelligent' system which can take over the work of civil servants. It is questionable if in this case it is possible to speak of an expert system as defined above.

The availability of expert systems, handling systems and advisory systems, of which a few concrete examples will be given in a following section, will increase in the coming years. It is however too early to indicate which forms and levels of administrative knowledge and expertise it will be possible to incorporate in computer programs. The limits of the potential area of applicability continue to expand. In those areas where knowledge systems obtain a footing, their application exerts a far-reaching influence on the functioning of public administration. This is evident from research carried out at the Ministry of Education and Science (Study Grants Directorate) and other organizations in Dutch public administration (1988; Van de Donk, 1988).

2.1 Some concrete examples of knowledge systems in public administration

2.1.1. The Dutch study grants system as handling system

All Dutch students from the age of 18 to the age of 30 receive a basic grant. Students not residing at home receive a higher basic grant than those living at home. In addition to the basic grant, students who do not have a sufficient source of income and cannot expect assistance from parents or a partner, can obtain interest- free loans. Students who are completely dependent on government grants are eligible for a supplementary grant.

A completely automated handling system has been developed to deal with these three forms of grants. In eighty percent of cases ('smooth cases') this system is capable, without human intervention, completely on the basis of the input of personal data of students, parents and partners yielded by the standard forms, of reaching the relevant decisions. The study grants of 600,000 Dutch students are regulated by this handling system. (Saat, 1984)

Another example of a handling system is the Norwegian system for Housing Aid described by Bing in this volume chapter 8. After the citizen has identified himself to the system by means of a personal identification number (PIN; this exists in Norway since 1964), the system quite independently either implements payment or informs the applicant, stating the reasons, of rejection of the application. "Using the PIN, the system accesses the central population register, which - according to the underlying rules - should be current within 8 weeks. Identifying the applicant, the system determines who else is registered as inhabiting the same housing unit as the applicant. These persons are known as a 'household' to the system. Due to the construction of the PIN, this also gives the system information on the age of the different members of the household, information utilized in determining whether the household qualifies for housing aid. Carrying the identifications of the members of the household, the system accesses the files of the central tax authority, retrieving income figures for all members of the household. The sum of income for all the members is the income of the household. Also carrying the identifications of the members of the household, the system will access the files of the National Insurance Institution, and determine their individual status with respect to a range of welfare schemes. The system returns with its information to its home base at the state housing bank, which operates the system. Based on information on the age of the housing unit, its location with respect to the center of a town, interest of bank loans etc, the final calculation takes place. (...) If the application is denied, the system will write out a form letter, specifying the reason for not awarding housing aid. If the applicant qualifies for housing aid, the system will print out a postal cheque, which is mailed to the applicant.".

2.1.2. The study grants floppy disk as advisory system

Citizen-friendly floppy disks containing menu-guided programs which make clear how a government regulation applies in a special case, and what are a citizen's rights under certain circumstances, are gaining in popularity, at least in Dutch public administration. Presently, citizen-oriented advisory systems are available on income tax, study grants, alimony after divorce, social security grants, rent subsidies and many other topics. More disks are being brought out commercially. Increasingly too, government authorities make such disks available (Van de Donk & Snellen, 1988). An anecdote worth mentioning is that the Study Grant disk brought out by government was vastly inferior to one which a student had developed for the student union.

The Ministry of Education and Science felt thus obliged to withdraw its own disk and to replace it by the one developed by the student.

2.1.3. The expert system on people sharing a dwelling

The development of expert systems in Dutch public administration is still in its early stages, and usually takes place in experimental projects in which software houses specializing in artificial intelligence, universities and government agencies co-operate. Up to the present, they have been especially aimed at complex implementation measures of the Dutch system of social security.

For instance an experimental expert system dealing with the 'regulation relating to people sharing a dwelling' was developed for the Municipal Welfare Department of Amsterdam which, like all municipal Welfare Departments, is entrusted with the execution of regulations, mostly drawn up by the national government, relating to the provision of welfare[1].

In this regulation - mainly drawn up with a view to economization - the question is to decide what adaptations, in view of his residential situation, are called for in the benefit a person receives.

This regulation was chosen since it was expected that especially in the case of complicated regulations an expert system might contribute to improved accessibility and application.

"The regulation relating to people sharing a dwelling shows qualities which are often viewed as characteristic for the area of legislation:

- Reasoning rests both on causal relationships and on analogies which point to comparable cases.
- Rules are sometimes incomplete, for instance due to the appearance of diverging situations which would involve a reduction of the benefit. Sometimes the rules are contradictory or ambiguous since they rest on poorly or vaguely defined concepts such as 'economic unit' versus 'cohabitation'.
- Concepts formulated in a complicated manner may be differentiated on the basis of new explanations or by the application of criteria, but this often leads to new questions which can only be solved by interpretation or common sense reasoning" (Van Dijck et al., 1987:29).

On the basis of an analysis of rules, official instructions and talks with civil service experts, a Prototype expert system concerning people sharing dwellings (PWES) was developed as an aid to officials charged with determining benefits.

An important conclusion of the experiment is that it would seem possible effectively to incorporate such regulations in an expert system, though this can only be put to optimum use when integrated within a system capable of giving more wide-spectrum support to officials.

3 Normativity in public administration

Characteristic of public administration is the fact that it must simultaneously meet diverging requirements deriving from various aspects of society. During the process of modernization in the past centuries, these social aspects have become completely independent of each other (Snellen, 1987). The political sphere has become independent of the legal sphere, the economic sphere of both these other spheres and of the scientific sphere relating to each of the other policy sectors. Each of these four spheres sets norms for the content of government action. Only when the demands of each of these spheres have been met can this action be considered politically, legally, economically and scientifically rational.

Political rationality means that the ruling group, whether or not a coalition, maintains its power. To this end, it will have to articulate and to a certain degree solve, the problems of the collectivity. Naturally, the solution to problems will be sought in the direction which the ruling group considers most desirable. Nonetheless, in all its actions and decisions, this group will constantly be obliged to take heed of limits which are dictated by the integrity of the society. Political solutions which endanger this integrity compromise the essence of politics as a means for peacefully conciliating differences and making acceptable the bonds of society.

Legal rationality in a constitutional state implies that government policy must have its foundation in law, must honour the guarantee function of the law, and must ensure equality before the law and legal security. And just as politicians and political parties uphold political rationality, so is it the task of the legal establishment, which occupies a guaranteed independent position with respect to politics, to preserve legal rationality.

From the point of view of economic rationality, norms for government action derive from the budgetary cycle within which all government allocations in the interest of the collectivity take place. In an era of economic growth, such as that experienced by western countries in the sixties, economic rationality does not place severe restrictions on government policy. This has however altered since the mid-seventies, when a growth policy had to make way for a policy of containment. Since that time, the limits placed by the economy on government action are no less rigid than those placed by law.

In addition to this, each sector in society recognizes its counterpart in a social-scientific or technological discipline, which provides this sector with its own scientific rationality considerations. In the area of the technical infrastructure of a country, technology plays a role, while medical or social-scientific insights are relevant to the welfare sectors. The demands of scientific rationality too must be brought into 'equilibrium' with the demands deriving from the other rationalities.

Government policy can be pictured as situated between these four rationalities, which remain at loggerheads with each other, indulging in a continuous struggle for precedence.

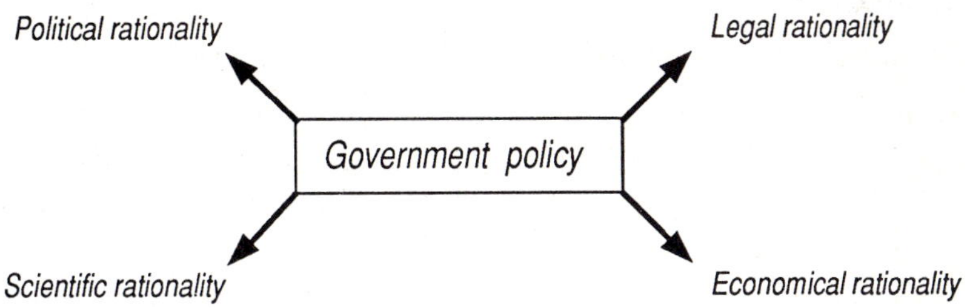

Figure 1 Four different rationalities

In the daily conduct of government policy, a sort of exchange relationship exists between these otherwise independent rationalities. Sometimes political desiderata will be satisfied at the expense of legal and economic rationalities; at other times, the interests of legal or scientific rationality will prevail at the expense of the others. This four-rationalities-model distinguishes public administration from private enterprise and from scientific or technological activities. Enterprises can in principle limit themselves to the scientific and economic rationalities. Scientific and technological activities are per definition based on a single rationality. Consequently, the application of knowledge systems in the business sphere or in a scientific or technological environment follows more naturally than their application in public administration. Knowledge systems which are applied in public administration must, in view of the specific nature of public administration, satisfy four different systems of norms which are moreover often difficult to reconcile.

The temptation will be great in the handling, advisory or expert systems only to take account of technological or scientific rationality. This would however be at the cost of other legitimate demands to which the use of knowledge systems might be subject.

When one realizes the intrinsic character of public administration, the limitations of the application possibilities of knowledge systems in this sphere come into view. Dominance of the technological and scientific rationality which is inherent in knowledge systems would mean an unacceptable neglect of the political, legal and economic demands to which every action of government is equally subject.

4 A first exploration of the norms that count

Introduction, development and utilization of knowledge-based systems in Public Administration.

The rationalities which were recognized in the previous section as setting the norms for every action of government, naturally also apply for the development and use of knowledge or expert systems.

These rationalities are important to knowledge systems at two levels. In the *first place* for the nature of the knowledge which is stored in the knowledge system, and the manner in which this was accomplished. In the *second place* for the use made of knowledge and expert systems by government, or which government permits citizens, advisers, intermediaries etc. to make of them. Norms of the former type might be termed *intrinsic,* while the second type might be termed *extrinsic* norms. In the development of these norms, the political, economic, legal and scientific significance of *knowledge* occupies a key role.

Knowledge, information, expertise, terms which are here used interchangeably, have different meanings in the four socially differentiated systems which were recognized in the previous section. We propose the following meanings:

a. Knowledge, information, is power

Knowledge is a recognized basis of power, a factor on which rests the power of an actor, and with the aid of which he acquires, maintains or enlarges his power (Kuypers, 1973). This applies not only to scientific knowledge, but to every form of knowledge relevant to one's own behaviour or to the behaviour of others. The greater is one's power if he is earlier and more adequately and completely informed as to relevant rights, obligations, chances, possibilities, plans, habits, usages etc. Only when one is well informed it is possible to develop the demeanour of power: that is to say, behaviour which motivates another to behave in accordance with the desires of the one exercising power. The demeanour of power may moreover be aimed at enhancing the base of power itself, in this instance information, by manipulating this in some way or other. Forms of manipulation are: withholding information, presenting only selected information, presenting biased information, flooding with information, etc.

b. Knowledge, information, is money

The post-industrial society is an information society in which information has become a dominant production factor, and consequently represents a central economic value (Feigenbaum & McCorduck, 1983; Bell, 1984). In the form of for instance technological inventions, organizational insights, developed process programmes and systematic knowledge of target groups, information is instrumental to economic production processes. The more advanced and complicated a society, and the more automated its production processes, the more crucial and valuable is the possession of information which makes possible productive and remunerative activities.

In the decision-making processes in public administration too, information will increasingly be expressed in terms of money (costs of development and maintenance of knowledge systems). This will in turn exert an influence on decisons regarding the availability, accessibility and use of information within these decision-making processes.

c. Knowledge, information, is a virtue

This proposition, which has been attributed to the Socratics, means that knowledge of cause-effect relationships in (societal) reality exerts an influence on purposive relations, the goals which people pursue and the instruments they employ to this end. In our opinion, the proposition does not imply that people are fundamentally good or desire good. It does however imply that (societal) reason may exert a regulating influence on the thinking processes of people and collectivities and on what they desire. This influence will not be lightly passed over. In Socrates' time, this position was not problematical. The point of departure of an, in principle, cognizable reality; of an ontological order in which everything had its own place, led to a, for experts cognizable, meaningful concept of justice. "Consequently, my friends, we must not so much worry about what people will say of us, but rather about what the expert on justice and injustice says, he alone, and truth itself" (Plato, Dialogues; Crito: section 8).

In our society too there is 'expertise' on justice. This however is no longer based on one fundamentally cognizable, ontological order, but on an evaluation of the content of decisions and of the procedures which must be followed in reaching decisions.

d. Knowledge, information is effectivity

Knowledge, especially of causal relations, is a prerequisite for effective action. Public administration calls for policy-area theories which encompass policy-relevant expectations relating to cause-effect relations in the policy area and regarding the presence of intervention variables in this area, and on which policy can thus be based. A prerequisite for effective policy, for instance with respect to the prevention of acidification of forests, is in this context an extensive knowledge concerning and insight into the chains of causes and effects relating to the question of acidification. Scientific-technological knowledge of the area with which policy is concerned is an important basis for the ultimate content of the policy itself. It results in policy theories which on the basis of causal and final (instrument is envisaged cause, object envisaged effect) relations, determine the structure and the instruments of policy.

In general, information technology offers vastly enlarged possibilities for collecting data relating to a particular policy area or to a concrete problem, and for employing them for analysis and research. In this way it contributes to a more adequate insight and more effective exertion of influence.

In the context of public administration, knowledge at one and the same time means power, money, virtue and effectivity. In an assessment of computer systems, with the aid of which knowledge is generated, converted into decisions or recommendations or disseminated, this multi-dimensionality of knowledge in public administration should be recognized.

Economic normativity and knowledge systems

Grimmer (1987; see also Maciejewski, 1987) has pointed out that automation drastically alters the temporal structure of decision-making and handling activities. This can certainly also be established with respect to the knowledge systems referred to above.

With the aid of a knowledge system, a decision can be quickly taken in each individual case. The marginal decision-making costs drop to zero. However, it is a time-consuming and costly undertaking to build up such a system (especially the development of expert systems is relatively expensive).

A considerable period consequently elapses before decision-making becomes possible. Regulations become inflexible. (The management contract for the implementation of the above-mentioned study grant system stipulates a period of nine months for introducing into the automated system any change in the legal rules).

The change in the temporal structure affects not only the civil service apparatus but also the citizen. More and more detailed data are required from the citizen. Filling in forms becomes more complicated and thus more time-consuming[2]. This share of the costs of decision-making is hidden, but should really be taken into consideration when assessing the relevant knowledge systems against economic norms. In a cost-benefit evaluation relating to knowledge systems, the following criteria should, inter alia, be taken into account:

- the time and investments necessary for development of the system, related to the rate of change in the relevant system of regulations.
- not only the marginal, but also the average costs per decision (or recommendation) resulting from the knowledge system.
- changes in decision-making costs of the citizen, inclusive of the development of the need for calling on intermediaries.

As far as we can see, these are the most important extrinsic economic norms of which account must be taken in the development and use of the various types of knowledge systems.

Intrinsic economic norms in a knowledge system relate to the effectivity and efficiency of the solutions in which it results. The existence of a system can in itself moreover exert an influence on the cost-benefit ratio of a decision. For instance, the rule 'de minimis non curat praetor' will yield different results due to the simple fact that the marginal costs of reaching a decision with the aid of a computer are almost zero, as was shown above. The 'de minimis' rule which also applies to decision-making and administrative costs, sets other limits if the case can be dealt with by computer. These limits will usually be more attractive to the citizen. For instance there is less reason for the Inland Revenue not to refund an amount to the tax-payer when the amount is under a certain limit.

Legal normativity and knowledge systems

It has often been argued that automation of legal decisions might serve to further legal security and equality before the law. This naturally applies especially to decisions where rightfulness completely coincides with lawfulness (Van de Voort & Van Wijk, 1986). In such instances, the applicable norms are so absolute and unambiguous that a decision 'mathematically' results from the conditions, rules and facts. (In this way the Dutch Ministry of Defence annually takes nearly a million decisions relating to conscription for military service).

A first legal requirement which such knowledge systems must meet is that the authority applying the rules be willing to make the system public, and that decisions taken with the system be fully documented, citizens being provided with all the relevant reasons for a decision.

If however the official or the organization implementing the regulation has been legally granted discretionary powers, there is then reason to devote extra attention to the possibility that special circumstances will arise. In such cases, the citizen must be given a hearing concerning these circumstances ('the citizen must be permitted to tell his story'; Hirsch Ballin, 1986), and the knowledge system must not assume the shape of a handling system for providing cut and dried decisions in a hundred percent of cases[3]. The use of an advisory system is then indicated.

But even where a completely automated handling process is employed (see Bing's example), the citizen should have the right to be heard. The assumptions regarding his or her situation which are derived from automated data bases must be made known to the individual if they have led to a decision.

Analogously, in the field of medicine, the problem of responsibility and liability in the case of 'decisions' taken by systems of this nature also arises (see for instance Bourcier, 1986:68).

Not only the executive, but also the judiciary may be served by expert and advisory systems[4]. Even to a greater degree than in the case of the administration, it is important that the citizen should be given a chance to be heard, and that every relevant fact relating to him or her be determined by the judge and not derived from computer systems without his prior knowledge.

Whether or not an expert system can be employed in the case of a certain law must in principle be determined by the legislature. This may be seen as a constitutional requirement. It would then be logical that the expert system in use in such cases has been provided or assessed by the legislature.

Political normativity and knowledge systems

The answer to the classical question "Who gets what, when and how?", defined by Lasswell (1936) as the essence of politics, depends to an important degree on the circumstance who or what group possesses the power to formulate this answer. Above it was argued that especially knowledge plays an important role in the acquisition, consolidation and expansion of power positions.

Public administration will in the future make increasing use of knowledge systems in deciding the answer to this question. In a sense, a share of power is delegated to technology, to knowledge systems[5].

In cases where a law is completely or partly implemented by means of computer handling systems (as illustrated by the Dutch study grant regulation and the example of housing aid in Norway), a potential problem exists as regards keeping power in check; on the one hand as regards the content of the system - the computer program - and the way in which this has been developed (the intrinsic norms), and on the other hand as regards the manner in which the system is used (extrinsic norms).

An interesting question in this context is whether parliamentary intervention in cases of this nature should cease after the text of a law has been approved, and whether it should not also see to it that the intentions of the law be adequately represented in the automated system.

A study as to the way in which the handling system for Dutch study grants discussed above was developed (Van de Donk, 1988) shows that during the technical design of the system[6] further choices touching on content must often be made in the interest of workability.

But also in the case of expert and advisory systems, the question is justified: *whose rules, whose expertise or recommendations* are ultimately incorporated in a knowledge system? In the sphere of public administration, a recommendation, a judgement of an expert and a decision of a handling system assume a political dimension. In this area knowledge is not neutral, but represents political choices, just as 'solutions' go hand in hand with the manner in which (and by whom) a problem was formulated.

With the introduction of the various types of knowledge systems a more subtle "(...) Mediatisierung der Herrschaft durch Vergegenständlichung in der Technik (...)" (mediation of dominance by objectivation in technology) has developed (Koenemann, 1986:183). A constant awareness of this political dimension is essential in the further introduction of the various types of knowledge systems, both as this applies to the civil servant - whose discretionary powers are reduced by the use of an on-line advisory or expert system or a handling system- and as regards the citizen whose position may be weakened, inter alia as a consequence of the reduced discretionary powers of the contact official. If he is still given an opportunity to tell 'his story' this is only possible, for instance in the case of semi-automated handling, by means of a 'standard mutation form' which can be read directly by the system.

On the other hand, it might be expected that advisory systems, which are at his disposal in increasing numbers, would provide the citizen more than formerly with the possibility (with or without the aid of a social counsellor), of preparing his arguments, and confronting the civil servant with the result of a 'try-out' with the aid of such a system.

At the moment in the Netherlands a large number of citizens who must fill in income tax forms already do this with the aid of the above- mentioned computer program. In the past year many of them sent the 'shadow forms' which had been prepared on their own printers directly to the Inland Revenue Service. (For the time being the Inland Revenue still requires that this be at least accompanied by a hand- written copy).

Technical-scientific rationality and knowledge systems

The development and use of knowledge systems must meet the norms applying to the knowledge itself which is incorporated in knowledge- based systems. The above-mentioned types of knowledge systems differ according to the nature of the knowledge they contain. Consequently the functions which these systems fulfill also vary. In our opinion, however, with respect to each of the three systems Ashby's "Law of requisite variety" applies. The knowledge (facts and relationships, rules, and in the case of expert systems heuristics) must make possible an adequate judgement with respect to the context in which it is used. In the case of a handling system, this for instance means that it should be possible to deal with a certain variety of cases without encountering any problems. In other words: the ratio of smooth cases to non-smooth cases should, also on the basis of economic-normative considerations, be as favourable as possible. This means that the knowledge with respect to legislation and execution practices incorporated in such a system must be very detailed. On the basis of legal normativity, there are also good arguments for this: the more detailed the description, the better the system will be able to deal with individual cases. For the time being it would appear that administrative-technical demands which attach to the development and use of knowledge systems are often at odds with the technological and financial resources available for the development of the various knowledge systems.

In addition to variety of the knowledge included in administrative knowledge systems, flexibility is also a requirement. In the development of larger knowledge systems in public administration, account must be taken of the fact that the interest of public administration for many complex problems will often to a large extent be found to be dependent on fluctuations in political priorities.

It should also be clear what is precisely the range (depth and scope) of a knowledge system, and where are the limits of competency of a system (Kwee & De Witte, 1987). The system must be able to recognize its limits and know when further judgement by an official is called for.

5 Concluding remarks

In public administration, the further introduction of information technology is really unchallenged, and is viewed as an important condition for the adequate execution of the tasks which public administration must fulfill.

This also applies as regards the products of the newest generation of this technology, the knowledge-based systems. The three types of knowledge systems distinguished in this chapter, namely handling systems, advisory systems and expert systems, will in the coming years be put to greater use in public administration.

This in principle gives rise to the danger that the traditionally closed nature of public administration will be intensified, while the distance between administration and citizen will be widened[7]. The picture of the citizen who no longer has the opportunity to defend his rights through personal contact with a civil servant, but is confronted with a difficult-to-read computer printout, is becoming increasingly a reality due to the introduction of -especially- handling systems.

It is clear that introduction of knowledge systems in public administration will call for careful weighing and testing against a number of norms which, as we have seen, are of a legal, political, technical-scientific and economic nature.

In this chapter we have attempted to sketch a general framework for this assessment. Naturally it was only possible to use a few examples, and further elaboration will be necessary. In this context an important question is how working with these knowledge systems is in keeping with the requirement that in public administration possibilities must in principle always exist for balancing of and integration between the four (coexisting) rationalities. How much scope will remain for this if, due to the implicit or explicit inclusion of the results of this process in knowledge systems, the process constantly threatens to anticipate itself?

References

Athanasiou, T. (1985). Artificial Intelligence. Cleverly Disguised Politics. In: T. Solomonides & L. Levidow (Eds.), (1985) *Compulsive Technology. Computers as Culture.* London: Free Association Books.

Bell, D. (1981) The social framework of information society. In: Forester, T.(ed.) (1981). *The Microelectronics Revolution.* Oxford: Basil Blackwell. pp. 500-550.

Bing, J. (1987, November). Computer assisted systems for public administration: impact on legal decision processes. *Contribution for The conference on New Technologies in Public Administration,* 13-15 november 1987, Zagreb (Yougoslavia).

Bonnet, A. (1987). *Kunstmatige Intelligentie. Verwachtingen en Werkelijkheid.* Amsterdam: Addison Wesley.

Bourcier, D. (1986). Intégration et décision, réflexions sur deux nouveaux concepts en informatique juridique. In: *Revue française d'Administration Publique,* no. 37, pp. 55-69.

Clifford, J., Jarke, M., & Vassiliou, Y. (1983, september). *A short introduction to expers systems.* Center for Research on Information Systems New York University.

Deijck, J.E. van, e.a. (1987). *Eindrapport Projekt Experimenteel Expertsysteem.* GSD Amsterdam.

Donk, W.B.H.J. van de, & I.Th.M. Snellen (1988). *Die Bedeutung neuer informations- und kommunikationstechnologien für vergrosserung der Verwaltungstransparenz und der participationschancen der Bürger.* Beitrag zur Seminarveranstaltung des Forschungsprojekts Verwaltungstranzparenz, Gelsenkirchen, 15 April 1988).

Donk, W.B.H.J. van de (1988). *And never the twain shall meet.....* Verslag van een vooronderzoek naar de dynamiek van wet- en regelgeving en de dynamiek van systeemontwikkeling bij de totstandkoming van de WSF 18 +. TIlburg/Groningen, juni 1988.

Feigenbaum, E.A. & P. McCorduck (1983). *The fifth generation.* Addison Wesley.

Glastonbury, B. (1985). *Computers in social work.* Hampshire: MCMillan Publishers LTD.

Grimmer, K. (1987). The Use of information technology in qualitative administration work - organizational, economic and service related aspects. *Paper for the international conference on "new technologies in public administration": socio-economic aspects from an interdisciplinary viewpoint.* Zagreb, 13 - 15 november 1987.

Hirsch Ballin, E.M.H. (1986). De legitimiteit van de selectie van informatie.In: *Ars Aequi,* 11, 726-730.

Inbar, M. (1979). *Routine Decision-Making: The Future of Bureaucracy* (239). London: Sage Publications.

Kevenhörster, P. (1984). *Politik im Elektronischen Zeitalter. Politische Wirkungen der Informationstechnik.* Baden-Baden: Nomos Verlagsgesellschaft.

Koenemann, J. (1986, juni). *Auswirkungen von Expertensystemem. Ansätze einer Technologiefolgenabschätzung auf dem Gebiet der Künstlichen Intelligenz.* Universität Hamburg - Fachbereich Informatik.

Kuypers, G. (1973). *Grondbegrippen van Politiek.* Antwerpen-Utrecht: Het Spectrum

Kwee, A.Y.L., & Witte de, J.J.S.C. (1987). *Kennissystemen in de dienstensector.* Alphen aan den Rijn/Brussel: Samsom.

Laswell, H. (1936). *Politics. Who gets What, When, How.* New York: McGraw Hill.

Maciejewski, P.G. (1987). Verändert die neue Bürotechnik die Entscheidungsprozesse? *Office Management,* 1987/3, 38-42.

Oskamp, A. (1986). Expert systemen en hun toepassing in het recht. In: *Ars Aequi,* 11, 692-705.

Saat, J.P (1984). Voorstudie-rapport met betrekking tot de invoering van een nieuw stelsel Studiefinanciering 18-27. *Rapport uitgebracht door de voorstudiegroep WSF+ aan de Centrale Directie Studiefinanciering, Ministerie van O&W.* (m.m.v. RCC en Volmac).

Snellen, I.Th.M. (1986). Computers in street-level bureaucracies, their probable consequences for the bureaucratic competence required of the citizen. *Paper presented to the conference of the EGPA*; Copenhagen 25 -27 august 1986.

Snellen, I.Th.M. (1987). *Boeiend en geboeid. Ambivalenties en ambities in de bestuurskunde.* (Oratie). Alphen aan den Rijn: Samsom H.D. Tjeenk Willink.

Snellen, I.Th.M. (1987). Informatisierung und ambtliches ermessen. *Beitrag zum Symposium "Aufforderungen der offentlichen Verwaltungen an die "Burokommunikation", insbesondere bei wenig strukturierten Aufgaben"*. Kassel, 1 bis 3 Juli 1987.

Snellen, I.Th.M. (1987). Informatization and the quality of governmental services. *Paper, presented to the conference of the European Group of Public Administration,* Valencia, May 1987.

Snellen, I.Th.M., & Donk, W.B.H.J. van de (1987). Some dialectical developments of informatization in public administration. *Paper for the international conference on " new technologies in public administration: socio-economic aspects from an interdisciplinary viewpoint.* Zagreb, 13 - 15 november 1987.

Vitalis, A. (1981). *Informatique, Pouvoir et Libertés.* Paris: Economica.

Voort, L. van de, en I. Van Wijk, (1986). De Computer wikt, de mens beschikt. Het geautomatiseerd nemen van beschikkingen en de eisen van de rechtsstaat. In: *Ars Aqui,* 2, pp. 79-86.

Weizenbaum, J. (1984 (1976)). *Computer Power and Human Reason.From Judgement to Calculation.* Harmondsworth,-Middlesex: Penguin Books Ltd.

Wester, P. (1988). Projekt Experimenteel Expertsysteem. In: *Kennissystemen,* nr 2, pp. 40-43.

Wild, A.H. de, (1986). Computers, logica en recht. In: *Ars Aequi,* 11, 714-725.

Wormer, J.M., Vreeman, F.G., & Vennix, J.A.M. (1987). *Expert systemen en beleid: een introductie in expertsystemen en de relatie met het beleidsproces.* Sociologisch instituut van de K.U.N.

Notes

1. The object of the experiment was to arrive at an assessment of the usefulness and possibilities for the application of expert systems within the Municipal Welfare Department. Van Deijck et. al. 1987; Wester, 1988)
2. Though in recent years, in the framework of attempts to arrive at a more client-friendly public administration, precisely also with the aid of information technology, attempts are being made to reduce these policy-making costs for the citizens. Many forms sent them by government will shortly have been for the most part already filled in by computer (for instance: the Dutch Internal Revenue).
3. Incidentally, studies carried out by Bing show that "(...) computerization is associated by a tendency to replace vague by strict criteria", which may be recognized as: "(...) an important way in which the technology is impinging upon legal reasoning" (Bing, 1987:10). See also Wormer, Wreeman and Vennix, 1987: Expert Systems and Public Policy (Dutch), Nijmegen: Catholic University Press.

4. In the Netherlands the traditional legal publishers have already for some time been active on the market for legal advisory systems. Supply varies from rapidly accessible jurisprudence to advisory programs relating to rent law, criminal law measures etc.
5. According to newspaper reports on the critical moments preceding the shooting down of the Iranian Airbus by the American cruiser Vincennes in July 1988, this was a case in point. "(...) some - anomymous - military experts (...) expressed the (...) view that the captain might have reached a different decision had he relied less on the computer analysis of electronic data and more on his own judgement" (Volkskrant, 12 July, 1988). See for a critical analysis of A.I.: Athanasiou, 1985)
6. Representation of the legal rules in the computer program.
7. See for example Laserre, Lenoir & Stirn (1987): La transparence administrative.

Expert Systems in Public Administration
I. Th.M. Snellen, W.B.H.J. van de Donk, J.-P. Baquiast (Eds.)
© Elsevier Science Publishers B.V. (North-Holland), 1989

Chapter 2

A methodological approach to normativity in expert systems

*Ignace Th.M. Snellen**

Abstract

Expert systems used for public administrative purposes have to honour the normative requirements that are applicable to any action of a public authority that acts for a collectivity for which it is responsible.
(van de Donk and Snellen in this volume).

To calibrate those expert systems in a normative sense it is necessary to know where and through which entries values and norms find their point of attachment in the (reasoning paths of) those systems.

In addition one has to realize that some expert systems are more prone to hidden value orientations than others.

I therefore start with an overview of relevant types of expert systems in use or in an advanced state of development with public authorities. After that I shall introduce the "praxeological table" as an instrument for a systematic detection inventarization and discussion of values and norms in expert systems.

The praxeological table will be explained with the help of a medical example that can easily be translated to public administrative practice.

---

* Department of Public Administration and Informatics Law, Tilburg University, P/O box 90153, 5000 LE Tilburg, The Netherlands

1 Introduction

For a few years already, the Institute of Electrical and Electronic Engineers (IEEE), an American organization, arranges annual conferences on "Expert Systems in Government".

During these conferences the Institute brings together specialists who have practical experience in building expert systems (E.S.)

The introduction to the Proceedings of the conference of 1987 mark the year 1987 as a *watershed year*, because for the first time in the history of expert systems users' needs are directing the market place. Or, as the introduction states:

> "Recent market surveys reveal less interest in what the expert systems technologists have decided to offer; consumers' needs are now dictating the trend".

The Conference of 1987 in Washington D.C. was also remarkable because a broad cross-section of agencies did attend and put to discussion their funding strategies with respect to expert systems - or, more generally, knowledge based systems - development.

Such a discussion with European national and European Community agencies, as potential users of E.S., on concerted actions with respect to the development of different kinds of knowledge based systems might be a useful initiative in view of the further opening of the Common Market after 1992.

Some of the contributions (a.o. Baquiast, Vittrup) in this volume point already in that direction.

In the 1987 volume of the IEEE conference proceedings one of the paper-givers, Takashi Gomi - a canadian specialist in the field -, presents an overview of the applications and possible applications of *non-military* expert systems in governments (U.S., Canada, Europe and Japan). Gomi states that, although there are "almost countless areas where expert system technology can eventually be applied ..... not many expert systems have so far been developed for *office* use". More are found - according to him - in "services in the field".

Outside the military field Gomi distinguishes three areas of application for which an actual system is in operation, under development or, at least, subject to discussion to develop a prototype expert system.

The three areas are: *administration*, *services* and *training*. (For a slightly shortened list see table 1).

It seems to me that for public administration the coming years, the applications mentioned in the services category - except a few - are the most interesting.

Takashi Gomi also indicates some promising applications in the near future for which no expert systems yet existed and in regard to which, uptill then, no actions were taken. Examples are: Protocols advisors, Notices generation and Criminal investigation.

Administration
- Office procedures consultant
- Document processing

Services
- Query processing
- Eligibility counseling and consultation
- Legal E.S.
- Transit dispatch
- Claims processing
- Weather forecasting
- Crime detection
- Knowledge based mail sorting
- Evacuation planning and management
- Decontamination

Training
- Job classification
- Job training advisor/planner
- Internal procedure tutoring

Table 1. Applications of (non-military) E.S. in Government (according to Gomi).

Another promising field for the application of E.S. suggested by him, might be *emergency management*. This seems to me a very sensible suggestion. Especially in situations of extreme stress, emergency or general panic, when even responsible people are prone to misjudgements, the availibility of an expert system, *that "keeps cool"*, might prevent accidents or chaos.

Norms and legal rules, that in such circumstances may be easily violated, will also be better protected, when the help of an expert system is available. From an European perspective it may be reassuring to notice that the United States and Japan appear to be not far ahead in the *civilian* applications of the technology concerned. For a representative overview of the situation in Europe (France) the contribution of Baquiast in this volume is very illuminating.

Against this background it may however look premature to emphasize the norms that have to be applied to expert systems used in government.

On the other hand, the sensitivity of expert systems to the normativity, that is so specific for *governmental* relations with individual citizens and with society at large, may be decisive for their acceptance and use in public administration.

Therefore, not only from a normative but also from a pragmatic point of view it is necessary to honour the specific nature of governmental relationships in the design, development and use of E.S. for governmental applications.

In the first chapter of this volume van de Donk and I have tried to demonstrate in a few pages this specific nature of public administration. We indicated that in a democratic constitutional state public administration is in a normative sense guided by four different and, often conflicting, "rationalities". By "rationality" is meant : a socially differentiated, internally consistent and self-reflective system of norms, that 1) regulates a basic aspect of society (such as politics, law, economy) and that 2) is maintained and developed by a specialised profession (such als politicians, economists, lawyers or professional sector specialists). (Snellen, 1987)

When expert systems are designed and developed for use in public administration, they therefore have to honor the special requirements put to democratic constitutional governments, as derived from the rationalities mentioned. For this purpose we have to find out in which way the norm-complexes, that are mentioned, may be applicable in expert systems, in which parts of these systems and to what extent.

When we try to get an idea where values and norms may "creep" into the reasoning, represented in the *knowledge base*, the *rule base*, or the *inference system* of an expert system, a specific instrument called *praxeological table* may be helpful.

A possibly useful praxeological table is (further) developed by a dutch colleague of mine to help advisors to public authorities to determine whether the normative aspects of their advice are adjusted to the circumstances of the case and acceptable to their client. (Brasz, 1976, 1986).

I translated the table in the sense I understand it. This praxeological table is an instrument by which a systematic and exhaustive presentation is extracted of all normative view-points, that are indispensable to come to an acceptable argumentation for a standpoint or an action.

The basic concepts of the praxeological table are : *giving of meaning*, *diagnosis* and *therapy*. These concepts are worked out dynamically and statically. Dynamically they are represented in lines of reasoning or argumentation and statically in degrees of concreteness. In general "meaning" supports the justification of (governmental) acts, a "diagnosis" determines, what is wrong in a situation, in the light of the values and norms that give meaning, and points into the direction of a given "therapy", as reasonable set of actions to improve a situation. So, in an argumentation a diagnosis on the one hand rests upon the values and norms, inspired by meaning, and on the other hand strengthens implicitly the normative aspects of meaning. In this way a diagnosis functions in public administrative reasoning as an intermediary between basic principles and therapeutic prescriptions and at the same time creates a normative foundation for these prescriptions.

Thus, a praxeological argumentation ideally follows a line of reasoning from *justifying* paradigmatic argumentation based on principles, via *relativating* argumentation based on factual descriptions, to *application oriented* argumentation, based on theories about effect.

In its static dimension every stage of argumentation is again characterized by layers of meaning, diagnosis and therapy. As a consequence the shape of the praxeological table can be represented as follows, see figure 1.

2 Values implicit in short circuit reasoning (expert systems)

Line of reasoning / ***Layers of concreteness***	*Justifying argumentation*	*Relevating argumentatiion*	*Application argumentation*
Meaning	1 Basic principles	4 Translation to case	7 Applicable theory
Diagnosis	2 Specifications	5 Practical limitations	8 Valuation of prescription
Therapy	3 Relevant criteria	6 Applicable parameters	9 Assumed context of application

Value loaded translation

Figure 1. The praxeological Table (Brasz)

It would go too far to discuss in the context of this contribution all the backgrounds of the praxeological table. It may suffice to give an example, to show:

1. What kind of steps are taken, or at least have to be taken, in argumentations on the basis of which practival advices are given;
2. What kind of values are always implied in the lines of reasoning followed to come to an advice.

This demonstration with the praxeological table will prove useful to illustrate step by step how values and norms are implicit in the design and the application of expert systems. It is important to realize, that these implicit values and norms are especially taken up in the short-circuit reasoning, related to diagnosis and therapy (or solution), represented in expert systems.

A concrete example, taken from the medical field, may clarify how the praxeological table makes it possible to identify the values and norms that are implicited in a practical argumentation.

This is not meant as a description and discussion with respect to medical expert systems. The only purpose is to give an easily recognizable description of the many value loaded translations that take place between the different steps in a practical decision oriented argumentation.

In this example we follow the praxeological table from step 1 to step 9, where a doctor examines a patient of a certain age. This step-wise analysis has an idealtypical character. In practice these steps need not be visible, although they always will be present (implicitly).

Step 1
The doctor adheres to some fundamental principles with respect to health and has some general ideas what health means. He may adhere to a very broad definition of health as the World Health Organization does, or to a more limited one (e.g. exempting social well-being as an element of health). As a matter of course values and norms are implied in this step, which are decisive for the whole reasoning process.

Step 2
The basic principles and general ideas of step 1 are translated into fields of application about which the doctor feels competent (e.g. he may define "problems at work" inside or outside his field of competence or as irrelevant).

The expectations of the doctor and the patient may differ from each other in this respect and contain value laden specifications of the basic principles for both of them.

Step 3
The criteria the doctor applies are on the one hand related to his fundamental view on health and on the other hand to his ideas about the relevant field of competence and his belief in the importance of some kinds of symptoms (e.g. physical symptoms more important than psychic ones) and of some kinds of medical treatment (traditional medicine, homeopathy, a.s.o.). In the criteria he applies the values and norms the doctor adheres to are made concrete.

As far as Expert Systems are concerned, the first column of the praxeological table is decisive for the domain characteristics that are taken into consideration by the systems. The first column enlightens at different levels of concreteness the paradigmatic and value dimensions that are implied by the domain characteristics.

Step 4
In this first diagnostic step the doctor confronts his general ideas and fundamental principles with the case at hand (a patient of a certain age). He translates his general ideas on health and well-being to the specific case and thereby realizes the *relativaty* of these ideas and principles. What is the *normal* condition of a person with the age of his patient?
The doctor approaches the health condition of his patient with his own spectrum of expectations and prejudices.
N.B. In this stage not only values and norms are coming to realization, but also a *power relationship* between doctor and patient.
The doctor in fact determines what the patient may expect as his (physical) well-being!

Step 5
The assumptions and expectations related to the specific case as determined in the former step will be translated to practical limitations, which the doctor applies to his intended medical treatment. Cost-benefit considerations of doctor and patient - which effort on both sides is worthwhile in view of the potential improvement, reasonably to be expected - will play an important role in this translation.
N.B. Against this "economic" background, the value loaded question arises, what care and cure the patient might *rightfully* claim.

Step 6

The foregoing considerations about feasibility and justified expectations result in *parameters* which are used in the therapy as goals that are to be achieved. As these parameters are an operationalization of those aspects of the case, the *doctor* finds relevant, they are marked by *his* value orientation.

These values are selected on the basis of professional standards, the power-relationship between doctor and patient, economic considerations, and in view of the acceptability and relevance of the complaints of the patient.

The diagnostic dimension of expert systems and the norms implied in this dimension are on the one hand related to step 4,5 and 6 and on the other hand dependent on the choice of the domain and of the application theory.
As such the diagnosis is value loaden by itself but also refers back to the norms involved in the specific domain and refers forward to the theory that is deemed applicable in an eventual theory.

Step 7

The therapy the doctor prescribes will depend on the symptoms he selected in his diagnosis as important and on the causal theories he deems appropriate. As we have seen many value loaded choices preceded his final diagnosis.
The causal theory he applies to the case again narrows down the relevant aspects which deserve treatment. So, further selections, limitations and value decisions with respect to curability, comparabele to the ones mentioned in the former steps, will likely be implied.

Step 8

The prescription that follows from the application of the causal theory will be subject to valuation by the doctor and the patient. These valuations may widely differ. The doctor may implicitely or explicitely make an estimation of the probable behaviour of the patient and his/her capacity to bear the consequences of the prescription. He values the prescription in view of the personal characteristics he ascribes to the patient.
The patient will also value the prescription. In his/her point of view considerations of costs and benefits will be taken up. The value laden self-image of the patient will in this respect play a dominant role.

Step 9

Finally the doctor will take into account some conditions in the specific situation of the patient, which he thinks may be decisive for the succes of his therapy.

It depends not only on the professional insight of the doctor, which conditions he takes into account as relevant, but also on his appreciation of the way in which the patient responds to those conditions.
Apart from professional insight the power of the doctor to take certain conditions into consideration or not, is in this step clearly visible. Other value aspects are: legitimacy (what kind of behaviour may be rightfully required from the patient) and economy (are the benefits of the therapy, in view of the conditions outbalancing the costs).

In the therapeutic dimension some of the values and norms are a consequence of the chosen domain-extension and the focus of the diagnosis, some others are directly derived from the practice-oriented thought processes that take place in steps 7, 8 and 9. These dependencies have to be taken into account when an expert system is evaluated as to its normative orientation.

As this example makes clear, the praxeological table can be useful to find out which values and norms, and what kind of conflicts between them, are present in a practical argumentation, on which an advice or a decision is based.

Expert systems, which are used for an advisory or case-handling function, will necessarily have the implicit value assumptions, which I unveiled going from one step to the other, in their domain characteristics, their knowledge base and their rule base.

The praxeological table is not presented here to discuss the structure of expert systems, let alone medical expert systems, but as a *heuristic device* to find out where in those systems what kind of normative assumptions may be hidden.

In this way the praxeological table could be applied to investigate the encounters between street level bureaucrats and their clients with respect to social security entitlements as to their normative dimensions.

In such encounters values and norms (co-)determine the domain for which the street level bureaucrat considers himself responsible and the scope of activities for which he defines a client-relationship.

E.g. in the Netherlands some social security offices at the municipal level practiced a model of "payment factory", while other ones combined this with a social counseling model.

As the first three steps of the praxeological table make clear the (paradigmatic) dimensions of the domain-choice have many practical value implications. When expert systems are used in social security offices, their domain specification e.g. would have to choose between a small scope and a wide one and would determine the kind of values and norms attached to them.

Furthermore, in his diagnosis of a case the street level bureaucrat will be guided by his ideas (assumptions, prejudices) about what the client in view of his life-situation might reasonably expect from the office in terms of help etc.. Steps 4, 5 and 6 of the praxeological table unveil the discretion the official has in determining what is problematic in the life situation of his client, and what is in his situation is to be accepted as unavoidable.

Introduction of expert systems will hedge this discretion in and at the same time fixate values and norms in the processing of the cases.

And finally, the outcome of the encounter of street level bureaucrat and client in the form of a therapy, solution or decision depends on the theory (e.g. about the content of the regulation) that will be applied on the case. Such theory regards on the one hand the kind of social benefit the client is entitled to and on the other hand the propable adequacy of the measures which fall within the scope of the regulation. Medical therapy and social care work share value dimensions, which by way of example are made visible in the analysis of steps 7, 8 and 9 of the praxeological table. The contributions of Rae and Olave in this volume are in this respect very enlightening.

3 Conclusion

The above-mentioned considerations are in my opinion logically convincing about the value implications of the use of expert systems. They make furthermore clear, that the "praxeological table" may be a useful instrument for the detection, inventarisation and analysis of the value dimensions and norms in (the application of) those systems.

In view of the normative requirements that are put to the acts and deeds of public administrations in modern societies the consequences in this respect of the use of expert systems have to be researched. On the basis of research with the help of the table mentioned a checklist could be developed to check the value premises in expert systems that are used in public administration.

References

H.A. Brasz, *Methoden van de Bestuurskunde,* 1976

H.A. Brasz, *Een kleine Methodologie van de Bestuurskunde,* 1986

Van de Donk en Snellen, *Knowledge-based systems in public administration: Evolving practices and norms* (Chapter 1 in this volume)

Takashi Gomi (1987) *Survey of non-military applications of expert systems in government.* Proceedings of the 1987-conference of the Institute of Electrical and Electronic Engineers. Washington DC (pp 224-242)

Snellen, *Oratie: Boeiend en Geboeid, Ambivalenties en Ambities in de Bestuurskunde,* 1987

Expert Systems in Public Administration
I.Th.M. Snellen, W.B.H.J. van de Donk, J.-P. Baquiast (Eds.)
© Elsevier Science Publishers B.V. (North-Holland), 1989

Chapter 3

Controversial Issues of Expert Systems in Public Administration

*Erik Frøkjær**

Abstract

The techniques and unsolved problems with computer-based expert systems in public administration are discussed. The character of such systems is illustrated by two different systems for handling legal issues. Fundamental problems of expert systems are uncovered in a discussion of the nature of human expertise. Technical and administrative problems of expert systems in public administration are characterized in terms of the different groups of persons involved in their development and operation. It is concluded that the useful potential of expert systems in public administration lies in their use as tools by highly skilled administrators, not as a replacement of such administrators, and that the establishment of such systems depends on the availability of highly skilled technical personnel within the administrations themselves.

1 Introduction

The aim of this chapter is to stimulate a discussion of controversial issues associated with the use of expert systems as tools in public administration. The issues treated are of importance to both civil servants, programmers, citizens, and politicians.

---

* Department of Computer Science, University of Copenhagen, Universitetsparken 1, DK 2100, Copenhagen 0, Denmark

First the perspectives and state of the art concerning expert systems in public administration are briefly illustrated by two examples. The idea of building expert systems to accomplish problem solving at a level corresponding to human experts is discussed and considered unrealistic. The claims currently made for such systems are based on myths without empirical or theoretical foundation. An alternative, realistic and interesting objective is to continue the work on more refined computer-based tools to support people in activities requiring expertise or professional knowledge. Such systems are more precisely characterized as "expert support systems" or "support systems for professionals". Yet, we shall accept the name "expert systems" as a synonym, because it is already in widespread use and is shorter.

Expert support systems are seen as a new type of computer-based tool within the group of decision support systems. Different types of decision support systems have been known in the Civil Service in Denmark for many years, for example, *The Law Model System* designed to show the economic impact of current and contemplated legislation (Økonomiministeriet, 1987) and *The Budget Model* to construct consistent time-series for activity and expenditures in different sectors (Frederiksen, 1983). Rather few staff people and programmers have been directly involved in the development and operational use of such systems. Their knowledge can be most valuable, however, with the possible introduction of expert support systems on a much larger scale in public administration. Vital to the success of these systems is that they support the users' intuitive understanding of the problem at hand and are convenient in the work of the people involved.

From this position, I will discuss aspects of quality and risks that the use of expert support systems in public administration can be expected to generate for various interest groups, that is, the owner organization, the operators, the system developers consisting of both domain experts and programmers, managers, clients, adversaries and society. This discussion is conducted in accordance with recommendations proposed by Peter Naur in the book *Concise Survey of Computer Methods* (1974), in a chapter concerning administrative and political aspects of large data systems.

I do not expect expert support systems in public administration to raise qualitatively new problems of an administrative or political nature. However, they may accentuate known problems, such as tendencies to monopolize knowledge, to avoid accepting clear responsibility, and to present problem solutions in a guise of objectivity and necessity. The main problem in utilizing expert support systems efficiently is seen as the ability to establish groups of knowledgeable system developers within the organization owning the system.

2 Expert systems in administrative applications

I will here try to give a brief idea of the perspective and state of the art concerning expert systems in public administration. As the area is characterized more by fiction than by fact, I will abstain from contributing my speculations and instead describe two of the best documented expert systems of relevance to public administration. The first example concerns handling of legal cases in actions for damages. The other is an attempt at formalizing a small legal area using logic rules and thereafter developing a computer program to assist in legal problem solving using this formalization as a basis.

Example l: Handling of legal cases in actions for damages

A group of scientists led by D.A. Waterman at the Rand Corporation in Santa Monica, California, has developed a system for legal decision making, Legal Decision-making System (LDS), and a special instance of it, System for Asbestos Litigation (SAL), used in cases where persons may be compensated for asbestosis (Waterman et al., 1986). It is expected that there will be a great demand for legal assistance in such cases, because there have been millions of cases, and it is projected that there will be 200,000 deaths in the USA within the next 30 years due to asbestosis. The main aim of LDS and SAL is to assess the amount of damages in connection with product liability. SAL is specialized to handle cases where a person has acquired asbestosis and therefore is suing the producer.

LDS calculates the damages due from the defendant on the basis of a description of product liability. The expertise of the system is made up of the formal knowledge of laws and regulations as well as informal rules and strategies used by legal experts. The informal knowledge has been collected from lengthy interviews with a few lawyers - the typical method to elicit or model knowledge in system development. The calculation of damages does not necessarily correspond to results of a court proceeding, but is a recommended estimate for a lawyer preparing the case either for the plaintiff or for the defendant. In the calculation, a number of factors are involved that are influenced by the description of the case as given by the user. The factors are the amount of damages, the likelihood of the defendant being found guilty, an estimate of the plaintiff's complicity, and other adjusting factors used in estimating.

Both systems are implemented in ROSIE, Rule-Oriented System for Implementing Expertise, a rule-based system development tool developed by Rand Corporation. LDS contains about 300 ROSIE rules.

The development reached the prototyping stage before it was decided that it would be more useful to specialize on cases of damages due to asbestosis. SAL contains 400 rules including rules of superficial medical contents, that is, rules and procedures for diagnosis without, however, any deeper knowledge of or model for the disease. SAL conducts a dialogue with the user to gather data and give explanations. SAL can explain why it posed a certain question, what the words in the question mean, how it reached a certain conclusion, and can give the rules employed in text form.

Example 2: Law and Logic Programming

The Logic Programming Group, headed by Robert A. Kowalski, at the Department of Computing at Imperial College in London has conducted many interesting studies on logic programming, some dealing with the logical analysis of legal texts on the one hand and the computerization of logic on the other. According to the team at Imperial College, a legal expert system incorporating the knowledge of a good lawyer in the form of if-then rules is conceivable. Instead of modeling the work process of the expert, here the lawyer, the team has strived to make the rules in the computer system correspond as closely as possible to the legislative text. Their ideas have been tried out using the British Nationality Act 1981 as an example (Sergot et al., 1986). A possible application of such a formalization of the act is to determine whether in a given circumstance a particular individual is or is not a British citizen. A large part of the act has been translated into a simple form of logic, that is that on which the programming language Prolog is based. Although Prolog logic is severely restricted, the project team claims it proved sufficiently high level to make the implementation resemble the style and structure of the actual text of the act. Such resemblance is vital because it helps increase confidence in the accuracy of the implementation and makes the implementation easier to maintain as the legislation changes and as case law evolves thereby augmenting the legislation.

But still there is a long way to go before we shall expect laws as logic programs in practical use. The project team at Imperial College seems to agree. The concluding paragraph in Sergot et al. (1986) reads:

> "The British Nationality Act 1981 has also proved to be a rich source of problems for the use of logic for knowledge representation. It has highlighted problems with negation as failure and counterfactual conditionals in particular. We believe that the formalization of legislation and the development of computer systems to assist with legal problem solving and decision making provide a rich domain for developing and testing artificial intelligence technology.
> More tentatively, the accumulated experience of managing complex systems of law may teach us something about maintenance of large bodies of complex software."

The logic programming approach to developing computer systems for legal problem solving have been severely criticized by P. Leith, Department of Jurisprudence, Queen's University of Belfast, Northern Ireland. In a paper Fundamental Errors in Legal Logic Programming, Leith argues

> "... that the logical methods are not appropriate for handling the law, since the real problem of law is not the clarification of individual legal terms from the legislation, but the control of the judiciary. If we wish the judiciary to apply rules of law with the purpose intended by the legislators, we cannot do so by giving them 'clear' rules of law since they will simply use 'common law' arguments to interpret these terms."
> (Leith, 1986)

The very idea of clear rules as the basis of judicial reasoning are criticized:

> " 'Rule based' philosophers of law posit that we can view the law as a collection of rules which seem, at least to me, to have 'an existence of their own'. It is not unfair to see these philosophers as agents of a formal or technical view of the law, since they hold that justice is best arrived at by 'applying the rules' in a formal and technical manner. The problem I see with this view of legal rules is that it ignores the social determinators of the process: by presenting a technical methodology as to how the judiciary ought to reason they present an essentially conservative view which bears little relation to empirical evidence. By empirical evidence, I mean the written case reports - the substantive law - which present a completely different story. By looking at how the judiciary actually adjudicate, we can see that there is very little evidence for the notion of a clear rule which they can apply without further thought. (...)
> This critique, it should be noted, does not say that the concept of a legal rule is without use. I am not saying that we should not speak of legal rules. What I am saying is that we should be careful to remember that legal rules are objects of discourse, not objects with a concrete nature which we can mysteriously formalise and 'find' in the legislation or the weekly law reports.
> I propose, then, that this view of law is not one which is consistent with computer systems based upon rule-based methods because these systems present only 'concrete' rules - they cannot present intuitively arrived at rule-breaking strategies. Neither, as a corollary, can they present rule-supporting strategies, which are, in both criminal and civil litigation, a necessary opposition to the attempted rule-breaking of the appellant's or defendant's counsel."
> (Leith, 1986)

Other sources to determine state of the art in this area

Examples of expert support systems in administrative work may be found in Proceedings of The First International Conference on *Artificial Intelligence and Law* (1987). In *Artificial Intelligence in the Legal Field* (Biagioli and

Fameli, 1987) an international survey and a selected bibliography to expert systems in this field is presented. The survey mentions approximately thirty systems, but most of them seem to be developed only to a prototype level and are not in operational use.

Research in the area of legal expert systems in the Nordic countries is, to my knowledge, primarily done by J. Bing, Norway, S. Hägglund, Sweden, and J. Karpf, Denmark [see (Bing, 1987), (Hägglund, 1988), and (Karpf, 1988)]. J. Karpf has conducted a research project much in line with the above mentioned logic programming team at Imperial College, London, using part of the Danish Inheritance Act as an example (Karpf, 1988). J. Karpf has been especially interested in studying equivalence between different logic models of a legal area. An example of a discussion of the social and organizational aspects of expert systems can be found in chapter 21 of *Computers and Democracy* (Bjerknes et al., 1987). For people wanting a concise survey of state of the art for expert systems in business, I recommend the Edp Analyzer report, *A Three-Year Strategy for Expert Systems* (Canning, 1987), and a report in Danish (Frøkjær and Pedersen, 1987). It is a well-known fact that the traditional software development methods, based on a certain specification technique and phases in a software life cycle model, are of little help when it comes to expert support systems. Prototyping techniques and experiments in the development process are essential (Walters and Nielsen, 1988).

Summary of problem sources in development of expert systems in administration

The legal area poses some special problems for expert system development. Three problem areas will be pointed out here. The first is the need for common sense reasoning, a need which so far has not been solved technically (McCarthy, 1984). It is therefore up to the user to add his or her common sense to the reasoning from the system. The second problem is the lack of a formal model of the legal process, so that deeper reasoning, like what is feasible in more formal, technical areas, can be performed. The third problem area concerns the complexity of the legal area. Both formal and informal rules are relatively complex, partly because the formal legal rules are expressed in natural language passages employing notions that defy precise definition.

In spite of these difficulties, it is widely expected that useful legal expert support systems can be developed within narrow legal areas.

Only very few expert systems have been constructed thus far. In the area of law and public administration a rough estimate would be approximately thirty. Most of these are not in operational use, but are developed to a prototype stage and are used for research experiments or to train staff in new subjects. I have not been able to find any expert system in this area performing at a level of competence comparable to that of experts or professionals. I can quote no instances supporting the idea of modeling human expertise in computer systems in such a way that the systems themselves can perform at the level of experts. Whether or not this will ever be possible has been a controversial issue in computer science for at least forty years. In the following section I will try to summarize some main trends in this more theoretical debate.

3 Computer programs and expertise

The belief that it is possible to build computer systems with expert abilities is subjected to a fundamental critique by the brothers Hubert Dreyfus, a philosopher, and Stuart Dreyfus, an expert in computer science and operations research. Two important books on this subject are recommended to anyone concerned with computers in modern society: *What computers can't do: a critique of artificial reason* (Dreyfus, 1972), and *Mind over machine : the power of human intuition and expertise in the era of the computer* (Dreyfus and Dreyfus, 1986). In the latter volume the authors join a number of eminent critics of recent work in artificial intelligence in arguing that in many areas of human endeavor computers will never perform at the level of human experts. See also Peter Naur (1985) and (1986), David Parnas (1985), and Terry Winograd and Fernando Flores (1986).

In the following is given a summary of the line of argumentation presented in *Mind over Machine* (Dreyfus and Dreyfus, 1986). The authors first consider the more than 2,000 years old differences between the rationalist tradition of philosophy (Plato, Descartes, and Kant), which maintains that the world is controlled by objective principles and rules, and the empiricist tradition (Pascal, Hume, and Ryle), which denies the existence of objective criteria and argues that human beings gain expertise through perception, intuition, and experience, rather than through following rules based on accepted facts.

In an analysis of human skill acquisition they emphasize the necessity of distinguishing the behavior patterns of the novice, who is often just following given rules, and the intuitively and fluently working expert.

Between these extremes we find other levels of behavior. They choose to distinguish between the advanced beginner, the competent individual, and the proficient individual. Their discussion is summarized in table 1:

Skill Level	*Components*	*Perspective*	*Decision*	*Commitment*
1. Novice	Context -free	None	Analytical	Detached
2. Advanced beginner	Context-free and situational	None	Analytical	Detached
3. Competent	Context-free and situational	Chosen	Analytical	Detached understanding and deciding. Involved in outcome
4. Proficient	Context-free and situational	Experienced	Analytical	Involved understanding. Detached deciding
5. Expert	Context-free and situational	Experienced	Intuitive	Involved

Table 1: Five Stages of Skill Acquisition.
(Dreyfus and Dreyfus, 1986: 50).

The decisive blow against the possibility of expert systems functioning at the level of human experts seems to be dealt in the column headed *Decision* in table 1. Experts are experts by virtue of their intuition, achieved by experience and years of work within the field. Their intuition is based on what the Dreyfus brothers call "knowing-how", that is, unconscious deep insight, which fundamentally seems to be only partly expressible. Before you reach this level of knowledge you build a "knowing-that" level characterized by the conscious, analytical knowledge that the field of interest is organized in a certain way. Fundamentally, the intuitive knowledge cannot be analyzed exhaustively and therefore can only be modeled partly .

Dreyfus and Dreyfus also do not expect expert systems to be able to reach the level of proficiency. In real world domains of expertise - as distinct from games or puzzles - the proficient individual will draw upon knowledge of extraneous situational facts impossible to predict or build into the computer. The currently popular expert systems approach based on knowledge engineering appears attractive because the difficulty of knowledge base construction can apparently be bypassed by asking experts to collect large numbers of facts and to suggest rules of thumb that will operate in given restricted domains.

However, the Dreyfus brothers argue that the enthusiasm about the expert systems approach is misplaced:

> "... given our five stages of skill acquisition, we can understand why knowledge engineers ... have had such trouble getting the experts to

> articulate the rules he is using. The expert is simply not following any rules. He is ... (instead) recognizing thousands of special cases ... That in turn explains why expert systems are never as good as experts." (Dreyfus and Dreyfus, 1986)

The Dreyfus brothers expect to see useful computer-based tools developed to support professionals and experts in their problem solving, for instance, tools like planning boards, management information systems, and training programs for professionals, but not as a replacement for professionals and experts. Computer systems will only be superior for some highly combinational problems where even experienced specialists have failed to develop complete understanding.

The fields of education and management are discussed rather deeply by Dreyfus and Dreyfus. Concerning the area of management they argue that computer models of business operations and decisions are necessarily based on facts and rules, but most important business decisions involve a deeper type of understanding.

> "... when the future can accurately be predicted using a model ... decision support systems have much to offer. They offer nothing but regressive thinking ... when the decomposed analytic model ... represents an understanding inferior to an expert's holistic involved intuition."
> (Dreyfus and Dreyfus, 1986)

Such views are strongly supported by the classical work of Henry Mintzberg, *The Nature of Managerial Work* (1973), and by T.J. Peters and R.H. Waterman with their book, *In Search of Excellence* (1982). If management and staff accept the idea that expertise is a matter of huge knowledge bases with facts and rules, there is a danger that this will impede their own process of developing skills surpassing the level of the machine systems.

To balance this severe critique of much artificial intelligence and expert system research by Dreyfus and other respected computer scientists, I will refer to assessments expressed by Bruce G. Buchanan. He is one of the founders of the expert system technology by virtue of his contributions to the development of the well-known Mycin project. In a paper, *Expert systems and the research literature*, Buchanan surveys state of the art in artificial intelligence and discusses the possibility of raising the actual level of expertise in expert systems.

In the section *Are these systems 'really' expert?* Buchanan (1986) argues:

> "It has been popular to argue against the very idea of artificial intelligence by claiming that even though AI programs appear at times

> to behave intelligently they are not 'really' intelligent. A variant of this argument has surfaced with respect to expert systems: that they only appear to behave expertly but are not 'really' expert. Use of the term 'really' is slippery, however, and hides the shifting criteria that are employed every time the behavior of programs improves. There is no reason to take this criticism seriously.
> However, three substantial criticisms of expert systems warrant brief discussion here. They are that expert systems are not going to pay off in the long run because they lack three kinds of knowledge:
>
> 1. Successively deeper layers of knowledge of their task areas to use when the shallow, compiled knowledge fails to reach a satisfactory answer.
> 2. Common sense to avoid errors due to reading the expressions of knowledge too literally or due to incomplete coverage of possibilities within the explicitly stated knowledge base, and
> 3. Knowledge about how to learn from experience.
>
> Expert systems of the current generation do lack these three kinds of knowledge, but that is not to say that future systems will. Nor does that lead directly to the conclusion that today's systems are not able to perform at the level of experts and contribute positively in well-defined contexts."

These three areas of criticism are discussed in the paper. Buchanan concludes that a result of the research in the past decade has been to make the building of simple, rule-based systems a straight forward task.

> "They can be important for helping people solve problems for which expertise is in short supply, or is not well distributed, or is not available around the clock. More complex problems will require more complex knowledge structures and reasoning methods, and may require knowledge of a qualitatively different kind. The next decade should prove to be a time of trying and testing many new ideas for extending the capabilities of expert systems".
> (Buchanan, 1986)

He seems not to see fundamental obstacles as do, for instance, the Dreyfus brothers. Using their terminology it is obvious that Buchanan does not accept the sharp demarcation line between intuition and analysis in problem solving. He expects that further research and experimentation will bring understanding and techniques allowing us to model still more of the problem solving skills known in human experts. Buchanan finishes his paper with this rather modest statement:

> "Expert systems are also here to stay. They have their weaknesses, but careful problem selection and design, explicit definition of context, and additional research will alleviate them.
> Even with their limitations, they can be applied successfully. Finally the successes will be all the stronger when the limitations are explicitly

noted as opportunities for experimentation and greater understanding." (Buchanan, 1986)

4 Quality aspects of expert support systems (ESS)

This section follows and partly paraphrases a discussion concerning administrative and political aspects of large data systems in society presented by Peter Naur (1974). I have found it useful to rethink Naur's treatment of large data systems, substituting large data systems by imagined expert support systems (ESS). Although they are not necessarily large systems, they will often be complex and used in applications of vital importance to the owner organization. This framework seems to be useful in our discussions of technical and administrative problems of expert systems in public administration.

People involved in expert support systems

In this section different persons and groups of persons shall be characterized in terms of their specific relation to an expert support system. The groups may overlap as the same individual may, in different contexts, belong to more than one group. Systems intended for use in more than one organization raise difficult problems of joint authority and management which are not treated in this text. We assume that the ESS is used by only one organization being responsible for the utilization.

The owner organization, or *owner*, is the organization or person who has initiated the construction of the ESS and has authority over it. By definition, the owner organization has had the data system constructed to reach certain goals.

The *operators* are the members of the staff that use the ESS in their daily tasks. They are in intimate contact with the computer, manipulating programs and data through its user interface.

The *system developers* are the people who have thought out the overall design and the details of the system. They develop the system through the activities: problem formulation, knowledge modeling (often denoted knowledge engineering in expert systems), building the user interface, validating, introducing, modifying, and maintaining the ESS. The activities are iterated and characterized by experimentation (prototyping). The system developers constitute a group of both experts and *programmers. Experts* are highly practised and skilful persons within the application area for the intended ESS. *Programmers* are highly practised and skilful persons trained within computer science, having some experience of programming techniques in artificial intelligence.

The *managers* will here be used to denote those members of the owner organization who are responsible for the activity of the field where the ESS is expected to be put into use. They must assume the responsibility of accepting the results of the system as correct and of using these results as the basis for further action. Managers can be staff or, in the public sector, politicians holding authority (in Denmark primarily a minister as head of a department of state or members of the municipal council).

The *clients* are the people outside the owner organization who communicate with the ESS in the manner intended in its design, for instance, in writing, in conversation with an operator, or using the system directly.

The *adversaries* are any persons inside or outside of the owner organization who try to use the ESS for their own benefit, against the interest of the owner. Depending on the kind of benefit they are trying to make, they may usually be classified as either embezzlers, vandals, or competitors.

Finally, *society* will be used to denote, in the usual vague sense, the collection of *citizens* who, though not closely connected with the system, may nevertheless be influenced indirectly by its operation. In a democracy, the citizens have some control possibilities concerning the politically selected authorities through elections. *Judges* make judicial decisions when legal problems concerning use or misuse of the ESS occur.

Adequacy and Convenience of ESS

The adequacy of a data system is a characteristic that indicates how well the system matches the overall needs of the organization that it is designed to serve. It is of concern, primarily, to the owner and the manager, in that an inadequate system will fail to provide the answers and perform the functions that might reasonably be expected of it.

The ESS can incorporate an interpretation of some legal rules or known good practices, but the quality of the interpretation can not be tested and validated to the same extent that we are used to with ordinary application programs like, for instance, payroll programs. In spite of the fact that such payroll programs will often contain a model of wage agreements in some form, of a complexity comparable to the legal model, expressed in rules, found in the most ambitious legal expert systems.

But typically, ordinary application programs do not offer the possibility to operate with uncertainty or for the operator to intervene rather freely during the execution of the system as seen in ESS. Much of the complexity in expert systems arises from the need to allow for a certain degree of freedom during their operation. From this follows that the assurance of the adequacy of the

ESS is much more difficult for the owner than what is usual. Again this stresses the need for competent operators and managers to apply the ESS in a responsible way. The system developers must be aware of the risks of improper use of the system due to operators having a too limited overall knowledge of the application area as well as the limitations of the ESS. System developers have to be directly engaged in the training and education of operators and managers. To summarize, the assurance of the adequacy of an ESS must be viewed as an ongoing process of awareness involving both the owner, managers, operators and system developers.

The convenience of a data system depends on how the system appears in direct contact. A system may be inconvenient for the operators or clients. ESS are normally supposed to interact with the operator very closely during a consultation, making the question of convenience vital. The system should model concepts and problem solving processes as transparently as possible, keeping to the operator in continuing contact with the model of reality embedded in the ESS. Model and reality should be compared in a systematic way, thus gathering information on how to improve the ESS and its application.

Reliability and Stability of ESS

A reliable data system is one that can be trusted to perform correctly. Part of the reliability thus depends on the degree of absence of programming mistakes in the system. Taking into account the fallibility of humans, the absence of mistakes in the programs alone will not ensure a reliable operation. Rather, one must view reliability in connection with the stability of the system, by which is meant the insensitivity of the system to random disturbances. Examples of random disturbances are: erroneous input, operators' mistakes, for example, misinterpreted or misselected data from the client or the system, typing errors, and many other factors. Reliability and stability are of primary concern to the manager, but are also important to the client and operator. In addition, stability influences the operators very directly, because it controls the consequences of the unavoidable mistakes by operators. To the client, the citizens, and society as a state governed by law, it is important that decisions made by the authorities can be checked.

Here expert systems may give rise to serious problems, if they are used directly to produce such decisions.

Security and Supervisability of ESS

The test of security of a data system is its ability to withstand attacks from adversaries. Since the system in many cases constitutes a central part of a large organization, its security will often be highly important. This holds true for an ESS as well, as it will typically be used in connection with important tasks.

I shall not discuss this point related to ESSs specifically; but let me quote from P. Naur a concise description of the problems concerning large data systems in general:

> "Several kinds of adversaries may be distinguished. Competitors may attempt to tap the system for secrets. Embezzlers may try to modify its operation in such a way that they improperly obtain advantages, for example high figures on their own financial account. Vandals may try to cause physical damage, either by actual bomb throwing or by changing the data more subtly, for example by exposing magnetic tapes to random magnetic fields.
> The security problem is particularly acute in relation to the operators and programmers of the system, since if they are also adversaries they are in a particularly favorable position to achieve their ends as such.
> On the other side, the security problem focuses on the manager. For him to assume the required responsibility, it is necessary that the large data system has been constructed to include an adequate degree of supervisability. This may take the form of special reports to the manager produced automatically by the system, and of means by which the manager may obtain summaries, averages, extremal values, and similar overall characteristic data concerning the data handled by the system, upon request."
> (Naur, 1974)

The relevance and the consequences of all such possible attacks on a particular system should be treated, primarily as a responsibility of the managers, in dialogue with the owner and the system developers, and the operators. The security investigations will pose very difficult political, administrative, and technical problems to the development and operation of EESs in wide-spread use in organizations, primarily because their operation is so difficult to control and so varied by virtue of their incorporated heuristics, their use of uncertainty, and the freedom in the interaction between system and operator.

Maintainability of ESS

In general program maintenance comprises

> "all technical activities related to a given program following its release for operational usage. Such activities are not limited to the correction of errors but may also include modification of the program to meet changing operational requirements, amendments to the program documentation, upgrades to the program, and so on."
> (Dictionary of Computing, 1986)

Maintenance of ESS is primarily the responsibility of the system developers and involves managers, the owner, and the operator, assuring that the system will continue to measure up to all the quality demands earlier mentioned. An ESS can be expected to be rather easy to maintain under the important assumption that the continuity in the group of system developers is kept.

Political effects of ESS
The ESS will have to be protected from adversaries. Detailed public knowledge of the rules built into the system can in some application areas cause refined speculations in the weaknesses of the knowledge model built into the ESS. Efforts to control such threats may prevent clients and the public from insight into the administration of the Civil Service and hereby intensify the impression that clients and citizens are treated in a mechanistic way by bureaucrats. Dilemmas of this type have always been central to all public administration in societies, but especially today these problems must be dealt with. We have seen strong political reactions against regulations that are unintelligible to the citizens. And we have to be aware that strict regulations are difficult to avoid in the highly organized, industrial societies we have created during the last century. (Again, one of the basic insights from programming is seen to have a much broader message: In programming, striving for simplicity is of utmost importance as the only way to cope with the unavoidable complexity of many programming tasks.)

Again, we shall learn that only if the operators obtain sufficient knowledge and training to master the new sophisticated tools, will it be possible to utilize the new technology effectively, and avoid wide-spread abuse.

5 Concluding remarks

Concerning the scientific problems

Though much research has been done since 1956, the situation today can basically be summed up as Maurice V. Wilkes, a leader and a pioneer in computer science, did it in his book *Automatic Digital Computers* (1956) in an appendix on the question "Machinery and Intelligence". He wrote:

> *"Although I have written about machines passing Turing's test* (my remark: a test to answer the question 'Can a machine think?' proposed by A.M. Turing in 1950. For a discussion see (Naur, 1986) and (Halpern, 1987)) as though this is a thing which might actually happen, I do not wish to give the impression that I think it will happen soon, or even that present lines of research, pursued competently, or even brilliantly, over a considerable period, will lead to its happening at all. On the contrary, every line of approach which has been tried up to the

present has proved abortive as far as this particular objective is concerned. Perhaps a genius will arise and turn the whole subject inside out. Until this happens I see a bright future for machines in executive capacities, but I do not see them behaving like human beings."

After more than thirty years of research all over the world without any serious breakthroughs on fundamental issues such as machine learning, common sense by machines, or the like, we should now expect more realism and humility in the many research and development programs in artificial intelligence. Still, these programs are characterized by claims of machine intelligence or even general intelligence, automated programming, machine learning, automated translation of natural languages, and similar uncritical and confusing uses of humanoid terms, raising false expectations among many scientists and in society as a whole. This impedes many important and more realistic research projects in this field. In my view, the ambition in applied artificial intelligence research projects, as also in the area of public administration, should be to develop useful computer-based tools to assist professionals or experts.

Concerning utilization of expert support systems in public administration

A wide-spread use of such complicated technical data systems as expert support systems in public administration handling tasks of direct importance to citizens carries definitely interesting perspectives, economic and organizational by making expert knowledge more explicit, easier to maintain, and by disseminating such knowledge beyond small privileged groups of civil servants and citizens.

There is a danger though, that unrealistic expectations of their potential and the need to decrease the public budgets will let their usage grow in a realm of false authority impeding human insight, creativity, and common sense in administration. Without a clear awareness of this danger we will in the long term see stronger political reactions against an inflexible bureaucracy.

In the short term, many skilful civil servants and programmers will be wasting their efforts in unrealistic development projects funded by governmental and private organizations. To convince yourself of the importance of this, you should talk carefully to people who have been directly involved in large research and development projects in computing; and read, for instance, the paper *Software Aspects of Strategic Defense Systems* by David L. Parnas (1985). In that paper, Parnas - in carefully written essays without technical jargon - treats a number of fundamental problems in software engineering, programming, and artificial intelligence; and explains why he believes the "star wars" effort will not achieve its stated goals. Also the role of the funding mechanisms in the US Department of Defense (DoD) is critically analyzed.

> "The people who end up making funding decisions in DoD are very often unsuccessful researchers, system builders, and people who enter bureaucracy immediately after their education. We call them technocrats. ... Most technocrats are honest and hard-working, but they are not capable of doing what is needed. ... I am convinced that there is now much more money being spent on software research than can be usefully spent. Very little of the work that is sponsored leads to results that are useful. Many useful results go unnoticed because the good work is buried in the rest."
> (Parnas, 1985)

He concludes that the DoD's overall approach to research management requires a thorough evaluation and review by people outside the DoD. I am convinced that this holds true for many research and development programs in Europe as well, both national programs or programs within the European Economic Community.

The key to avoiding such pitfalls is to build data systems that are understandable to their users, clients, system developers, and management. Otherwise, the systems cannot be mastered. I could give you quite a few concrete examples, where this elementary principle relating to large data systems has not been respected. Some are treated in a paper *Problems in Controlling Data Processing in Public Administration in Denmark* (Frøkjær, 1987). From discussions abroad with people within public administration or computer science, I am under the impression that the state of affairs elsewhere is not much better.

In many organizations using computers, there is a growing understanding of the need to attract and keep a staff of knowledgeable programmers to implement and maintain data systems in accordance with changing demands. This was stressed as a key problem in (Frøkjær, 1987), and has later been stressed in answers to a questionnaire on the utilization of data processing submitted to a number of governmental institutions by the Danish Ministry of Finance. In a recent report, surveying problems in the Danish public sector as a whole, the results of this investigation are summarized in the following way (Finansministeriet, 1988):

> "The institutions all identified one key problem relating to their problem solving, namely the difficulty of attracting and keeping qualified computer personnel. The main cause, they held, was the salary situation, and especially the limited possibilities of giving a satisfactory salary to the most qualified employees."
> [Translated from Danish]

One should recognize that the institutions are stressing that the core of the key-problem is retaining the most highly qualified people, showing that there is an understanding that they cannot be substituted for by a number of less knowledgeable people. In spite of such clear statements from the governmental institutions, the officials in the Ministry of Finance summarize the situation concerning the data processing competence level in the governmental sector as follows (Finansministeriet, 1988):

> "The technical and commercial advances in the computer market mean that standard systems for numerous tasks, including system development, are constantly being improved. In addition, the growing technical standardization has as a consequence that the computer field as a whole is rendered simpler and more coherent, modifying the need for technical specialists.
> These certain and long term trends makes the task of problem solving less burdensome, partly compensating for the problem of attracting and keeping computer personnel."
> [Translated from Danish]

Such predictions are based on wishful thinking, superficial speculations without empirical foundations, or just echoing the claims of computer firms overselling their latest or coming products as the answer to the software crisis recognized as early as 1968 (Naur and Randell, 1969). So far, this software crisis has persisted for twenty years.

One of the reasons the software crisis is still with us is that we are solving, or trying to solve, more and more complex problems with help of computers. Expert systems are one good example. Another source of difficulty in programming is the need for more efficient data interchanges between man and computer. A third important source of difficulty is the rapid development of new and more powerful hardware and software techniques, renewing the need for new or modified standards. Within none of these areas, do I see any reliable indications that we are reaching the limits of our demands.

The Ministry of Finance in Denmark is creating illusions or is simply naive when diverting the growing attention in the governmental organizations from the seriousness of the main problem: How to raise the level of computing competence, also in-house, as a necessary basis for further efficient utilization of data technology. Most organizations need experienced system developers who are familiar with their requirements in order to make responsible choices in organizational development.

Expert support systems reinforce the problem of raising the level of computing competence. A study of some of the few systems of this type that have surpassed the stage of prototypes for experimentation and have grown into operational use shows that their development has been a complex task drawing on the full range of programming techniques and working methods from software engineering; not just a few techniques from artificial intelligence. Expert support systems are complex data systems and demand the most qualified and involved civil servants and programmers for their development, implementation, and maintenance. The scarcity of such skilled system developers will continue to be a most critical problem in the foreseeable future.

References

Artificial Intelligence and Law (1987). *Proceedings of The First International Conference on Artificial Intelligence and Law, Boston 1987,* Center for Law and Computer Science, Northeastern University and ACM SIGART, ACM-Press, New York.

Biagioli, C., and E. Fameli (1987). "Expert Systems in Law: An International Survey and A Selected Bibliography", in: P. Mercatali, "Artificial Intelligence in the Legal Field", part one, *The Journal for Integrated Study of Artificial Intelligence, Cognitive Science and Applied Epistemology,* Vol. 4, no. 4, pp. 323-359.

Bing, J. (ed.) (1987). *F*KUS, Knowledge based systems for public administration, Complex,* Oslo.

Bjerknes, G., P. Ehn, and M. Kyng (eds.) (1987). Computers and Democracy - A Scandinavian Challenge, Avebury, chapter 21, "SAFE Expert Systems", *report by the Conference Group on Expert Systems,* pp. 419-434.

Buchanan, B. G. (1986). "Expert systems: working systems and the research literature", *Expert Systems,* Vol. 3, no. 1, pp. 32-51.

Canning McNurlin, B. (1987). "A Three-Year Strategy for Expert Systems", EDP Analyzer, *United Communications Group,* Vol. 25, no. 3, 16 p.

Dictionary of Computing (1986), second edition, Oxford University Press.

Dreyfus, H. L. (1972). *What computers can't do: a critique of artificial reason,* Harper and Row, New York. Reviewed in Computing Review, review number 23,463, July 1972.

Dreyfus, H., and S. Dreyfus (1986). *Mind over Machine,* The Free Press, New York. Reviewed in Computing Reviews, review number 8709-0747, pp. 478-481, September 1987.

Finansministeriet (1988). Redegørelse om den offentlige sektor 1988, (Survey of the public sector 1988), in Danish, *Statens Informationstjeneste,* København, chapter 17, pp. 277-285.

Frederiksen, J. (1983). *The Danish Budget Model in a User Perspective, Ministry of Finance, Denmark.* Presented at the Conference on Automated Decision Support Systems, Denmark, September 13-15, 1983, International Council for Automatic Data Processing in Government Administration, 13 p.

Frøkjær, E., and G. Schmeltz Pedersen (1987). *Ekspertsystemer,* in Danish, Forlaget Kommuneinformation, København, 51 p.

Frøkjær, E. (1987). "Styringsproblemer i det offentliges edb-anvendelse" (Problems in Controlling Data Processing in Public Administration in Denmark), in Danish, *Politica,* Vol. 19, no. 1, pp. 31-56.

Halpern, M. (1987). "Turing's Test and the ideology of artificial intelligence", *Artificial Intelligence Review,* Ablex Publ. Corp., Vol. 1, pp. 79-93.

Hägglund, S. (1988). *Emerging Systems for Computer-based Knowledge Processing in Office Work,* Institutionen för Datavetenskap, Universitetet i Linköping, October 27. Submitted for publication in Office: Technology and People.

Karpf, J. (1988). *Legal Logic Programming Techniques,* Paper presented at The Fourth International Congress on Law and Computers, Rome, Institute of Computer and Systems Sciences, Copenhagen Business School, 17 p.

Leith, P. (1986). "Fundamental Errors in Legal Logic Programming", *The Computer Journal,* Vol 29, no. 6, pp. 545-552.

McCarthy, J. (1984). "Some Expert Systems Need Common Sense", in *Annals of the New York Academy of Science,* Vol. 426, pp.129-137. Invited presentation for the New York Academy of Sciences, Symposium on Computer Culture, New York, April 5-8, 1983.

Mintzberg, H. (1973). *The Nature of Managerial Work,* Harper and Row.

Naur, P., and B. Randell (eds.) (1969). Software engineering, *Report on a conference sponsored by the Nato Science Committee,* Garmisch, Germany, 7th to 11th October 1968, Scientific Affairs Division, Nato, Brussels, Belgium, January, 231 p. Reprinted in Naur, P., B. Randell and J. N. Buxton (eds.): Software Engineering: Concepts and Techniques, Petrocelli/Charter, New York, 1976.

Naur, P. (1974). *Large Data Systems in Human Society,* chapter 17 in Concise Survey of Computer Methods, Studentlitteratur, Lund, pp. 288-293.

Naur, P. (1985). "Review 8502-0062 of D. Michie: Machine intelligence and related topics", *Computing Reviews,* Vol. 26, no. 2, pp. 101-104.

Naur, P. (1986). "Thinking and Turing's Test", *BIT,* Vol. 26, pp. 175-187.

Parnas, D. L. (1985). "Software Aspects of Strategic Defense Systems", *Communications of the ACM,* Vol. 28, no. 12, pp. 1326-1335.

Peters, Thomas J. and Robert H. Waterman (1982). *In Search of Excellence,* Harper and Row.

Sergot, M.J., F. Fadri, R.A. Kowalski, F. Kriwaczek, P. Hammond, and H.T. Cory (1986). "The British Nationality Act as a Logic Program", *Communications of the ACM,* Vol. 29, no. 5, pp. 370-386.

Walters, J. R., and N.R. Nielsen (1988). *Crafting knowledge based systems,* Wiley.

Waterman, D. A., Jody Paul and Mark Peterson (1986). "Expert systems for legal decision making", *Expert Systems,* Vol. 3, no. 4, pp. 212-226.

Wilkes, M.V. (1956). *Automatic Digital Computers,* Methuen & Co. LTD, London. Appendix: "Machinery and Intelligence", pp. 289-293.

Winograd, T., and F. Flores (1986). *Understanding Computers and Cognition: A New Foundation for Design,* Ablex Publishing Co., 207 p. Reviews on this book in Artificial Intelligence, Vol. 31, 1987, pp. 213-261.

Økonomiministeriet (1987). *Lovmodel - Overview of the Danish Law Model System,* in English, København, Oct., 31 p.

Part 2

Evolving practices and norms

Expert Systems in Public Administration
I. Th.M. Snellen, W.B.H.J. van de Donk, J.-P. Baquiast (Eds.)
© Elsevier Science Publishers B.V. (North-Holland), 1989

Chapter 4

Knowledge, rationality, normativity in legal expert systems

*Danièle Bourcier**

Abstract

The development and use of expert-systems, and especially of legal decisionmaking aid systems, reformulates the traditional debate on rationality in new terms.

If rationality is intrinsic to persuasive argumentation and necessary to foresee the consequences of a decision, can we speak of an "intelligent" machine being rational?

The notion of legal rationality must thus be situated not in relation to the textual codification of the law but in the context of the resolution of problems or the making of decisions. It thus becomes important to ask, what consitutes the "communicational knowledge" which enters the administrative process. Starting from the example of a mayor's decision in the field of public order, we will examine the different norms involved in a legal decision: norms of identification and evaluation of facts, technical and legal norms, standards and vague concepts.

We will see that these norms are subject to different successive treatments in the model we propose, BRUITLOG. But are the norms we start with left unaffected by this process? Likewise, doesn't the modelling procedure introduce new normativities? Finally, we will examine the problem of the relation

---

* Director of the interdisciplinary research team "Computer Law Linguistics", National Center of Scientific Research, Conseil d'Etat, Palais Royal, 75001, Paris, France

of the margin of choice in legal decision-making (discretionary power) to the number of rules necessary to represent this process.

Two traditional concepts in the philosophy of law, rationality and normativity (Hegselmann, 1979) are involved in the development of legal knowledge-base systems.

First we will see how these concepts have to be reformulated in relation to decision making processes. Then we will examine concrete problems of modelling set by three types of knowledge in a legal expert system.

1 Legal practical rationality and decision making processes

Traditionally, the problems of representation of the norm have been essentially discussed in relation to the internal rationality of legislative discourse.

Yet laws are only logical representations of the reality of positive law. Some authors have even compared the form of the law to a programming language thereby justifying the use of such a language to construct the production rules of an expert system.

We will deal less with the problem of the homeomorphism of the logic and of the law than with how certain notions at play in this logical representation can be seen in a different perspective: a decisional procedure of problem-solving.

Thinking about legal rationality involves two perspectives.

Firstly, to find what is rational in a discourse or a practice is to try to establish a necessary and non contingent link which would allow the emergence and the setting-up of relations between the elements of this practice or of this discourse (Lalande, 1926). In this sense we can say that the law puts forward its rationality as a criterion of its legitimacy. The logical model based on the principles of the unity of the legal corpus, the univocal meaning of the law as well as the unity of the legal administrative system suggest the image of the rational legislator.

The free and rational elaboration of a universal and scientifically founded norm (Bourdieu, 1986) becomes the deductive application of a rule of law in a judge's practice. The judge thus corresponds to the rational legislator, rationally applying the rule of law following syllogistic reasoning.

For some authors (Ost, Lenoble, 1980) this rationality is merely a fiction and stems from the mytho-logical presupposition which gets rid of the "surface antagonisms" and guarantees "the intelligibility of the norm". When we want to construct an expert-system, this first rationality, the rationality of "as if", seems incapable of describing the cognitive process involved in a given situation. Neither formal logic nor even a "logique du raisonnable" are enough to account for the real determinants of legal reasoning. For this reason, we propose to analyse a different sort of rationality, beyond this first internal rationality: a practical rationality of decision making.

This account of this opposition between the rationality of the legal corpus and that of the practice has been important for some years thanks to the new problematics and models which have been produced by the human sciences: decision-theory, psycho-cognitive approaches to decision making processes, economic models, and organisation theory (Roy, 1983). For some time now, legal theorists have developed not only a theory of law based on the ideal of a selfsufficient and autonomous system "purified of all the uncertainties and lacunae tied to its practical genesis", but also work-tools "adapted to the urgency of practice: legal source-books, standardized documents and soon information retrieval systems" (Bourdieu, 1984). Should expert systems be closer to the first or the second rationality? We would like to stress that at present all softwares are closer to a literal and exegetic translation of the rule of law in "pseudo-rules of law" (Waline, 1971) and model decisional processes reduced to what legal theorists call "pseudo-decisions" (Frayssinet, 1981).

This opposition between two rationalities has become central to a fundamental philosophical debate ever since technology and science began to play such a crucial role in all areas of administration and politics.

Weber has already formulated a distinction between a rational law which is predictable and calculable in contrast to a magical formalism of legal text or ritual.

Likewise, legal theorists (Aarnio, Alexy, Peczenik, 1981) have attempted to establish a theory of legal reasoning in a wider sense and to include sociological and historical aspects in their considerations based on the theory of science and to reconcile the doctrines based on the analytical school and legal realism.

The same position is held by Habermas (1968) who opposes a pragmatic model to a decisional or technocratic model, these latter both excluding any rationality which would not be scientifico-technical. His pragmatic model would describe "a dynamical process of reciprocal adjustment where the solution of a problem would result from an iterative movement ending up in a progressive determination of the problem in relation to the solutions which it is possible to find". Habermas is trying to go beyond that weberian rationality where he concept of rationalization allows "the free-flow of communication" thanks to a community of rationally-argued convictions (Habermas, 1987).

These different approaches allow us to analyse the two concepts of rationality and normativity in a new way, and to see the limits and the openings in relation to the specific field of administrative decision making.

The concept of administrative expert systems thus leads us to introduce a practical rationality based on the hypothesis thas it is possible to construct a normative system capable of providing a legally acceptable solution for each examined case and a legally acceptable justification for this solution given the chosen strategies.

This solution would not only be the application of a set of rules to a personal situation (individual assessment, sanctions etc...). It would also be a general legal decision putting forward a new norm and thus subject to the rules of the establishment of the norm.

But it would belong to the category of "acte particulier" (Dupuis, Guedon, 1986), which is actually a sort of general decision applicable to the case in question: for example the banning of the showing of a film, the closing of a disco or the regulating of the noise of a lidt.

Here again, we should stress that in all the current expert systems, the result of the decision making process will lead to the elaboration of the individual assessment of cases. These measures will concern one or several specifically designated subjects: for example, the liquidation of a pension or the calculation of sick-pay in the case of illness.

The result thus requires the representation of the *knowledge necessary* for the domain in question and also the rules for handling such knowledge.

Knowledge in the field of law involves legal norms, that is imperative, prescriptive, hypothetical, classificatory and argumentative statements belonging to the legal system and valid in this domain of reference.

The rules of *handling knowledge* are the rules of legal methodology (the evaluation of priority, the import of a norm, the treatment of vague concepts...), of reasoning (the forbidding of extensive or analogical reasoning, the forbidding of the creating of norms in the field of penal law...) or communicational interaction (definitional requirements, examples, undecidability, strategies, choice and procedure control). It is thus necessary to translate the operations of discursive transformation into decision-making rules. Some authors (Alexy, 1978) founded their theory of legal argumentation on such "jumps" in discours.

The objective will thus be to formalize this set of *resolution rules* into *production rules* which are acceptable by the inference mechanism.

We will then distinguish three levels of translation rules in law as well as a fourth result which can be a norm (decree).

Legal corpus and practice	Normative dispositions Analysis of practice and experience (precedents)
Analysis	Resolution rules
Formalization	Production rules (PROLOG)
Solution of the problem	General decree Assessment of individual cases

Figure 1: Levels of normativity

It is important to describe the different sources of norms involved in these levels. Thus rules from statistical analysis can be used in the resolution rules.

Likewise, one can add know-now, anancastic rules (Von Wright, 1986) and even rules of common sanse to the normative dispositions.

Indeed the results of the decision can be a norm but it can also involve procedural, technical and argumentative aspects. It can be translated in the form of commands but also as recommendation or advice. Care must be taken as distinguish the normative solution from other solutions.

Finally, the search for a suitable model necessitates taking into account not only these instrumental rules (legal technique) implying conditional specifications but also strategies based on standards, on value systems or on general maxims (Habermas, 1968).

Legal corpus and practice	Value systems Maxims and standards
Analysis	Priorities, alternatives, preferences in relation to norms or solutions
Formalization	Ranking, meta-knowledge guiding resulotion procedures (mechanism of control)
Results	Choice of resolution and decision procedures in relation to strategical criteria and desired arguments

Figure 2: Treatment of strategies.

These strategies involve a type of rationality which is not the *rationality* of norms: decisional policies in the field of administrative action or jurisprudence.

The construction of knowledge-based systems for legal decision making thus implies that one studies the question of the practical rationality of decision making processes: types of norms (implicit or explicit), criteria for the determination of *normative sub-systems,* and formulations of strategy.

These determiniation criteria can be reached by different methods: methods of literal interpretation when one is dealing with a normative statement but also by teleological methods when values have to be determined.

But other methods can be used here too: mathematical or statistical methods when it is a question of interpreting a jurisprudential norm stemming from precedent.

By introducing the notions of representation of legal knowledge, the concept of normativity takes on *another meaning*. It is no longer a question of knowing what a legal norm is or of characterising normativity in law but of formulating the means of solving the following problem: what are the rules which found a juridical decision or a new norm?

Finally one cannot undertake a study of resolution norms and a modelling of legal decisional processes - especially when one is dealing with an administrative decision - without posing the following question: the administrator can no longer limit himself to the simple production of an administrative action, based on the division of work organized in relation to the different levels of competence and bound by determined rules (my emphasis); there is a real structural change brought about by the *objective constraints* of technologies and by new communicational strategies.

Indeed, this debate on the rationality of law takes on a new social significance when the process aims at validating and reproducing a model. The field of artificial intelligence contains its own objective constraints (inference mechanisms, languages, man-machine dialogue). Likewise, the administrative decision takes on political import when it is made by an elected local authority acting in the field of its own competence. It implies that the bureaucratic strategies or the positions of the authorities involved in this process (state administration, local authorities) will not remain unaffected. This brings up to the question of the *interprete-decideur's* margin of choice in relation to the rationality involved in the choice of the methods and objectives already determined *by other authorities.*

2 Discretionary power of the decision-maker or how to rationalize the process of making administrative decisions

We will examine the concrete problems posed by the modelling of three types of rationality from the experience of MAIRILOG (a project described in the following chapter): assessment of facts, technical expertise, discretionary power of the decision-maker.

2.1. Facts and values: the rules of description and evaluation

One of the first problems to be analysed when we want to build an expert system is that of the relations between, on the one hand, the notion of *fact* and *situation,* and, on the other, the truth-conditions of the norm and the pertinence conditions of the description of the precedents.

Next it is necessary to see whether rules of description of "triggerind facts" exist which would bring in other implicit *normative orders* such as a *logic of value.*

A major difficulty is encountered throughout the different stages of construction and brings us to the following paradox. When we want to build an expert system which would describe the various factual and normative elements we run the risk of "normalising" and removing the dynamical aspect of the interaction. We have thus tried in the MAIRILOG project to elaborate a model in which modules of choice of evaluation or of rationality are integrated: indeed it is impossible to impose a global and deterministic rationality. The decision-maker must be able to choose different *types of reasoning*, and *models of choice* for each particular decision-making act.

Let us examine the first question: what is a fact for the law? The question is situated more on the side of science than that of philosophy. In fact the response to this question will determine the observational model of "reality" and the legal identification of the problem.

Even before artificial intelligence, this simple question seemed not to have received many replies: legal theorists either referred in term "fact" to the rubric "law" or 'act" (Dictionnaire d'Eguilles, 1988); or it was situated essentially on the side of proof (Perelman, 1976).

Certain authors have elaborated the notion of pure fact. For Gaudemet (1972) the statement of facts in jurisprudence does not have a descriptive importance but rather a strategic and even a prescriptive one. In giving such a central place to the elements of pure fact and in insisting on the particular circumstances surrounding the emergence of a dispute, the decision maker limits the import of the decision he makes: he thus shows that the factual data were essential and that the solution chosen was above all a function of the facts involved. However we should note that in the more specific field of legal responsibility, the facts (understood as an pure argumentation) are determinant. This leads us to the following formulation: *a detailed consideration of the facts by the judge may mean the absence of norms and the illegitimacy of generalisation.*

However is it not ultimately in legal decisionmaking that one would be surest of attaining this "regional determination" (Granger, 1988) of the facts, indispensable for a scientific formulation of law. Contrary to the "exact" sciences, the legal method leaves open the material and conceptual means which would allow it to build up the class of facts to be defined.

The notion of fact must thus be expanded to that of a *group of facts, circumstances and situations.* But should it be expanded in the way suggested by authors like Geny (1954) who see the power of individualising and thus of assessing the facts, that is, all the "contingencies of life" in the "libre recherche" of the judge? For Geny, the judge needs to introduce certain elements unforseen by the law, without which he would be unable to grasp the facts.

For many authors, working mainly in private law, the notion of 'fact" is important in theorising law, but they fail to set a dividing line between the two. The problem has often been approached exclusively from the standpoint of the control that the Cour de Cassation exercises in a legal organisation. For Rivero (1961), one of the only authors in the field of French public law to evoke this notion, this disctinction of fact is merely functional: it is used to measure the *extent of discretionary power.*

To sum up, what interests an administrative authority confronted with a situation of real or potential disorder requiring its intervention, is to link "the diversity of aspects, circumstances and behaviour to *categories*" (Husson, 1974) in the same way as a judge.

In general these categories correspond to the *conditional elements* of the rule of law. Thus, in the rule according to which "the use of loudspeakers on the public highway is forbidden without special authorisation" (ord. 5 June 1969 of the Préfet de police de Paris on noise), "the use of loudspeakers" would constitute the *fact* conditioning the norm of interdiction. Thus, on the one hand, the *fact* is the equivalent of the *term* or the *identifier* (in the sense of the PROLOG clause, for example) but it is also the *concrete* circumstances which will be stored as facts in the *"facts base"* during each session with the computer.

Let us pause for a moment to examine this functional distinction. Firstly, the circumstantial element is singled out by the system to be converted into a *positive, negative or absent* fact: it is the "individual reality" of a particular case. The fact, now in the system's memory, can also be *undecidable* when it is a doubtful or vague fact. The memory will be requested to instantiate the different conditions of the rule. Between the facts base and the rule base, a *transformation* has taken place: we have passed from concrete to abstract and then on to instantiation.

It seems that we encounter the same elements in the organisation and logical machanisms of the system as we do in the cognitive operation of subsumption well-known to jurists, but it is the machine which constructs its resolution procedures in a dynamical and non-deterministic fashion.

Often, the facts stem from perception: we call them *material* facts. In the example of the loudspeaker, it is enough to note that such an *object* is involved and that is has been *used* (the behaviour). But when the first article of the same edict indicates that 'all noise caused without necessity is forbidden" or that in the juridictional field the judge has to decide whether a husband was guilty of "grevious insult", it is a question of another operation. This operation, again well-known to jurists, is that of qualification, which some authors have called the interpretation of facts (Ivainer 1988). In this instance, we cannot juxtapose an experience and a system of norms. Indeed, as Husson points out: "whether the applied notion has been received by the law or forged by it and whether, in this latter case, it remain technical or, on the contrary, became vulgarised and has given rise to a precise legal or jurisprudential definition, or is confided to the discretion of the interpreter, there is always a confrontation of the material facts with a certain schema or model. It is thus no longer a question of a simple matter of fact:" (Husson, 1974).

Let us take as an example the general notion of the "practice of activities of games which are *not adapted* to residential areas" being forbidden.

Confronted with a situation (not defined in the text in question) such as the daily practice of piano playing in an appartment which irritates the neighbours, the decisionmaker will exercise a *normative* and not merely *schematising* competence. In fact, he will categorise this activity according to criteria stemming from *beliefs* on *tolerations* connected to *ways of life.*

How can one represent these primarily cognitive and then normative operations when one has to eventually state them in the form of rules? We suggest a series of operations (identification, characterisation, calculus...) which aim to provide a solution in terms of the decision-making process. Certainly, in many areas the decision-maker, like the judge, can base his qualification on such modes of assessment as measurement, technical norms or on expert's advice (we will examine these questions later). But in the field of *morality,* for example, one can ask by what local criteria a mayor could justify the claim that a film is particularly likely to breach public order in his district.

For many jurists the progress of law is in "making the system of its categories tighter, thas is, both more precise and more nuanced, in multiplying the specifications and in clarifying the criteria of application" (Husson, 1974). Can expert systems help these requirements and even rationalise the procedures involved?

Two elements can help us with this representation: a systematic analysis of jurisprudence starting from the control of legality by the judge, or an integration of the different interpretations, both attested (circulars, authors' opinions) and implicit (correlation analysis).

Facts for jurisprudence will thus be considered as *describers,* correlated to the various types of decision. In the case of noise from a disco, the emission of noise until four in the morning in a residential area, together with the noise produced by parking, would constitute a group of *relevant facts sufficient* to characterise a possible breach of public order. The uniform repetition of such a situation would allow one to formulate a *descriptive "norm" from the set of facts*. But how would one deal with a decision which led to the legality of a decree of the mayor authorising on Sundays the construction of a motorcross course in a quarry only a few meters from a country house used only on weekends. In this case, it would be less a question of a *characterisation of the facts* (circumstantial standards) than of a *global assessment* (normative standards) bearing on the importance of *leisure policies* for young people in relation to the standard of *public peace*. The norm to be extracted from this decision would be a *priority* between two standards, not a collection of facts.

Yet no value judgement can be put forward as a unique, normative order founding a progression in the identification of a fact; it can only be "decided". The categories of language carry with them value judgements; the choice must be left to the decision maker[1].

We can set out the various levels of *normalisation* of factual situations in the following table.

Knowledge	Description of the circumstances of a situation (jurisprudence) Legal conditions Guidelines of administrative interpretation of factual situation
Analysis	General schema of identification Cognitive sub-trees Semantic networks
Formalization	Terms and identifiers in the knowledge base Relations (hierarchy, classification)
Results	List of facts introduced or inferred constituting the base of facts of a specific situation to be dealt with

Figure 3: Levels of normalisation of facts

To construct a pragmatic model for the rational identification of the facts, it is thus necessary to:

- find the truth-conditions of the application of the norm, the *pertinent* descriptive elements of the case and its precedents, looking for the values and standards which are set in opposition for each group of facts by a factorial analysis (Bourcier, 1988);

- identify the facts by their juridical (normative) denomination, in order to avoid homonymic disparities of meaning and ambiguities, and to respect the structural spaces specific to law;
- construct semantic networks of facts and a general schema of the structure of the situation;
- take account of the consequences of qualifications to eventually change the denomination of a fact in the interaction with the decision-maker.

2.2 Technical expertise and legal decision-making: status of technical rules of expertise.

In the process of elaborating an administrative decision, there is an area of rationality which can be modeled more easily: the field of scientific and technical knowledge involved in the determination of legal decision-making. But is this form of knowledge more rational? Isn't it the reckoning ground of the implicit norms or institutional strategies which would put its universal validity and hence its direct utilisation in question in the knowledge base?

Another question would be to determine how such expertise is used, and its integration in the resolution of a legal problem, given its status in relation to legal decision-making.

Finally one can ask whether the technique itself of expert systems cannot be conceived - as its name suggests - as a new avatar of the technocratic ideal and the "scientificisation of politics", using the authority of technical knowledge and the objective knowledge of things (Max Weber) to spread political and bureaucratic domination. This latter aspect is particularly important in the field of decisions made by decentralised authorities in France. It is the role itself of the local elect as administrative authority that runs the risk of being modified by a more or less *occult* technical administrative supervision; in accepting his role as a mere user of the system, doesn't the mayor become the *relay* of policies and choices formulated by the central administration?

Likewise, is it the future-orientated aspect of the mayor's function which will be stressed by the expert system (e.g. by the scientific assessment of the risks and consequences of his actions) rather than the circumstantial aspect of his interventions? What risks being normalised in a definitive fashion here is the definition itself of the standards, for instance, that of the upholding of public peace, independent of the temporal or structural changes which might modify their content of their finality.

The use of technical and scientific knowledge in politico-administrative decision-making preceded the age of the expert-system: it even seems to characterise the evolution of our societies over the last twenty years.

When a local administration wishes to make a decision (urbanism, public health for example), it is constrained by a specific technical knowledge. Thus in the case of the regulation of noise, the mayor can either seek the advice of an expert or apply the technical norms contained in the regulations. Let us analyse the role of the expert in the making of a legal decision.

There is both a *legal* and a *technical* sense to the term expertise.

The appeal to a technical expert is an integral part of legal procedure. For example, in a matter of construction, the judge will call in the expert in the context of an inquiry to determine the nature of the problems, their origin, their gravity and the elements needed to allow a resolution.

This first function accorded to expertise has its origin in the hypothesis that a judgement is the end term of the operations consisting of "the perception of the data, coding, integration, relation, weighing up the facts" (Mullet, 1980). In reality, different *participants* are involved in the preparation of a decision, whose role is to establish the *reality of the facts* according to several different types of logic. The decision is thus an accumulation of judgements where verifications from diverses sources are ordered together.

In order to establish the facts, the administrator must also appeal to other forms of knowledge. For Sadran and Dumas (1982), the expertise which they analysed in the framework of administrative decision-making in a local context consisted of "the insertion of a specialized professional knowledge above decision processes, tending towards the rationalisation of policies by the production of norms or models of behaviour, added to the legal regulations".

With expert-systems, it is thus necessary to situate the appeal to technical expertise at *the level of the establishment of the facts,* whether it is a question of measurement, calculation or diagnosis.

Expertise is considered as a source of the production of true or verifiable knowledge and as a means of establishing a consensus between professionals. But a study carried out for the Ministry of Justice (de Bonis, Bourcier, 1987) has shown that the consensus was far from being agreed on between experts in the fields of construction or psychiatric expertise. Indeed, certain implicit, non-technical factors can enter the determination of various results. The study also showed that out of two populations, one made up of experts, the other of judges, the consensus between legal professionals was greater than that between technicians.

One must thus assess the results of technical appraisal carefully when one knows that the appeal to the experts takes place within institutional strategies where the search for truth is not the only criterion in the interpretation of the facts.

1 Determination of the technical critreria of the acoustic nuisance

Class of effects to be taken into account:
Acoustic level in decibels
Point of reception
Point of emission
Time of day

Operations:
Calculation of additional criteria in relation
to the number of decibels (technical rules)

Result:
Technical diagnosis of the acoustic nuisance

2 Determination of jurisprudential criteria (choice of strategies)
Internal result

3 Discretionary choice of the mayor
(Interaction in the form of a question)

4 Regulation of the choice
in relation to other aspects of the situation(technical, factual)

5 Possibility, if the contradiction persists, of the proposal
of a charge in the qualification

6 Proposal of argumentation given by the facts and measurements

Figure 4: Table of the treatment of technical rules in a decision making process

With technical expertise, there are technical rules which have been integrated into the legal universe (ratification of instruments or procedures and also normalisation stemming from scientific discoveries or technical apparatus). But they are not enough to legally qualify a situation (emergency, difficulties etc...). The status of the technical rule is close to that of the ratification relating to technical expertise. In legal procedure, ratification of the expert's report and the conclusions of the expert can be articulated by the judge if the latter does not modify any of the proposed argumentation.

With administrative decision-making involving the power of the mayor's regulations, technical argumentation cannot be used exclusively to constitute the base of a legal argumentation. This rule is confirmed by the case in which the mayor was able to forbid the running of a kennel even though the noise levels were lower than that allowed for by the technical regulations. The integration of technical rules in the decision-making process has been formulated by BRUITLOG as shown in figure 4.

A final point on the determining role of technology in the modelling of cognitive activities.

Techniques are not neutral: they imply the choice of models, constraints which risk creating problematic feedback related to the finalities of socio-political systems. Will they not then have the second effect of depriving the decision-maker or administrative agent of his own discretionary margin in interpreting the situation, the rule or the finality of his assignment or of stopping him from judging in equity, from deciding with his own conviction? The French law "Informatique et Libertés"[2] took account of the dangers that such practices could present by examining all files based on human behaviour patterns in each individual case. But are we aware of the dangers of the arbitrary, the importance of the inequality of treatment or the non-decision to which human behaviour often leads?

2.3 Discretionary power and the formulation of rules.

The rationalisation of decision-making processes can thus come into play at the time of the objectification of the relevant problem, the definition or the qualification of the facts. But the simulation of the decision also implies that certain *institutional and communicational rules* be fitted into the mechanism itself, without giving rise to any rationalisation in the form of production rules. It is a question of clauses relating to the notion of discretionary power and what is known in French as "intime conviction" or "appreciation souveraine". Let us take for example the notion of emergency. This is a standard, that is, vague concept used to structure a reasoning process or to justify a decision. But the emergency can only be defined in terms of necessary or sufficient conditions.

There are many other standards in the field of a mayor's regulations (public order, public peace, public health, security...) It is within his power and his competence to correlate these standards to the particular local circumstances from which he will elaborate his decision. It is thus up to him to furnish each of these terms with a decisional content.

The system thus cannot reason as if it knew what emergency was, and *universalise* often very specific criteria. People have tried to solve this question of the "unformulated knowledge in the form of rules" in different ways.

For BRUITLOG, the emergency will be *inferred* from a positive response to a series of synonymous or specific formulations found in law or jurisprudence: serious breach of public peace, serious pollution, imminent danger. Then the qualification will be compared with other data collected during the course of the session. If there is any inconsistency, the system will indicate this.

For LOG-EAU, an expert-system for decision-making in the field of threats to water cleanliness where the emergency determines the emergency interim proceedings, the district experts (health inspector) have been able to determine very few reliable criteria (epidemics) or sets of criteria varying according to the situations (irreversability of the situation, naturre of complaint, visibility of insalubrity, nature of the damage). In the case of buildings close to collapse (IMMLOG expert system), although the notion of emergency allows one to determine the normal procedure or the procedure for imminent danger, no criteria are available; the rule of law only indicates that the assessment of emergency lies with the mayor and secondarily with the expert who certifies the state of the premises; as for jurisprudence, a statement in the "code pratique de la construction" tells us thas "legal decisions giving exact details of the degree of acuteness of danger which would justify emergency procedure have not been published". Emergency is thus actually a standard implying the *discretionary* role of the mayor in this diagnosis. No formalism can be substituted for the supreme choice of the decision-maker.

It is thus not possible to define the notion of emergency with deductive or even statistical rules (the variables are difficult to locate). On the other hand the system can help to single out certain inconsistencies in the whole situation under scrutiny. The system can also indicate how certain agreement upon criteria can be excluded. Finally, the system can start from implied consequences (competence, procedure to be followed, responsability) to suggest the qualification of emergency to the decision-maker.

One question thus remains central: standards *naturally* allow the exercise of a discretionary power. But there are also other types of norm, the *textual formulation* of which leads to a completely discretionary *choice of action:* hence the expressions "the administration was not obliged to..." or "the mayor might...". In the case of advertising openings for a job connected to a public

- go back over the decisional tree if the space of possible responses according to an evaluation is not adequate (back-tracking).
- control the consistency of certain responses.

We can thus insist on the interest of studying the *cognitive* aspects of the legal decision, allowing us to distinguish the various stages involved in the decisional process. The stake of this type of system is clear, as it which works to systematise the drawing up of legal and cognitive rules for the working-out of the decision.

For Geny, discretionary power belongs to "libre recherche", in that these two notions are "the two branches of the samen capacity of the law to adapt to particular situations". An expert-system can clarify the law and, in so doing, contributes to the progress of the formalisation of the rules and processes of judgement, but it cannot be based on *artificial rules* and define a level of precision which borders on illegality.

Inaccuracy and vagueness are the basic characteristics of legal language. Can the decision of the legal decision-maker involving such vague information integrate the contributions of decision analyses, the specific constraints on the legal field and the methodology specific to expert-systems? It is necessary to study, beyond the classical expert-systems, a *new concept of aid to legal decisional expertise* which includes a theory or argumentation. The characteristics of this type of system (Saunders, 1989) might be the following in the field of law: a choice between solutions or different argumentations, the influence of contradictory criteria on decisions, the introduction of subjective factors into the rules and the use of standards and values. Even in law, one cannot assume the existence of one single valid solution; as in all situations connected to decision-making, there is no single optimal solution (Roy, 1983) which is neutral in relation to the decision-making process itself.

Can an expert system be considered as a "rational" human expert, when its choices refer to a normative context which is technical, evaluative and legal?

References

Aarnio, Aulis, Alexy, Robert, Peczenik, Aleksander. (1981) Le fondement du raisonnement juridique in Rechtstheorie 12, Berlin: Duncker & Humblot, (traduction Grzegorczyk), séminaire de théorie du Droit, Paris X).

Alexy, R. (1978). Theorie Juristischer Argumentation, Francfort-sur-main.

Bonis (de) Monique et Bourcier Danièle. (1987). *Expertise et analyse du processus décisionnel judiciaire. Droit et sciences cognitives,* Tomes 1 et 2, Rapport ronéo, UA 962 CNRS, Paris.

Bourcier, D. (1988). Analyse des standards de la police municipale: approche décisionnelle, thèse d'Etat, Paris.

Bourdieu, Pierre. (1984). *La force du droit - Eléments pour une sociologie juridique.* In Actes de la Recherche en sciences sociales n° 64, Paris: Minuit.

Braibant Guy. (1984). Le droit administratif français, Paris: Presses de la FNSP et Dalloz.

Dupuis, Georges, Guedon Marie-Josée. (1986). *Institutions administratives, Droit administratif,* Paris: Colin.

Dictionnaire de théorie et de sociologie du Droit (dit Dictionnaire d'Eguilles. (1988). Paris: L.G.D.J. Story scientia.

Frayssinet, J. (1981). *La bureaucratique,* Paris: Berger-Levrault.

Gaudemet, Yves. (1972). *Les méthodes du juge administratif,* Paris: LGDJ

Geny, François. (1954). *Méthodes d'interprétation et source en Droit privé positif,* Paris: LGDJ.

Granger, Gilles Gaston, (1988). *Pour la connaissance philosophique,* Paris: Jacob.

Habermas, Jürgen. (1968). *Technick und Wissenschaft als Ideologie,* Frankfurt am Main.

Habermas, Jürgen. (1987). *Théorie de l'agir communicationnel,* Paris: Fayard.

Hegselmann, R. (1979). *Normativität und Rationalität,* Frankfurt am Main.

Husson, L. (1974). *Nouvelles études sur la pensée juridique,* Paris: Dalloz.

Ivainer, Théodore. (1988). *L'interprétation des faits en droit,* Paris: LGDJ.

Labetoulle, Daniel. (1978). *Le pouvoir discrétionnaire en matière d'urbanisme et d'interventionnisme économique.* In: Le pouvoir discrétionnaire et le juge administratif, IFSA, cahier n° 16, Paris: Cujas.

Lalande, André. (1926). *Vocabulaire technique et critique de la philosophie,* Paris: PUF. (4e éd.).

Mullet, Etienne. (1980). *L'activité clinique de jugement,* Thèse, Paris V.

Ost, François et Le Noble, Jacques. (1980). *Droit, Mythe, raison. Essai sur la dèrive mythologique de la rationalité juridique,* Bruxelles: Facultés Universitaires Saint-Louis.

Perelman, Chaïm. (1976). *Logique juridique,* Paris: Dalloz.

Rivero, Jean. (1961). *La distinction du fait et du droit, la jurisprudence du Conseil d'Etat français.* In Le fait et le droit, Etudes de Logique juridique, Bruylant: Bruxelles.

Roy, Bernard. (1983). Introduction in *La décision, ses disciplines,* ses acteurs (Actes du colloque de Cerisy, 1980) in Sciences des systèmes, Lyon: Presses universitaires.

Sadran, Pierre et Dumas, Jean. (1982). *L'expertise dans l'administration locale.* In De la décision administrative en milieu local, IFSA, Paris: CNRS.

Saunders, Michael. (1989). *Les systèmes experts sont venus combler une lacune.* In Lettre de l'Intelligence artificielle, n° 46, fevrier 1989, Paris: EC 2.

Von Wright, Georg-Henrik. 91986). *La fondation des normes et des énoncés normatifs* (transl.) in Cahiers S.T.S. n° 12, (ed. D. Bourcier) Paris: CNRS.

Waline, M. (1971). *L'autorisation du pouvoir discrétionnaire.* In Revue du Droit public, Paris: p. 1224.

Weber, Max, *Wissenschaft als Beruf* (1919) transl.: Le savant et le politique, Paris: Plon (1959).

Notes

1. Administrative decisions, contrary to judiciary decisions, have little effect on the interpretation of behaviour. Cf. Th. Ivainer, who cites the decision of a court of appeal where a judge inferred from the return to living together or a husband and wife during their divorce case that the original greivances could no longer be considered. This is an example of a real value judgement "shared by the intersubjectivity of the social group".
2. Loi n° 78-17 6 janvier 1978, J.O.R.F. 7 janvier 1978 et rect. J.O.R.F. 25 janvier 1978.
3. C.E. 28 mai 1954, recueil Lebon p. 308.

Expert Systems in Public Administration
I. Th.M. Snellen, W.B.H.J. van de Donk, J.-P. Baquiast (Eds.)
© Elsevier Science Publishers B.V. (North-Holland), 1989

Chapter 5

The expert system BRUITLOG and the MAIRILOG project

*Danièle Bourcier**

Abstract

We shall summarize here the main characteristics of MAIRILOG and BRUITLOG which were elaborated as a part of a research program on the methodology of expert systems applied to law.

1 Introduction

The BRUITLOG system is a decision making system for the mayor concerned with the policy of noise and public tranquillity. Its purpose is to represent legal knowledge and to simulate the mayor's reasoning. It covers the whole concerned positive law, i.e. enacted law, regulations, interpretation notes and administrative case law.

MAIRILOG is an expert system project elaborated from the experience acquired with BRUITLOG.

The principal function of MAIRILOG is individual decision support and it is mostly intended for the community administration. But we have noticed that a large number of services outside of community administration may also be interested, and it may be used at various hierarchical levels. Besides, the system is not limited concerning security (in its widest sense) and with respect to

* Director of the interdisciplinary research team "Computer Law Linguistics", National Center of Scientific Research, Conseil d'Etat, Palais Royal, 75001, Paris, France

the competence of the mayor. When the mayor is not competent, MAIRILOG indicates to which authority the right to act and the rules to apply should be given.

MAIRILOG will cover the whole domain of the mayor's decision in the matter of policy (safety, salubrity, tranquillity).

2 Development

The MAIRILOG project has been developed by the research team "computer science, law, linguistics" (Council of state, France).

This research team, associated to the CNRS since 1973, was created by Lucien Mehl, honorary Councillor of State, and is now directed by Danièle Bourcier. This team gathers workers, from various research fields such as mathematics, law, computer science, linguistics, who share an interest in law and/or Artificial Intelligence. Its main orientations are:

- research on the impact of Artificial Intelligence on law and the analysis of legal decision.
- applications : legal and administrative expert systems
- conception of data base retrieval systems with a natural language interface (SPIRIT).

The support from valorization organisms enables the team to try out and distribute its projects.

BRUITLOG was sponsored by the Department of valorization (CNRS) and by the Agence nationale de valorisation (ANVAR). The system was dealt with a market research in relation to local authorities. Researchers, computer scientists, mayors and local civil servants have taken part in this project.

3 How does the system work?

BRUITLOG is an expert system that helps to make diagnosis and to find texts which can be applied in the area of noise policy ("BRUIT" means noise in French).

During the dialogue with the computer (PC/AT) the responses are fed into a fact base where the juridically relevant elements are recorded, categorized and combined automatically. To do this, BRUITLOG asks questions to determine the characteristics of the town (geographical, juridical, etc.) and how serious the noise is (with respect to qualitative or quantitative criteria).

It then attempts to identify : where the noise is coming from, where the noise is heard, the type of noise produced, the causes, the circumstances.

At the end of the dialogue, BRUITLOG provides the relevant provisions for the described situation in terms of the competence (or not) of the mayor, the range of his powers, the motives and visas that should appear in his decision, and even the timeliness, effectiveness of his decision and the possible alternatives (urbanism).

BRUITLOG has several services at its disposal outside of identifying the situation and looking for a solution : during the dialogue one can interrogate a service of definitions of examples, graphs of position in the tree structure, and jurisprudence for the most complex aspects of the domain.

Finally it is possible to use the base of applicable provisions as a simple documentary file by subject.

BRUITLOG is written in PROLOG II and comprises a knowledge base of about 500 clauses and an inference engine SYSEXPERT. This motor allows, among other things, forward and backward chaining with back-tracking on the terms and the rules, and appropriate reasoning for the jurist's approach.

In the future the system will be connected to an editor which will output a municipal pre-decree with legal mentions (signatures, motives, enactment).

BRUITLOG is a decision support system: it is also an document retrieval support system (direct access to the applicable clause base through identifiers). It is also used as a learning system.

A depth-first backtracking, at both rule level and term level, is integrated to manage alternatives. But the strategy can be completely combinatory with the possible adjunction of metarules. Paths which have been examined are marked in the database (control of reasoning).

The logical operators of SYSEXPERT are and, or (inclusive, exclusive), not (negation), nor (on terms and propositions). The mathematical operators are add, substract, multiply, divided, equal, different, superior, inferior. They allow to process numeric variables which are necessary when evaluating the accoustic inconvenience.

The sytem is fully interactive whether during the creation of the factual base or when consulting the active base. It can handle indecidability and uncertainty during the dialogue.

The clause-editor allows the lawyer to control the writing of clauses in PROLOG, and to modify and update them himself.

4 Future users

- Central administration and local administrature services
- Local governments (mayors, legal and technical services)
- Public or private organisms in charge of hygiene, health, environment, safety (experts).

5 Evaluation and methodological problems

The working out of a decision aided system in the domain of public law had a methodological, theoretical and practical purpose. The first point was the use of the expert system methodology to formalize a field of law which has various legal origins and which is not well structured. We were also interested in finding out the different ways of representing the "open-structured" undetermined concepts and standards (urgent, disturbance, ...)

The conception of such a system allowed the research team to keep on analyzing the decision process (legal cybernetics, decision tables, expert systems) and studying the role of analogy in Artificial Intelligence.

The different problems are met during the following steps : text comprehension, formalisation of knowledge, the communication interface, reasoning simulation.

Text comprehension poses the traditional questions of the analysis and interpretation of texts in law. A text taken at a moment t can be modified, developed in its application at a moment t'. Reading must therefore lead to translating the text into universal rules. Here we refer to the difficulties inherent in analysing texts where the links between passages are implicit or refer to passages dispersed between several authorized sources.

Law is an experimental field for the study of cognitive processes. It is admitted that the goal of law is not only thruth but also justice. This means that although truth is expressed by the answer yes or no in the expression of a proposition, justice is an operational concept that requires taking into consideration and expressing conflicting values and objectives. Rather than repeating the law that such and such an abstract norm is true, the lawyer must immediately find himself in a situation where he must settle conflicts between the general and the specific, the state and the individual, the facts and the law.

Legal questions have no single correct answer. This is why lawyers may not agree on certain difficult questions : the legal text contains the elements necessary for several interpretations (order and disorder in BRUITLOG for example).

Formalisation poses more technical problems : what is the most adequate model for the presentation of knowledge from a given field? Should we use structured semantic networks or production rules?

In BRUITLOG we chose to represent knowledge in the form of rules "if x, then y". But it was necessary to see how one can unse and superimpose propositional logic and predicate logic.

Another cognitive question involves the fact that although legal texts are normative they do not always reflect representations in the form if implicational rules. Thus legal reasoning is based on texts whose elements are not one-dimensional. The technical concepts of law are open-structured concepts, standards whose definition may be changed using meta-rules, or "topoï" not always easily expressed as a universal rule of law. For example, what does a disturbing noise consist of? It is not sufficient to quantify the technical norm, one needs to know what criteria are used by the decider. How can one represent this cognitive parameter, the axiological aspect of every choise? And above all, are these rules valid rules of the law?

One may equally wonder whether all the production rules that a legal expert system needs are simultaneously rules of law. Is there not room for rules of law practice, of law management, which are never expressed as such in the "droit positif"?

Another problem concerns the level of language used in lawyer-machine communication. Should one use the vocabulary of the raw facts or the vocabulary of the legally qualified facts? BRUITLOG has adopted the second solution until the system is capable of interpreting the user's natural language using other software.

As far as reasoning simulation is concerned, one must distinguish reasoning based on the rule of law from reasoning based on logical rules (deduction). Law is an activity that is not mechanically governed but rather guided by rules. Rules are not the end of all activity, they are only the means by which an action is justified. This is a fundamental aspect of administrative law. For example, the mayor's goal is not to apply the law but to settle a conflict opposing order on the one side and individual freedom on the other and to make a valid, adequate, effective decision.

The latest orientation of current work in artificial intelligence and law suggests that the concept of a prototype may be useful in clarifying the classification techniques so valuable to lawyers. Indeed, it has been noted that classification criteria are often independent of lexical categories : in fact the labels only constitute indicators of categorisation activity. It is therefore necessary to know how one can use the work on typicality in order to develop reasoning based on categories.

References

Lettre de l'Intelligence Artificielle no. 1, january 1985.

Bourcier, D. (1985). "About Intelligence in Legal Information Systems", in Computing Power and Legal Reasoning, ed. Ch. Walter, New York : West Publishing.

"BRUITLOG, une banque intelligente sur Micro" in Intelligence Artificielle, Oct. 1985, no. 8.

Bourcier, D. (1986). "Intregration and decision, two new concepts in legal computer science", in Revue française d'administration publique, Jan.-March 1986, no. 37.

Bourcier, D. (1986). "Le droit médiatisé", in Cahiers STS, no. 12, Ordre Juridique, Ordre technologique, Paris : CNRS.

Bourcier, D. (1988). Analyse des standards de la police municipale. Approche décisionnelle, thèse, Paris I.

Bourcier, D. La décision artificielle, Paris : PUF (à paraître).

Fierens-Vialar, V. (1989). Les Systèmes-experts pour les professions juridiques in Lamy Informatique.

Pigeon, D. MILOG, Technical Report, in Revue Telecom, fall 85, no. 65.

Expert Systems in Public Administration
I. Th.M. Snellen, W.B.H.J. van de Donk, J.-P. Baquiast (Eds.)
© Elsevier Science Publishers B.V. (North-Holland), 1989

Chapter 6

Modelling law and legal expert systems

*Roland Traunmüller**

Abstract

Legal regulations have a decisive role in any action in public administration. So every supporting system aimed ad public administrators has as its central point the facility of modeling regulations. A lot of different approaches have been made in addressing this question now with the onset of legal expert systems reaching a climax. So an overview of the subject of modeling law and legal expert systems is given and historical development, present state, problems, and prospects are presented. Based on these findings, integration of legal expert systems in information systems and their use in public administration are considered.

1 New awareness for the subject matter of modeling law

1.1 Modeling law as a matter of broad application

Modeling legal regulations is a subject matter of broad application caused by an almost ubiquitous presence of legal norms in data processing applications of public administrations. Furthermore there is an increasing interest in the theoretical background of formalization of legal regulations

* Department of Computer Science, Johannes Kepler University, Linz, A-4040 Linz-Anhof, Austria

and in the use of computer assisted instruction for teaching law subjects. The issue has recently attracted growing attention through a new interest in expert systems which can be applied in legal professions as well as in public administration.

The new awareness of that subject matter in question has its different drives from supply and demand as well. From the supply side computer science in the meantime is able to provide a lot of sophisticated tools for developing expert systems with reasonable effort. From the user side there is an urgent need for creating more intelligent functions in office information systems.

1.2 Modeling law as a non-trivial problem

Law can be considered as an application of high complexity and interdependence comprising high principles and down to earth facts as well. So modeling law is a complicated task taking into account a lot of peculiarities of the subject in question: vague notions (often on purpose); open-textured notions; rules as well as precedence cases; decisive role of analogy; understanding as a key issue in law ; representation of everyday knowledge. Consequently representing law in legal expert systems is by no means a trivial task.

1.3 Modeling law as a subject of longstanding interest

Applying information technology to law is a subject of longstanding interest dating back as far as 1949. Its focus has shifted with new technological possibilities and user's demand for novel applications. The shift in interest and focus roughly corresponds with the alternations of generations of information processing. Subsequently the following topics have emerged (with corresponding generations given as Roman Numerals):

Implicit Modeling of Regulations (I, II)
Formalization of Legal Regulations (III)
Dedicated Application Packages (III)
Legal Decision Support Systems (IV)
Legal Expert Systems (V)

1.4 Legal Expert Systems in public administration

Further difficulties occur whenever pilot expert systems are transferred to real environments and supposed to operate on every day tasks. Also transferring legal expert systems to the realm of public administration is an audacious enterprise urging particular procedures, ways and precautions. On the other hand there are factors that make public pdministration a promising field for the use of expert systems.

2 Early attempts of modeling regulations

2.1 Implicit representation of legal regulations

There is nearly no application in law and public administration that would not be determined by legal regulations. Nevertheless, regarding the historical course, at the beginning of applying computers to such fields there ws no explicit consciousness of this fact. The legal regulations were only taken in account in an implicit manner.

Jurimetrics
Statistical analyses of law were the first application of computers to law (dating back as early as 1949) performed with computers of the first generation. In jurimetrics norms play a major role, but are only considered implicitly.

Juridical Information Retrieval
A typical application of the second generation of information processing is juridical information retrieval. Although only simple structures are requested as descriptors and their boolean junctions a complex mental model is underlying the search strategy of the user.

Simulation Programs
In most simulations for public administration concerning financial planning and distribution, legal norms were a framework of decisive power.

2.2 Implicit modeling in administrative programs

In the beginning modeling of legal regulations in data processing applications was done in the crude way of straightway programming a piece of legislation. Its aim was to construct working systems without major theoretical ambition. This had been done for a wide range of applications, ranging from tax law to educational allowances.

Legislation with reference to information processing was a further way of implicit modeling and an approach coming from the turning side. The idea that legislators should pay attention to programming by obeying to guidelines when drafting legislation serve as basis for this approach. This idea was proclaimed during the sixties but was never enforced. Nowadays we think that it is the computer which should adapt to the humans and not otherwise. So the whole idea is not en vogue any more. Nevertheless, it must be said that using strict guidelines and adopting some sort of discipline in the drafting process would not be a too bad advice.

2.3 Formalization as an answer to theoretical considerations

The subsequent period of third generation computing was characterized by a hughe qualitative and quantitative growth that lead to a divergent development. On one hand the researchers were looking for a theoretical background and tried to use different stringent formal models (e.g. sets, propositions, graphs, nets) to serve as a basis of formalizing legal regulations. This development has big merits in theoretical understanding the ways and problems of representig law in a stringent way. In the following only sketches are given and reference is made to the literature for details (cf. Fiedler et al, 1984 and Fiedler and Traunmüller, 1986 for an overview).

2.4 Formalization with logical models

Logic and law have a long and rich common history. There were a lot of early attempts to use logic for modeling that recently on the new basis of AI and Prolog find a new revival:

First order predicate logic has been used as a means for juridical reasoning, thus giving a real renaissance for predicate logic as a means for modeling with the use of Prolog now.

Deontic logic was studied extensively and very sophisticated considerations have been made representing deontic logic in programs. In recent years programs representing deontic logic are developed for expert systems.

2.5 Formalization with mathematical models

There was a wide range of mathematical formalisms used. These attempts were interesting, but because of the toy size examples of no practical impact. Nevertheless, it encouraged research in methodological aspects and so eventually have influenced the building of decision support systems (presented in the next section). Typical mathematical models used were:

Set theory was used to solve legal inconsistencies.

Graph theory was used for modeling rules of inheritance.

Net theory was used for modeling sequences of activities as strictly regulated by civil procedures.

2.6 Dedicated application packages for public administration

In third generation information processing formalization was only one topic. In addition, there was a growing interest in improving the large application packages aimed at all major administrative applications. These developments were paramount in quantitative terms making public administration to a giant user of data processing.

All this brought big maintenance problems and so the need for an enhanced structuring of programs with regard to the rules to be modeled arose. Whereas most of the body of the law was still embodied in the programs themselves, the contoures and shapes of the regulations were better seen now. In that way in case of legal alterations maintainabilty was to be secured. There was a large fan of methods and techniques used for getting better structured and better maintainable programs. So in representing the features of the law, diverse methods and techniques were used: decision tables for complex case distinctions; parametrization of values; modularization of tasks; graphical representation for documentation.

In spite of some progress there has remained a shocking misproportion. The hughe amount of legal norms involved could in no way be compared with the rather meager efforts to represent the norms in a sound methodological way. It was the age of the software crises which also struck fully the realm of public administration.

3 Decision Support Systems and Expert Systems in law

3.1 A new pace in methodological progress

The year 1976 saw a fine harvest bringing major progress in the matter of modeling law. Pivotal systems as LEGOL, TAXMAN, ASVG-DEMO, and OECD-CERI were developed. They all set the pace for further progress.

Progress in these fourth generation systems came along in a twofold way: First, these systems were based on sound methodological concepts adapted from different fields of computer science (data bases, artificial intelligence, etc.) to the specific task of modeling regulations. Given the fact that examples of modest real size were modeled, a clear advantage compared to the toy size formalizations with graphs and sets was reached. As a second advantage, the systems developed were aimed at problem solving in support of concrete decision situations. Although some of these systems were created on different occasions and with varying scopes, they can all be summarized under the header of decision support systems and can be seen as forerunners of expert systems.

With seventies going on eighties a new quantum leap occured and fifth generations computing brought a revolution in concepts. Data bases were replaced by knowledge bases and automatic reasoning as well as logical programming became new powerful ways of building systems. Surely, the incoming products were still aimed at decision support, but they got a new label. They were baptized expert systems to show the high level of aspiration.

In the following part some pivotal systems are mentioned. More examples are given throughout this volume and in the literature (e.g. Susskind, 1986; Erdmann et al., 1986; Fiedler, Haft, Traunmüller, 1988).

3.2 Legal decision support systems

LEGOL (Stamper, 1976) was intended as a description lanquage for law and as tool for the systems analyst doing the translation as well. Its formal structure comes from relational data base languages comprising entities and entity definitions. The relational model is augmented by rules and implicit time attributes. So the LEGOL system was especially successfull in cases with pronounced time structures or recursive facts (inheritance decisions and family allowances rspv.).

TAXMAN I (McCarty, 1977) intended to solve a legal problem by means of artificial intelligence problem solvers. This is done by matching different templates in search for common patterns. Although test cases (commercial code taxation liabilty of bonds) were rather small the origin from artificial intelligence rendered TAXMAN the fame of being the most legitimate forerunner of our recent AI-based expert systems.

ASVG-DEMO (Lucas et al., 1979) can be evaluated as a very early example of sophisticated dialog guidance. The system was intended for social security problems and automatically asked for the case in question all missing data in a clarifying dialog.

OECD-CERI was a large project launched by OECD (Paris) and headed by the author (Strigl and Traunmüller, 1974). It was an educational information system at university level based on purely administrative data, such as grades and study regulations. From the text of the study regulations an elaborate translation program was created automatically to evaluate the study progress of the individual student. The resulting objectivated data were used for administrative purposes as well as for planning and counseling.

3.3 Legal expert systems

TAXMAN II (McCarty, 1980) has quite different scope compared to its forerunner TAXMAN I. It has the theoretical ambition to investigate the open texture of dogmatic juridical questions. Through the definitions of prototypes and in operating deformations legal concepts can be evaluated, so providing insight in various levels of the legal abstraction process.

OBLOG II (Gordon and Quirchmayr, 1986) is designed as knowlwedge representation language for legal applications. According to the common structure of regulations based on rules and exeptions the description language contained these concepts as well as subsequent non-monotonic reasoning.

LEX (Haft et al., 1988) is a natural language based expert system. All relevant texts of some significant offences of traffic law are given and handled by linquistic and logic modules, thus enabling a very fine natural language dialog.

The Logic Programming Group at Imperial College has modeled in Prolog the British Nationality Act, so giving a fine example for the use of Prolog in building expert systems. This project is now followed by the DHSS-project which in a much larger volume will model legislation on supplementary benefits (Kowalski and Sergot, 1986).

BRUITLOG is a recent example for expert system aimed at public administration and presented in this volume (chapter 5). It is also an example of current interest and vigorous efforts in France where a goverment agency (French Interministerial committee on computer science and office informatics) is active in promoting expert systems for public administration (chapter 19).

4 Obstacles and prospects for legal expert systems

4.1 Deficiencies of existing legal expert systems

In regarding current legal expert systems severe deficiencies can be located. These deficiencies pertain partly to general shortcomings of present day methods and techniques, partly they are caused by intrinsic difficulties of the subject matter in question.

The part of the reproaches due to the general state of present day expert systems technology comprises shortcomings that occur in pilot projects for other subject matters as well. First of all, critics focus on the fact that the scope of existing expert systems is very small. At present, success is largely determined by the fact that useful applications can be found comprising both, complex structure and a small scope, simultaneously.

4.2 The intrinsic difficulties of the subject matter law

Furtheron there are obstacles pertaining to the intrinsic difficulties of the application field. The reason is that law is a particulary complicated subject matter:

In law understanding is a key issue because the human consciousness of means and ends is an ever underlying assumption. Applying law needs common sense as well as a lot of everyday knowledge, which seem evident even for children, but both are very complicated to represent in computational models.

Law can be viewed as an application of high complexity and interdependence that comprises very common principles as well as very detailed rules. It is necessary to apply these rules to real, factual situations which induces the necessity of additional assumptions for modeling the environment.

Many notions are deliberately open textured (i.e. they are not conclusively defined and comprise possibilities of exemptions) and often vague on purpose. Rules are not the only way expressing norms and precedence cases and analogy play an important role too.

4.3 Prospects for legal expert systems

At first sight, law as a typical expert profession can be regarded as suited for expert systems, but abovementioned points rendered to be major obstacles. So it highly depends on the skill of the person in charge of locating applications if obstacles as mentioned before can be avoided. So in the near future progress may only come bit by bit with intelligent modules in the right portions. This may not be the big bang dreamed of by some computer scientists, but it will surely make acceptance much easier.

4.4 Legal expert systems in public administration

There will be better prospects for applications in Public Administration based on two rerasons One point is the fact that in some way complex tax codes (cf. TAXMAN) may be more suitable than criminal cases solved by first year's law student. The reason is that the tax case belongs to a coherent body of law where it is avoided that within an application reference is made to regulations in other fields of law.

A coherent body of law is a decisive point in finding suitable candidates. If the application does not refer to a coherent body of law systems turn to be very clumsy and complicated. So it will be very difficult to build expert systems for the general lawyer's office. Under these aspects public administration will be a promising candidate for the future progress in legal expert systems.

Second, there are economic reasons in favour of public administration. There is a spread of tasks that cannot be coped with by a mere augmentation of manpower. Also in public administration a particular development will be used in multiple ways for a great many local agencies so that development costs will have a high return. As an additional fact, public administration as a powerful user will always have a good bargaining position.

5 Requirement features for future legal Expert Systems

5.1 Systems for broader areas of legal knowledge

First of all future legal expert systems will have to cover a much broader area than present systems aimed at a very narrow sector of the legal body. So current systems can only answer with a very limited scope. It is that not only the sector of regulations covered has to be enlarged. Moreover it must be possible to reach norms scatterred over different regulations. A broad diversity of documents including different categories have to be included.

5.2 High level description languages for law

Coping with complex features of regulations will need a high level description language. It will be based on common sense categories may be as trivial as space, time, mass and on more complex categories as action, permission, purpose, cause reaching higher concepts as intention, belief and so on. Some of the current research already cited (TAXMAN, OBLOG, LEX, etc.) has already established pivotal elements.

5.3 Advanced forms of integration

Integration has to be performed on different levels: The basic form of integration is the integration with the usual professional problem solving. Interleaved human-computer-problem solving will be necessary and so the use of natural language becomes desireable in a high degree.

As a second step the integration into existing office functions will lead to global office information system. In that way also connection with external sources is provided.

That is why integration of data as well as relying on existing data collections is very important. Furtheron textual data have to be included in the integrated system as well.

Last, but not least norms have to be included in the system, both as texts of the rules and as algorithms whenever necessary.

6 Integrating expert systems in information systems

6.1 The role of expert systems in information systems

Most novelties coming up can be seen in a twofold way as revolutionary events as well as continuity of the existing field. Some researchers coming from artificial intelligence stress the novel way of machine intelligence. To others - as in the case of the author who has been working a quarter of a century in information systems - a more evolutionary attitude is common. They view expert systems as a new method and very powerful technology inheriting fourth generations decision support systems. So the name is neither justified as an impressive label nor by mere desire for novelties. Only the need for better solutions can be accepted as justification.

Consequently, knowledge technology is used when problems exceed the common algorithmic and data base approaches used in information systems technology. In that way always two levels of abstraction - the global information systems and the particular intelligent function - have to be taken into consideration.

6.2 Selfcontained systems vs. embedded modules

When speaking of expert systems selfcontained stand-alone solutions are imagined first. In some mode its an analogy to thinking of science fiction like robots when speaking of robotics. In reality the common way of using expert systems will be building intelligent parts into standard applications.

Very often expert systems will make their success as intelligent modules enhancing common application programs. Therefore intelligent modules are a natural way of application enrichment. This is now already the case for the example of text processing. Here we meet a forced enrichement through the integration of intelligent modules for spelling, hyphenation and stilistic guidance within standard editor programs.

6.3 Organizational solution and appropriate hardware

Expert systems on mainframes was the solution as in earlier days the computing power necessary for artificial intelligence algorithms was only available on mainframes. But now in choosing the appropriate hardware organizational considerations will prevail: That is why mainframe solutions are considered only when centralization is to be enforced on specific grounds as organizational constraints, availability of data or security reasons.

Expert systems on workstations is the normal situation for developing, but too expensive for applications.

Expert systems on PC is desirable for economic reasons with the consequence that development is performed on workstation with following downgrading of the operative software to PC level.

7 Expert systems in information systems for public administration

7.1 Information systems in the realm of public administration

A priori the procedure of designing an information system should not depend on the nature of the information system in question. Consequently, the scientific discipline of information systems has developed methods and tools to provide support in building information sytems in a sound way. Nevertheless there are features peculiar for the realm of public administration that have to be taken into account (cf. Reinermann et al., 1988)

7.2 Expert systems as part of information systems

As discussed before two levels of abstraction have to be regarded. On the global level expert systems are part of an integral information system and have to be designed according to the specific methods of the discipline (e.g. Olle et al., 1988). On the other hand expert systems have very specific features that are best solved with specialized methods, techniques, and tools. So expert systems and intelligent modules have to be designed and constructed with regard to the appropriate technology of knowledge engineering (e.g. Kowalski, 1979).

7.3 Implementing expert systems in public administrations

Compared with design, implementation is generally underestimated in resources and importance. It is a hell of work to fill the empty knowledge base with rules and to combine them with the factual data. It is a still greater effort to test the filled rule base and get rid of all inconsistencies and flaws. Not supported by full endorsement and heavy cooperation from the prospective users the task will fail.

Public administration is a case sui generis where some problems are further aggravated due to particular features of public administration. Some of them are:

Expert systems have to be properly integrated in the overall organizational flow of tasks.

Organizational complexity and bureaurocratic attitude advice very cautious procedures of implementation.

It is necessary to have expert systems filled and maintained centrally that afterwards work decentrally in various copies on different sites.

So parts of rules or of the factual data have to be adapted to the particular site. Also in case of changes to the legal norms sophisticated procedures are to be established.

References

Erdmann, U., Fiedler, H., Haft, F., Traunmüller, R. (1986). *Computergestützte Juristische Expertensysteme*. Tübingen: Attempto.

Fiedler, H., Barthel, T., Voogd, G. (1984). Untersuchungen zur Formalisierung im Recht (UFORED). Opladen : *Forschungsbericht Land Nordrhein-Westfalen.*

Fiedler, H., Traunmüller, R. (Ed.) (1986). *Formalisierung im Recht und Ansätze juristischer Expertensysteme*. München: Schweitzer.

Fiedler, H., Haft, F., Traunmüller, R. (Ed.) (1988). Expert Systems in Law. Tübingen: Attempto.

Haft, F., Jones, R., Wetter, T. (1988). A Natural Language Based Legal Expert System for Consulting and Tutoring - The Lex Project. in: *Fiedler/ Haft/ Traunmüller* (1988). Tübingen: Attempto.

Kowalski, R. A. (1979). *Logic for Problemsolving*. New York: Elsevier.

Kowalski, R. A., Sergot, M. (1986). A Logic-based Calculus of Events. *New Generation Computing*, Volume 4, pp 67-95. New York: Springer.

Lucas, P., Izbicki, H., Kalod, G. (1979). *ASVG-DEMO: An Experiment in Application Programming*. TR 25.148. Wien: IBM Laboratory Vienna.

McCarty, L.T. (1977). Reflexions on TAXMAN: An Experiment in Artificial Intelligence and Legal Reasoning. *Harvard Law Revue* 90, pp 837-893.

McCarty, L.T. (1980). Some Requirements for a Computer-Based Legal Consultant. *LRP-TR8*. New Jersey: Rutgers University.

Gordon, T., Quirchmayr, G. (1986). OBLOG - eine Programmiersprache fr juristische Expertensysteme. in: *Erdmann/ Fiedler/ Haft/ Traunmüller* (1986). Tübingen: Attempto.

Olle, T.W., Hagelstein, J., McDonald, I., Rolland, C., Sol, H., Van Assche, F., Verrijn-Stuart, A.A. (1988). *Information Systems Methodologies - A Framework for Understanding*. Wokingham: Addison-Wesley.

Reinermann, H., Fiedler, H., Grimmer, K., Lenk, K. und Traunmüller, R. (Ed.) (1988). *Neue Informationstechniken - Neue Verwaltungsstrukturen?* Heidelberg: Decker-Müller.

Stamper, R. (1976). The LEGOL-1 prototype system and language. *The Computer Journal* Volume 20, p105ff.

Strigl, K., Traunmüller, R. (1974). *Measuring Student Success: A Systematical Statistical Analysis*. Paris: OECD.

Susskind, R. (1987). *Expert Systems in Law*. Oxford: Oxford University Press.

Expert Systems in Public Administration
I.Th.M. Snellen, W.B.H.J. van de Donk, J.-P. Baquiast (Eds.)
© Elsevier Science Publishers B.V. (North-Holland), 1989

Chapter 7

Expert systems and future tax administration

*Jorma Kuopus**

Abstract

Despite the technological complexity involved, the utilization of Expert Systems is spreading through the administrative machinery. As with the earlier stages of administrative automation, the large mass administration is acting as a pioneer in developing sophisticated software. But simultaneously, private software producers are expanding the factual scope of computerized public administration.

The article deals with the societal changes brought about by the newest, emerging software technology and, especially in taxation, by fiscal expert systems. Comparative material from Finland, Sweden, the Federal Republic of Germany and the United States of America offers a basis to sketch a possible trend of tax technology development. The threat of a possible paradigm shift away from the Rule of Law introduced in the field of taxation by the Magna Charta (1215) is discussed.

1 Introduction

This article is based on my jurisprudential doctoral studies during 1983-1988. In May 1988 I defended my thesis "The Rule of Law and Computerized Administration of Taxation" at the Helsinki University Law Faculty[1]. Artificial Intelligence and Expert Systems, as its emerging branche form an essential part of my doctoral scrutiny.

---

* Office of the parliamentary Ombudsman,
00102 Eduskunta, Helsinky, Finland

The societal and in particular the legal impact of the computerization process within the realm of public administration - especially in the social security system - has recently been subjected to critical analysis by various scholars[2]. As an example of computerized mass administration I have chosen the tax administrations of Finland, Sweden, the Federal Republic of Germany and the United States of America.

Administrative automation only covers some 10 percent of all legal studies in the business-oriented research field of Computer Law. However, in the respective German literature the scope of Administrative Informatics ("Verwaltungs-informatik") is reasonably wide enough to cover the growing administrative automation and its societal implications.

Despite the terminological vagueness, it seems reasonable to equate Administrative Automation with *Mass Administration.* The latter concept, "Massenverwaltung" in Weberian rationalization jargon[3], is used in many situations and by researchers of different scientific orientation. In a wide sense, mass administration has been considered (e.g. by the CDCJ Committee of the Council of Europe in May 1987) to involve, on the one hand, the dispersal of results or negative effects of administrative activity or mass production (e.g. nuclear power plants) simultaneously over wide sectors of interest. On the other hand, it covers the actual proceedings by authorities, in which a large number of similar albeit separate administrative decisions are produced over a limited period of time. In my nomenclature, which is rooted in Administrative and Information Law, "Mass Administration" includes the last-mentioned aspect - the computerized, "assembly-line type" production of similar, simultaneous administrative routine decisions, involving different subjects of administrative action.

Since its conception by Marvin Minsky et consortium, the *concept of expert systems* tends to be relatively vague. There are at least three functional *types of legal expert systems:* 1) "job aids" systems featuring AI, 2) consulting i.e. apprentice systems (DSS) or 3) human decision making imitating true expert tools (intelligent utility)[4]. Furthermore, the definitions vary. Also grouping of expert systems can be made as follows: case management, monitoring, legal interpretation/ prediction (such as Expert Tax System), and document generation[5]. Much of the available literature on expert systems and knowledge elicitation presumes an academic or working knowledge of artificial intelligence, employing terminology that is often unintelligible for potential commercial and administrative users of information technology. Managers in public administration should be able to evaluate the performance and the limitations of the information technology in order to create a citizen-oriented administrative service culture. Consequently, I will not make a sharp disdinction between different systems because of their functional variety and the modular and shell developments within AI technology.

The emergence of *fiscal expert systems* is connected with this rationalizing development and has significant additional functional aspects as well. So far, they have merely been evaluated as administrative machinery tools such as instruments for government tax policy analysis, but not within the context of taxpayer - administration relations. The tax administrations of many countries have future plans on expert systems for the 1990's, but the actual development of expert systems is for the time being implemented by private auditors and accountants (tax packaged software)[6]. My aim is not only to discuss the present status of expert systems applications, but also to challenge the final aims of such systems and their societal consequences. The proliferation of legal expert systems in governmental administration such as taxation may have the effect of dehumanizing the decision making process.

2 Computerization of the administrative decision

Governmental computerization may be viewed as a rationalization process, a branch of the western rationalistic tradition. The development of information technology goes through various stages, which can be described in terms of 1) software/hardware (device) 2) human participation 3) organizational process and 4) "output" i.e. performance. We are here especially interested in the organizational and functional aspect, i.e. the actors involved.

Types of Decision	*Traditional*	*Modern*
Programmed: routine repetitive decisions	- Habit - Clerical routine - Organization structure	- Computers - Management science
Non-programmed: one-shot, ill structured novel, policy decision	Judgement Intuition Creativity Rules-of-thumb	Heuristic Interactive computers Artificial intelligence

Figure 1: Decision making techniques

Even within computer science, computerization has primarily been studied from an administrative point of view. The "deontic" application of legal rules within the environment of modern public administration may be classified as follows, see figure 1[7].

The substantial *differences between human cognition and computerized performance* [8] have caused many adjustments: factory-line type production of administrative decisions vs. individual scrutiny of cases; programmed interpretation of norms vs. human discretion; ADP-appropriate legislation vs. case-specific individual norms; co-operation within Information Systems Management vs. scrutiny made by an individual decision-maker; compilation of relevant events by means of ADP-blanks vs. human interaction between citizen and civil servant etc.

The list could be continued, but the essential feature is clear: mass production and decision support systems (DSS) have created pressures on both fact estimation and rule formulation. At the present stage of computerization there is a mutual adjustment process going on at both sides of the "barrier" - between the automated mass production of administrative performances on the one hand and traditional lawyer-type scrutiny on the other hand. However, the information administration based on ADP-architectures (data, information system, telecommunications and device layers) is not capable to cope with societal demands for structuring of the new technology. In addition, the lack of legal experience in programming and information systems design may explain the low degree of legal normativity of data processing architecture patterns. In my view, the sectoral concept of Data Protection emerging in the 1970s is only the first step on the way to a well-structured information society. Thus, the Data Protection is one part of the effort needed to organize data flows, information systems architectures and the information structure of public administration.

3 Diffusion of fiscal expert systems

A contemporary feature of present-day public administration is the spread of information technology and Intelligent Knowledge-based Systems (IKBS) to the field of practical applications. This new technology per se, together with software development offers new opportunities for the utilization of information industry commodities and the solving of knowledge-based problems. Finnish public administration at both municipal and state level can rely on the support of business firms with a keen interest and R&D-knowhow in expert systems.

The rapid progress of information technology cannot be explained on purely theoretical grounds. *Practical cases* and concrete instances of the application software are called for. One such an example is the system designed by the Technical Research Center of Finland for the National Board of Housing on the basis of the "GURU"™ commercial expert system package. This "AATU" (Adam) system enables local authorities to evaluate applications for housing allowance, and assist them in making housing allowance decisions. This modularly C and assembler designed application software was put on the market for the use of Finnish local authorities in July 1988 at a housing fair. Preliminary trial results in the communes of Vantaa, Nurmijärvi and Järvenpää show that the calculation of housing allowance is made quicker and with no "bugs" when the basic data is correct. The calculation of the housing allowance has become quicker. The most significant change has been that even inexperienced or "deskilled" civil servants have been able to give advice and make decisions on housing allowance. As an advertisement for expert system shells states: "Expert systems are a revolution in the re-use and communication of undocumented, vulnerable expertise and know-how which has important benefits for real business practice. Don't rely on feelings!" However, this slogan might cause many disputes with regard to legal normativity involved. Figure 2 gives an outline of the system structure:

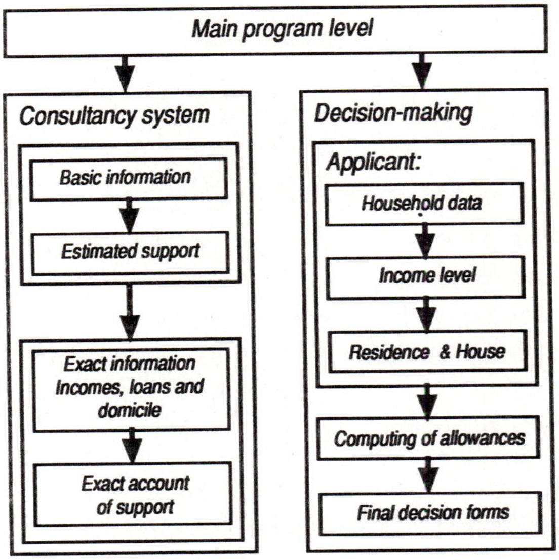

Figure 2: The outline of a system structure

Several Finnish PC-based application software products have been created using the English XiPlus™ expert system environment - a second generation development tool - e.g. for bank loan estimation (inter alia "MATIAS" used by OKO Bank for estimating farming loans). In the words of an expert, a human decision maker can remember only some 100-200 applicable rules, whereas an estate or farming loan decision involves more than 2 000 intrinsic rules applying simultaneously. The profit motive is central in this field. In the future, the third generation of development tools with graphics generating, hyper-text databases, object-oriented languages, customer-oriented tailored microchips, wafer scale integration etc. are due to rush the design of expert system applications. A norm-based thesaurus describing the legal domain in a way which will make it easy for a lawyer to identify what part of the domain is relevant for his or her problem, and accessing the text retrieval system through this structure, or through hypertext, is expected to revolutionize the legal profession[9].

One brand-new software knowledge application produced by Finnish Nokia Data together with the National Board of Taxation is of special interest to the present topic. The tax administration has tried this prototype since Fall 1988. This rule-based system is generated on 50 rules and applies to inheritance tax assessment. The system will assist in the assessment of individual shareholders of death estates and in evaluation of inheritance values. The application software will also be helpful when an estate is situated in different countries (e.g. 60 per cent of stocks in Sweden and 40 in Finland). The potential key areas of fiscal interest might be taxation of real estates, forestry/agriculture and international business transactions. However, the spread of expert systems has so far not been subject to strict normative guidance of the Ministry of Finance nor has - despite the in 1988 launched large FINNSOFT -effort - the Finnish Technology Development Center issued any written overviews or cost-benefit estimations of expert systems in use.

The general idea of expert systems in taxation is that the utilization of such systems is confined to the taxation administration itself. This narrow view is probably reflected in the range of connected legal problems identified. Figure 1 above gives some background on administrative automation within organizations and their connections. An additional aspect appears when we combine the administrative organization, in this case the tax administration, with information systems users and interest groups.

There are many reasons for the growing use of computerized applications and especially of *expert systems particularly in the field of taxation:* [10]

- taxation is based on monetary performances, like Electronic Funds Transfer (cf. in the international respect the SWIFT) and computable values
- tax legislation is already clearly distinct and its internal conception is artificial (clear taxonomy, e.g. avoir fiscal)[11]
- the fiscal area is fully regulated, even overregulated

- administrative actions follow yearly repetitive, legally programmed routines
- there are standardized information forms and growingdata bases of tax administration and private organizations
- the administration must be rational and cost-effective
- the tax system has an endogenic tendency to combine the levying of different kinds of taxes (one single Master File for each taxpayer) and finally,
- many of the straightforward accounting functions, such as payroll, in organizations have been computerized for the last twenty years.

4 A scenario for the emerging tax administration

In the general business practice, the information system's host treats his system as an economically profit-generating investment. With regard to administrative automation private citizens, business firms, private taxpreparers and banks are all users of the public computerized information system in large. E.g. the Finnish tax advisers use a standard return form of the Inland Revenue or tax administration compiled in their spreadsheet tax calculation software, such as Symphony™.

At the conceptual level, it is possible to evaluate the "driving forces" of Information Technology at external output or organization, or internal, physical computing level. Simultaneously, the development *within computer science* offers a rough theoretical basis for a comprehensive evaluation. The multidisciplinary field of "Information Systems" is concerned with the development and use of computerized information systems as well as their impact on the individual, on society as a whole and on organizations. Within the microcosms of AI area there is a phenomenon labelled "Distributed Artificial Intelligence" by R.G. Smith (Stanford Ph.D. doctoral thesis, USA 1978). ADP specialists are speaking not only about neural computers and Knowledge Engineering but also at the field of DAI about "Contract Net Frameworks", which at least raises curiosity[12] with a legal inspector who happens to be outstanding. Consequently, it might not be misleading to expect that Information Technology will create combined networks of various organisations and telematics also in the IKBS-area. Single computers and terminals will be linking not only their numeral raw data but more widely their expert knowledge: "a network (VAN/ISDN) is an enterprise", as the saying goes.

One example of state-of-the-art tax applications is the Danish *"ST-Tele-Tax"* on-line fiscal system where private taxpreparers use a tax calculation system designed by the tax administration itself. The prototype was produced in spring 1987. The complexities introduced by the reform of the Danish tax system in 1986 focused the authorities' attention on the need for at least one functional, although in practice incomplete, system for the preparation of tax returns and filling in of forms. The computerized information systems were required to be compatible, guiding and - by means of an intelligent interface - operator-friendly. Private citizens and business organizations use the tailored software of the tax administration itself. The private sector is typically short of own expertise in tax law, but still using high-level applications of computing.

In Sweden, on the other hand, legal constitutional problems arose when the National Tax Board (Riksskatteverket) expanded its use of information systems inside private organizations and tried to audit ADP-supported, standardized accounting. The U.S. fashion of the Internal Revenue Service is to audit electronic bookkeeping documents by portable microcomputers and auditing software. In Sweden, the problem was solved through some specific amendments to the tax law (see Reg.prop. 1987/88:65 and Swedish Legal Code SFS 1987:1228-1232). However, new problems are bound to arise when public authorities use for their electronic auditing private software protected by copyright: public and private interests will come into conflict with each other.

The U.S. tax technology also includes paperless information processing, optical scanners, electronic funds transfer, high level program generators, audio response systems for the handling of managerial and inquiry problems, satellite communications and CD-ROM archives (FAISR)[13]. Expert systems, besides being a major technological source of legal problems, are an important factor in the informatization in public administration.

To give a general idea of the changes taking place in taxation, one could mention the U.S. trend towards electronic filing, bound to increase especially in the 1990s. As a result of automated tax processes, rationalized tax administration refrains from the use of *signed tax documents* and urges private tax consultants and taxpayers alike to "scratch paper" without limiting the use of paper forms (form 8453)[14]. The Internal Revenue Service from time to time puts the professional taxpreparers to test in order to assure that they have sufficient skills in electronic filing. Successful candidates submit the test to the I.R.S., it will send them an acceptance letter - "*their 'driver' licence for the fiscal network*" - and, ultimately, a password for the use of the information system at the main roads of Information Society. Under the present conditions, it is easy to write a simple tax calculation program on BASIC, and, commercial software products featuring AI are available for the use in tax assessment[15].

In the U.S., it is the taxpayer and not the tax authorities who runs the tax system and prepares his own public services by means of his own information systems. Tax administration only supervises and makes sample audits of the processes of a computerized society. In the U.S., an essential part of the Self-Assessment tax system since the 1960s has been the mechanical validity check of tax returns by means of a statistical Discriminant Function System (DIF): only some 2 to 3 percent of all annual tax returns are audited manually. The prominent U.S. Tax Reform of 1986 has initiated reforms in many European countries and in other OECD member countries. Through this reform we are getting not only beneficial and simplifying amendments of the tax legislation but we are also sliding - in the name of the official service-culture - towards business-like, computerized tax routines which are hard to combine with the traditions of public administration.

I wish to stress that the design of a societal infrastructure based on an information technology, which in this case is dominated by the United States, may also bring *intrinsic and underlying managerial ideas* to bear on the structure of Information Management and Public Administration. As the constraining normative structure at various levels is expected, e.g. because of unwillingness to make stringent regulations for telecommunications, also to remain weak, one may presume that with time, new technologies will develop into extensive networks, which remould and consolidate managerial business ideas as well as their own administrative structures. Imported technologies linked to telematics networks and supposed to adapt to changes in management will to a large extent shape the management of public administration into their own ramifications. European public administration - at least in the Scandinavian perspective - was as late as the 1980's - despite its limited economic resources citizen- and service-oriented rather than extensively cost-effective in the managerial sense.

5 Conclusions: From the Rule of Law to the Rule of Technique

The Administrative Law of many European welfare states is still essentially based on the ideas of the human implementation, manual procedures and age-old legal traditions developed within the framework of the Rule of Law. The legal atmosphere is undergoing substantial change in the emerging information societies. Consequently, where does this leave the traditional German "Rechtsstaat" model? The familiar elements of our present-day administrative normativity are, since the days of Otto Mayer, Walter Jellinek, and Ernst Forsthoff, the civil servant's legally regulated responsibility and the Rule of Law. This is the very statutory basis of the traditional citizen-orientation, of the citizen's legal safeguards.

On the basis of my professional and study experience it seems to me that information society is bound to forge ahead out of reach of any sufficient regulation and control. There are two leading reasons for this situation: firstly, the lag of top administrative managers in information technology knowledge and secondly, the general unwillingness of IT designers to mould their structures in a normative form. Consequently, this development should serve as a fresh impulse for some legal conclusions. The traditional, legally ruled governmental body operates by the Rule of Law. In my view, the real importance of governmental normativity in large might well diminish under the system of self-assessment in taxation. Modern public administration will grow less transparent, when the instrinsic supervisibility of Information Systems is getting more and more separated from the traditional administrative organization and its legal protection system. The constitutional equality between *citizens* before the law may also be endangered by economical inequality. The poor and unskilled are not able to utilize sophisticated computer systems or hire tax consulting professionals to handle growing needs for electronic filing[16]. Not even well-to-do taxpayer are accorded individual tax treatment (in Finland more than 93 % of private tax cases are processed by means of computerized, simple, form- and database-oriented assembly-line routines). In spite of these inevitable realities, the *traditional legal safeguards including citizen-asserted remedies* are still basically constructed to deal ex post with correction of individually implemented decisions - not to cope with masses of computerized cases or with technical utility structures.

The impact of information technology on the *civil servants* of the tax administration is two-fold: 1) the need for centrally guided fiscal networks will probably reduce the independence of street-level-bureaucrats 2) the factual importance of lay-men boards will be reduced. The reasons for the first tendency are many: growing mechanical auditing based on AI technology, direct and indirect taxation by computers[17], need to create computer networks and compatibility for centralized information systems. The computerized but still incredulous tax administration tends to rely more on its various prerecorded tax data bases and statistical average business information material than on individually delivered taxpayer information (tax returns). The ambition for the assessment work is to focus - also by means of fiscal expert systems - on the most interesting taxpayers. The second tendency is greatly enhanced by the growing discontent with the inconsistencies of local taxation -a computerized tax office would bring about uniform, tax practice, even though without any case specific features. Simultaneously, as expert systems become increasingly sophisticated, computers will participate in an interactive decision making process of taxation.

To all appearances, in many European countries[18] taxpayers or their representatives will - despite restrictive but sectoral Data Protection - get more and more involved in electronic filing and surveillance of tax evaders. Consequently, the supervision of legality and the part of normativity will diminish and get watered down through a situation involving a lax normative structure of managerial information administration. Private ADP-experts hired by computerized tax administrations will strengthen this tendency. The market for ADP-experts is thus indirectly responsible for the injury inflicted to the legal position of individual citizens in their capacity as customers of the computerized public administration.

Are there in the end any legal constraints ("Rahmenbedingungen")[19] acting to *control the developing system of computerized taxation?* The Rule of Law, being created within the framework of the eighteenth century, will possibly be abolished and relegated to the role predecessor of future methods of fancy software technology, network protocols and Information Systems Management. A rational and predictable enforcement of modern exhaustive legislation will need not only the Separation of Powers but also a balancing of the distribution of advantages of the sophisticated information technology among the taxpaying citizenry.

Expert systems are designed to capture the knowledge and decision-making capabilities of experts and make this knowledge available to others in organizations. They may also lead to rationalization of overlapping administrative routines and to greater transparency of legal rules through forward- and backward-chaining implementation. Developmental trends indicate the possibilities of a more or less totally automated process from the taxable event to the final payment of taxes. My message and caveat is however: Expert systems must be viewed as an important stage of fiscal technology which indirectly changes the patterns of processing taxation information and the levying of tax. I thus envisage a future where expert systems through their intrinsic determinism will bring about - both in the material and the procedural sense - a gradual alteration of *the total tax system design,* which according to the democratic standards should be a matter of a political, multifaceted controversy and decision-making[20].

References

Campbell, D./Connor, S. (1986). On The Record - Surveillance, Computers & Privacy. The Inside Story. London: Michael Duncan.

Hamfelt, Andreas/Wahlgren, Peter (1988). Datorstödda beslut - Artificiell intelligens och juridik. Stockholm: IRI/University of Stockholm.

Kravitz, Janet (1987). The IRS's Computer Generated Assessments and Notices - Are They Valid? Capital University Law Review 16/87, pp. 87-104.

Kuhlmann, Stefan (1986). Formalisierung des Handelns öffentlicher Verwaltungen am Beispiel der Interaktionen von Verwaltung und Bürger. Kassel: Gesamthochschule Kassel.

Kuopus, Jorma (1988). *Hallinnon lainalaisuus ja automatisoitu verohallinto.* Jyväskylä: Finnish Lawyers Publishing Company.

Kübler, Hartmut (1987). *Informationstechnik in Verwaltungsorganisationen. Einsatzbedingungen, Chancen and Risiken.* Stuttgart: Kohlhammer.

Magnusson, Cecilia (1988). *Kunskapsteknik och juridik i offentlig förvaltning.* Stockholm: Statskontoret, Report 1988:11.

Magnusson, Cecilia/Torvund, Olav (Eds. 1988). *Myndighetsdata och rättssäkerhet.* Lund: Norstedts förlag.

Moran, Dick (1988): *The Tax Man Calleth.* UNISYS/Solutions March/April 1988 pp. 8-9.

Phillips, Lothar (1986). Rechtsmodule. *Computer und Recht* 2/1986, pp. 113-115.

Quinlan, J. Ross (Ed. 1987): *Applications of Expert Systems.* Reading: Addision-Wesley Publishing Company.

Riksskatteverket (1988). *Skatteförvaltningens ADB-strategi inför 90-talet.* Stockholm: Riksskatteverket, Report 1988:4.

Schartum, Dag Wiese (1987). *The Introduction of Computers in the Norwegian Local Insurance Offices, Corepoints and Context.* Oslo: Universitetsforlaget.

Susskind, Richard (1987). *Expert Systems in Law.* Oxford: Clarendon Press.

Svensson, Carl-Göran (IFA Congress 1988). National Report of Sweden. International Fiscal Association Congress, Amsterdam 1988. *Seminar A, Data Processing in Taxation. Background Information.* Amsterdam: IFA.

Tomeski, A./Lazarus, H./Sadek, K. (1983). *People-oriented computer systems. The computer in transition.* Florida: Malabar.

Weber, Max (1928, 1985). *Wirtschaft und Gesellschaft.* Tübingen: C.B.J. Mohr Verlag.

Winograd, Terry/Flores, Fernando (1987). *Understanding Computers and Cognition.* Reading: Addison-Wesley Publishing Company.

Notes:

1. See in detail Kuopus (1988) with an English Summary. In addition, see an article “Förvaltningsautomation i skatteväsendet -exempel från Finland, Sverige, Tyskland och USA” in The 5th Nordic Annual Yearbook of Legal Informatics (Magnusson/Torvund 1988: 81 pp.)
2. See at the doctoral level inter alia Kuhlmann (1986), Schartum (1987) and Magnusson (Statskontoret rapport 1988:11). The British Alvey-project also includes a part DHSS-Demonstrator Project centered on IKBS (e.g. “policy drafting”).
3. Cf. Weber (1985:128).
4. Cf. e.g. Winograd/Flores (1987:151-153), Quinlan (Ed. 1987:23) and Hamfelt/Wahlgren (IRI-rapport 1988:12-16).
5. See in detail Waterman, Donald A./Paul, Jody/Peterson, Mark: Expert Systems for Legal Decision Making in Quinlan (Ed. 1987:43-44).
6. Cf. the Swedish Report Riksskatteverket (RSV Rapport 1988:4, pp. 25-26). (IRI-rapport 1988:12-16).
7. See the figure by Tomeski/Lazarus/Sadek (1983:177).
8. See in detail Winograd/Flores (1985: 12-13).
9. A such system for legal information retrieval is studied at the Oslo University/NRCCL within the Norwegian research effort “F*KUS”.
10. See also Susskind (1987:50-53).
11. For the legal informatics discussion on the topic of Mechanical Jurisprudence (since Roscoe Pound) and the use of normative modules based on the use of Expert System Toolkits, see inter alia Phillips (Computer und Recht 2/1986:113-115).
12. Cf. e.g. Tom J. Schwartz in AIWEEK March 1, 1988, pp. 3 and 9 on commercial neural nets.
13. See e.g. The Journal of Taxation 1/1985, p. 7.

14. See e.g. Moran (UNISYS/Solutions 1988:8-9). Cf. Kravitz (Capital University Law Review 16/87:103-104).
15. I refer to the Tax Advisor (U.S./Canadian) as well as IRS Interest & Penalties Calculator, CPAid's Tax Planner, Estate Plan Analyzer, PerTAX and Tax Calender developed in the USA; For more detail see The Tax Executive July 1981, pp. 314-325, Taxation (GB), 22 of February 1986 pp. 410-412, Attorneys Computer Report September 1987 pp. 10, idem. May 1988 p. 8 and idem. June 1988 p. 9. We are able to base our argument on the analysis of practical applications and not only on the theoretical TAXMAN I and II prototypes (corporate tax problems) developed by L. Thorne McCarty at the end of 1970s.
16. See also Svensson (IFA Congress, Amsterdam 1988:14-15). Information Systems in the Tax Administration will also be the subject of the 23rd CIAT (Inter-America Center of Tax Administators) General Assembly (10-14 April, 1989, Montevideo, Uruguay).
17. Operating systems for collection of traffic tolls exist in Norway (Bergen and Ålesund) and plans for a similar system were discussed in last spring in Helsinki. The systems are based on detectors, computerized intelligent systems, EFTS, television supervising, moment-by-moment assessment of debit balance and lack of human interaction. There are European Community plans for the computerized taxation for heavy traffic (see the document of the Council COM (86) 750 on Vehicle Taxes, Fuel Taxes and Road Tolls, Brussels December 1987). There is in Sweden a computerized system for the taxation of professional vehicles (trafikskattelagen); c.f. Campbell/Connor (1986: pp. 190-196) and the spatial INMARSAT/STANDARD-C satellite communications system to prevent thefts of heavy vehicles on international routes.
18. Cf. the German Steuerberater-organization and their computerized services (Fern-Kolleg, LexINFORM and since 1971 DATEV e.G.).
19. See e.g. Kübler (1987: pp. 19-20).
20. A project at the Sloan School of Management of the Massachusetts Institute of Technology ("MITs Management in 1990s") started in 1985 and sponsored inter alia by the I.R.S. is working on the task of drafting and planning tax technology of the next decade. Within the IRS the National Office for Data Processing (!) is making plans for the Future Tax System Redesign; see Internal Revenue Service Strategic Plan, Document 6941 (5-84), Washington D.C. pp. 161-166 and the IRS: The 1985 Annual Report, Washington D.C. 3-86 p. 86.

Expert Systems in Public Administration
I. Th.M. Snellen, W.B.H.J. van de Donk, J.-P. Baquiast (Eds.)
© Elsevier Science Publishers B.V. (North-Holland), 1989

Chapter 8

Computer-assisted systems for public administration: Impact on legal decision processes[1]

*Jon Bing**

1 Introduction: The Norwegian System for Housing Aid

To introduce some of the issues discussed in this chapter, the Norwegian system for housing aid may serve as a reference[2]. This system was introduced in the early '70ies by a plenary decision in parliament[3]. Its objective is to give certain households, qualified by the plenary decision, a supplementary benefit which corresponds to a fraction of the difference between what - in the language of the decision - are "real" and "reasonable" housing costs.

The scheme was conceived and realized to be implemented by a computerized system. The subsidiary legislation broke down the rather general language of the plenary decision, until a highly computerized system was realized, where almost all activities necessary to decide an application were executed by the system.

Somewhat simplified, the system is initiated by an applicant, who identifies himself or herself by the personal identification number (PIN)[4]. Using the PIN, the system accesses the central population register, which - according to the underlying rules - should be current within 8 weeks. Identifying the applicant, the system determines who else is registered as inhabiting the same housing unit as the applicant. These persons are known as a "household" to the system. Due to the construction of the PIN, this also give the

* Norwegian Research Center for Computers and Law, University of Oslo, Niels Juelsgate 16, N-0272 Oslo 2, Norway

system information concerning the the age of the different members of the household, information utilized in determining whether the household qualifies for housing aid.

Carrying the identifications of the members of the household, the system accesses the files of the central tax authority, retrieving income figures for all members of the household. The sum of income for all the members is the income of the household. Also carrying the identification of the members of the household, the system will access the files of the National Insurance Institution, and determine their individual status with respect to a range of welfare schemes.

The system returns with this information to its home base at the state housing bank, which operates the system. Based on information concerning the age of the housing unit, its location with respect to the center of a town, interest of bank loans etc., the final calculation takes place.

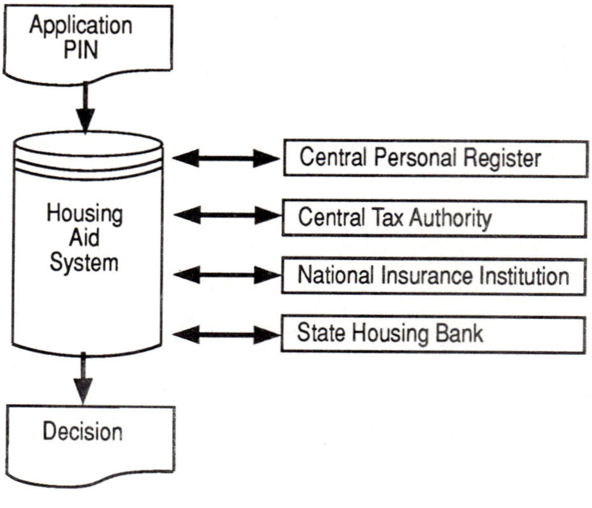

Figure 1: Simplified outline of the Norwegian Housing Aid System

One will remember that the language of the underlying plenary decision implied that "real" housing costs should be taken into consideration. In fact the system uses the information mentioned above to calculate the average or typical cost of the housing unit in question - no determination of actual costs takes place. Similarly, the plenary decision indicates the "reasonable" housing costs as another decisive criterion. This would seem to imply an expert judgement[5], but this is also calculated, using the same data as for calculating "real" costs, but taking properties of the household into account.

On this basis, the final decision is computed. If the application is denied, the system will write out a form letter, specifying the reason for not awarding housing aid. If the applicant qualifies for housing aid, the system will print out a postal cheque, which is mailed to the applicant.

This system decides approximately 100,000 applications every 6 months. An application is retained in the system until explicitly withdrawn. In a country of 4 million inhabitants, it is a major example of a mass administrative system which could not have been realized without computers.

As discussed below, such systems have several properties of interest to lawyers. The discussion may indicate a critical attitude to such systems. It may therefore be prudent at the very outset to state that it is my belief that such systems are necessary for mass administrative solutions. We need, however, to improve our understanding of their qualities in legal terms in order to secure that they are designed to maintain and strengthen our conventional ideals associated with due process and the rule of law.

One will notice, that such a system is quite similar to an expert system. The ad hoc process of representing the rules contained in the relevant legal instruments for the housing aid system, will in an expert system be replaced by the systematic knowledge acquisition, where a knowledge engineer cooperates with experts.The datafiles of the different governmental institutions will in an expert system correspond to a knowledge base. The ad hoc rule representation in the housing aid system, will correspond to the inference mechanism of an expert system. And the communication with the housing aid system corresponds to the dialog module of an expert system. This correspondence has considerable interest in principle. It demonstrates that many of the problems today perceived in the design of artificial intelligence systems for legal domains are not theoretical issues, but are very much part of a modern public administration. It also demonstrates that research in legal expert systems is urgent in order to achieve the necessary insight to adequately apply computerized systems to legal domains.

2 From language to programs

To construct a system like the system for housing aid, the system designers have to study the relevant legal instruments written in natural language. Based on this material, and possibly on supplementary discussions with experts, they must arrive at an understanding of the rule[6] structure of the legal domain in question.

Converting the representation of rules to a programming language will raise several issues relevant for this paper. The basic representation of a rule is a "IF ... THEN ..." statement. The antecedent will contain one criterion, or a set of criteria joined by conjunctive or disjunctive operators, or negations. We will presume that all normative structures may be represented as such statements at some level of complexity.

2.1 Syntactical ambiguity

Natural language has several features which make the meaning more or less vague. Programming language is by its very nature not vague. The semantic of a programming language is determined by the compiler or the interpreter converting the high level language to machine code. There is no room in this process for ambiguity as in natural language.

This is, however, restricted to the elements of a program consisting of programming language, the defined words of the programming language constructed according to the syntax of this language. But the program will also incorporate variables defined by the programmer, given tags often of a mnemonic nature. Such variables may be "income", "age", "negligence", etc. Though the variables are part of the program, their meaning is not defined by the compiler or interpreter, but rather by procedures set out in the program itself: The value of the variable is introduced through a keyboard, retrieved from a file, etc.

In the next section something will be said of ambiguity and variables. In this section, we will restrict ourselves to a comment on syntactic ambiguity.

Natural language has features which allow some syntactic ambiguity to seep into the meaning. Statutory text in natural language should be drafted in such a way that this type of ambiguity is rare, and - indeed - it is less frequent here than in normal prose. It is, for instance, amusing to see that "and" - being a conjunctive operator - in general prose often is used as a synonym for a disjunctive operator, for instance in a sign proclaiming,

IT IS PROHIBITED TO BRING FOOD AND DRINK INTO THE CINEMA.

Statutory language is drafted more carefully[7]. But there are, nevertheless, no problems of finding examples of ambiguities. As an example, one may take sect. 8-3(1)[8] of the Norwegian Social Security Act, in which some of the criteria for being entitled to an invalid pension is set out. This includes that,

> "... earning ability after therapy, training, education, or other forms of rehabilitation which are seen as appropriate, still is permanently reduced ..."

For programming purposes, the disjunct set of criteria may be specified,

a -> therapy
b -> training
c -> education
d -> other forms of rehabilitation which are seen as appropriate

The logical structure implied by the natural language text would seem to be,

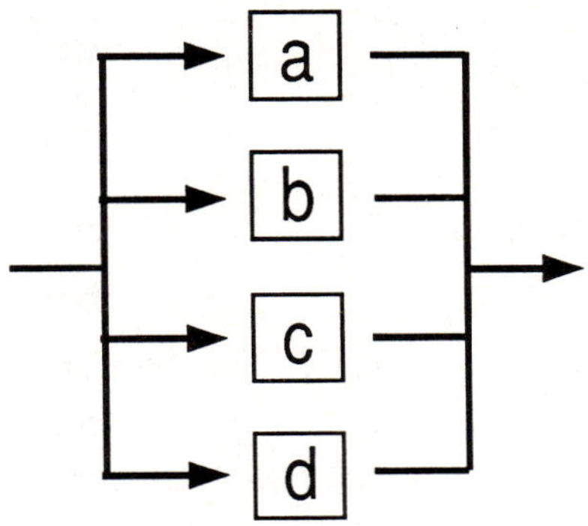

Figure 2 : Structure of antecedent - SSA Sect. 8-3(1)

In this case, the program would represent the rule in such a way that if an applicant had taken any of the options, this part of the rule was satisfied. But it is likely that the statutory provision is interpreted differently. One may imagine a case in which an applicant has had an operation resulting in everything less but a success. The applicant cannot return to his former job, but his general background makes it quite certain that he may be trained for another equally well paid and satisfying job. In this case, an argument along the lines that "therapy" has been undertaken, and consequently that "other forms of rehabilitation which are seen as appropriate" cannot be required, probably will fail. Therefore, the diagram above should be retraced.

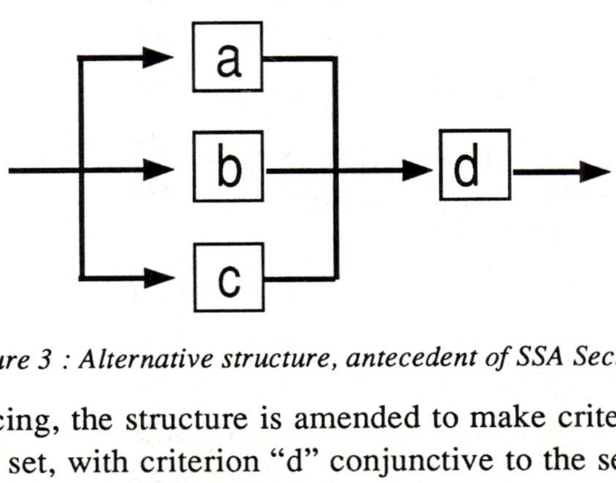

Figure 3 : Alternative structure, antecedent of SSA Sect .8-3(1)

By this retracing, the structure is amended to make criteria "a", "b", and "c" a disjunctive set, with criterion "d" conjunctive to the set, reflecting the probable interpretation of the statutory provision.

This is one small example of how the programming of systems for legal decisions requires the system designer to interpret the legal instruments. The programming is by its very nature a legal decision, where the designer makes permanent decisions of the law. The resulting system will become a framework in which the decision makers have to work, and will be confined them to the options set out by the program designer. The impact on legal decision making is crucial, and emphasizes the point that the design of such system is a task requiring legal expertise.

2.2 Vague and strict criteria

To decide a certain case, the variables of the program have to be assigned values. The values may be Boolean (truth values as above) or quantitative values (as for "age", "income" etc.) In this section, we shall dwell upon another possible distinction between types of criteria, that between strict and vague criteria. It should be understood that this is a distinction between two ends of a spectrum, with many intermediary examples of "less strict" and "less vague" criteria.

2.2.1 Types of strict criteria

By a "strict criterion" is indicated a criterion which by itself refers to a rather unambiguous fact, a fact which different persons with high probability in different contexts would determine in an identical way. Strict criteria are used very frequently in statutory texts, but would seem to fall within one of three categories.

(1) Quantified criteria.

Here are indicated the types of criteria which refer to some sort of object or process which may be measured - like sums of money, age, weight, speed, etc. There may be instances of doubt, a radar speed trap may have a certain known leeway for its measures, the age in years of a person at his or her birthday may be subject to dispute - but nevertheless, the value of such criteria may be determined without much doubt.

(2) Natural status.

This may be seen as a variation of the first criteria, but with binary values. A major example of a natural status is sex, which can be determined with little room for doubt. But also other natural statuses are used in legislation. The legislation of construction will, for instance, have different fire regulations relative to whether the construction is of wood, brick, cast iron, concrete, etc.

(3) Legal status.

Most interestingly, the law also simplifies the rule structures by using legal status as a criterion. Whether someone is a medical doctor, a judge, etc, is not determined by examining the basic qualifications of the person, but by determining whether the person is licensed as a medical doctor, has been appointed a judge, etc.

One will note that the legal system relies heavily on the use of legal status. An example may be speed limits for a road. There is a set of rules governing the speed limits which the highway authority should assign to different stretches of road. The authority makes a decision, and posts the traffic sign. A motorist exceeding the speed limit, will not be heard with the defense that the highway authority has misinterpreted its rules, and assigned a too low a speedlimit to the road. The decision will not go beyond the fact of the traffic sign (with exceptions for blatant misjudgments).

This is an example of a two-step decision, in which the first legal decision assigns a legal status to an object, a person or a process, and further legal decision does not go beyond this "fact" to apply subsequent rules.

2.2.2 Vagueness through language

Though the law abounds with strict criteria, it also abounds with vague criteria. Of these, two categories will be mentioned.

Words and phrases as occurring in natural language are by their very nature vague. We are not concerned here with homographs, but with general words and phrases. Their meaning is not exact, though their interpretation is constrained by the overall context.

The traditional example is demonstrated by the question, "When do several trees become one forest?" But there are numerous other examples, where the person, applying a rule, employing such criteria, has to classify the facts of the case according to them[9].

One will notice that such criteria require some background knowledge of the person applying the rules. Mainly, this is a background knowledge of the usage of languages, common to persons within a certain culture. But as the criteria are employed within the context of a rule structure, it obviously also requires some understanding of this legal context.

One has observed a tendency computerizing in legal domains, to replace vague criteria with rule structures employing strict criteria. Strict criteria do not require the same understanding of the context, as they are of more stable and independent of the rules in which they occur.

An example may be found in an amendment of the form used for collecting data prior to calculating old age pension in Norway. One of the provisions makes the old age pension in some cases relative to whether the applicant supports a spouse. Formerly, this took the form of a question asking whether the applicant supported a spouse, leaving to the applicant the rather subtle problem of deciding what "supporting" really implied. Obviously, the overall economical situations might vary widely between applicants; two applicants in different general circumstances might respond differently to the question though the spouses had an identical income. Such relativity a legal concept is quite common.

The form has been revised, replacing this question with a simple question on the annual income of the spouse. This is then supplemented, "behind the stage", so to say, by an extra rule specifying that if the income of the spouse exceeds the basic amount[10], the spouse is not supported. In this way, a vague criterion has given place to a rule structure, employing strict criteria only ("income" and "basic amount").

If it can be maintained that computerization is associated with a tendency to replace vague by strict criteria, we have identified an important way in which the technology is impinging upon legal reasoning. We would have to study the issue further to determine whether this is advantageous. Use of strict criteria will in general promote certainty in law, but generally also require larger normative structures, as marginal cases cannot be excluded by common sense classification according to vague criteria, but have to be explicitly excluded by an exemption. Humans may find it difficult to cope with a complex structure of rules defined by strict criteria, while computers have no problems in this respect, while vague criteria may limit the possibilities of computerization.

2.2.3 Expert judgements

The uncertainty implied in the vagueness of language originates outside the legal system itself, and is related to the fact that legal instruments are written in natural language. But though the language is a natural language, employed in a legal instrument it also becomes a technical language, where different rules for the interpretation of words and phrases are applied than those part of the common language culture.

A major example is supplied by those words and phrases indicating that a certain type of legal decision process shall take place: an expert judgement. Such a word is "negligence" in the law of damages. A general requirement to find a person liable, is that this person has been negligent.

Any lawyer will know what "negligence" means. There is no vagueness associated with the term similar to the vagueness associated with "forest". But there is considerable uncertainty associated with the term, as the term initiates an expert judgement, which may be seen as a subordinate level of the rule structure. On this level, a new set of relevant facts is identified, using the rules associated with the expert judgement, derived from case law, legal literature, etc. Such facts may, in the case of negligence, be the age of the person in question, whether the act was part of a job, whether security regulations were observed, whether the person or object suffering damage presented a typical risk, etc. Such subsidiary facts may either favor negligence or non-negligence, and may be associated with weights indicating the relative importance of the presence of the subsidiary fact in this case[11].

Based on the underlying theory of norms, two interesting features of legal expert judgements should be emphasized. (1) It is not possible in advance to specify an exhaustive list of all potentially relevant, subsidiary facts. (2) It is not possible in advance to specify the relative weight which will be assigned to a subsidiary fact when occurring in a given case.

The underlying theory of norms is, of course, open to criticisms[12]. But if this theory is accepted, one has identified two absolute limits for the representation of legal norms in computer programs. An expert judgement cannot, by definition, be part of a computer program, as the program requires the predefinition of the subsidiary facts and weights, or - at the very least - a method for modifying its current set of subsidiary facts and associated weights. Obviously, an expert judgement may be approximated by a program, and such an approximation may be sufficient to decide the large majority of cases in an adequate way. But in principle the program cannot include expert judgements.

To the extent legal decisions are being computerized, expert judgements have consequently to be excluded. This may imply amendments of the relevant legal instruments, which by itself is not a trivial process. Therefore, system designers may opt for the solution of involving a human to make the expert system, and present the system with the result in the same way in which values are specified for other types of variables.

One will, however, appreciate that the process of classifying the facts of a case according to such a variable will be different both from the classification according to a strict criterion, and to a criterion where the vagueness is associated with natural language rather than legal norms.

For the user, however, it may often be a difficult issue to identify what sort of decision is to be made. A major reason for this is the migration of criteria from one category of vagueness to another. A criterion may start out as part of a statutory text, which may involve some sort of rule for "forest". The first time a case is decided on the basis of this provision, the judge is faced with the problem of classifying the facts of the case according to the guidelines found in the usage of the word "forest" within the legal context. But when the decision is made, most legal systems will qualify this as a relevant legal source which may or must be taken into consideration the next time a case is decided on the basis of the same provision. In this way, the dynamics of the legal system may qualify the criterion further, and remove its understanding from the general context of language to the more specialized legal context. In this process, the term ceases to be just a word part of natural language, it becomes a reference to a subsidiary expert judgement where the previous cases create the legal norms relevant for the classification of facts with respect to the criterion.

This process may take place without any amendment of the legal instruments themselves. A person presented with the task of specifying a Boolean value for the variable "forest", would require sufficient background knowledge to be able to perceive whether the vague criterion safely may be understood within the context of text alone, or whether there are additional legal sources to be taken into account.

Again, computer systems may be designed to support such a situation. But it will require methods more akin to the current expert system technology, which will allow the user to access detailed explanations and also exit into the text of the basic legal instruments, rather than the current technology where the user is presented with a formalized interface (a "soft copy" of a traditional form) with scant explanation and relying heavily on conventional documentation associated with all the traditional problems of updating and access.

3 Specifying the variables

The values of the criteria imbedded in a computer program have to be specified. In principle it may only be specified by two methods: Either based on a rule utilizing values of criteria which already are known to the system, or by original input by a human, who has a knowledge of the facts of the case.

In practice one may also include the access of another system which has relevant information. In that system, however, the information has to be the result of one of the two basic processes.

In this section, we will briefly examine some of the issues related to original determination of the values by human-machine interaction, and through the matching of files from different systems[13].

3.1 Human-machine interaction

In principle such a systems may work in an interactive mode. The computer processes the information available. Each time a value for a variable is missing, a query is produced on the screen of the decision maker, who then specifies the correct value by examining the documents of the case, or initiating supplemental research.

As mentioned above, this presumes some background knowledge of the user. The user must be able to understand the identifiers of the variables as references to the criteria in the proper legal context. In typical mass administrative situations, the users will be specialized and may be presumed to have sufficient background knowledge to make correct classification also according to vague criteria and expert judgements. System designers may want to develop systems to require only specification according to strict criteria, which would make it possible to use less qualified decision makers, and - which may also be of interest - make it possible for one decision maker to handle a broader spectrum of cases. If specialization mainly is a strategy to ensure sufficient expertise in the decision maker, it may be advantageous to lower the requirements. This would perhaps make geographical decentralization of the decision making system easier, and would make it possible for an applicant to have several types of cases handled by the same decision maker.

Above, we also mentioned that rule structures emphasizing strict criteria will be more certain, and thus strengthening the element in the ideal of the rule of law related to certainty of the decisions within the legal system. In the same way as such rule structures reduce the requirements of background knowledge of the decision maker, it would facilitate the development of advisory systems or expert systems designed to be used by the applicant to gain insight into his or her personal situation, for planning purposes or for preparing an application within a certain area.

One should therefore be careful not to discard the development of rule based systems emphasizing strict criteria. It is true that such systems will be less flexible, and will reduce the possibility of the decision maker to take into account features unique to the case at hand. But such system would increase certainty, and also allow development of rule structures with a finer mesh than can be supported by a wholly manual system. It would seem, therefore, that an assessment of a development towards less vague criteria and increased computerization, cannot be made in general, but will have to be made case by case, taking into account the nature of the legal domain in question.

One should note that though such a development may favor *geographical* decentralization, it most certainly would increase the coordination and control of some central agency with respect to the system as a whole. The computerized case handling system will be a far more powerful tool for coordinating a public administration which is geographically distributed throughout the country, than the traditional tools of circular letters, instructions etc. Again, it is difficult generally to assess whether this is an advantage or not with respect to the ideals of the rule of law - it certainly may increase the possibility to have a case decided in the same way, irrespective of where in the country it appears, thus strengthening the unity of the legal system. But at the same time local independence and the freedom to modify, within certain restraints, the norms to suit local conditions have been seen as advantages, emphasized by the political ideas of decentralization throughout the last few decades.

In this way one may argue that the quality of computerized systems is not implied by computer technology, but by its application; the design of the system within a certain domain of law, and the implied dynamics initiated by introducing the system within that area.

One of the basic requirements is that the system is able to reflect the conceptual structure of the criteria employed by the rules governing the domain in question. This is by no means a trivial requirement.

In Norway one has seen the development of two parallel systems for case handling at the local social welfare offices, one based on a local solution, one based on a regional solution. In our context, the interesting thing with this situation is that there exists two parallel computerized solutions for the same area of law.

Both systems rely for certain tasks on a man-machine interaction, where the decision maker specifies values for certain criteria indicated on the screen. One of the applications is sick leave benefit. The rules coordinate the welfare benefit with certain tax consequences, and must therefore distinguish between categories of employees. Obviously one needs as many categories as there are different consequences. As the rules are identical, one would expect that the two parallel systems specify the same categories.

This is, however, not the case. One of the systems displays 6 alternative categories, the other 9[14]. The decision maker is invited to set Boolean truth values for the alternatives. The display does not include the possibility of adding an unspecified category, or otherwise escape the guidance imposed by the system.

The philosophy of the system designers may have been that the system only should handle the large majority of the cases; if the applicant does not fit into the predefined categories, the case has to be settled manually. But obviously the decision maker will have difficulties perceiving that the system is incomplete. To discover this, the decision maker has to rely on his or her background knowledge, and if this does not include an understanding of the limitations, the system is not designed to disclose these.

In this case it would seem difficult to avoid the conclusion that at least one of the systems is designed inappropriately, and will have an effect on the law in action not justified by the underlying normative structure.

One may also mention that when introducing computerized systems, one also introduces documentation - manuals and other types of user documentation designed to help the user cope with the system. Much of this will be of a technical nature with little legal relevance. But the example mentioned above demonstrates that if the user actually has difficulties with defining the applicant with respect to the displayed alternatives, he or she may refer to the manuals. These explain when to choose which alternative, but emphasize the technical aspects - the legal problems are not discussed. To disclose these, the user has to refer to the traditional set of legal sources. One therefore has a situation where the computerized system is accompanied by a new type of literature, which is legal in nature, but which has been developed within a technological context. The relation between this new type of documentation and the conventional circulars, instructions and regulations issued by the competent administrative authorities also has to be discussed, and one will have to find a more satisfactory solution than the one currently employed.

3.2 Matching files

A tempting solution for determining the values of criteria imbedded in the computer program, is access to an external system in which values for the same criteria can be retrieved. An example has been given initially, illustrating how the system for housing aid extracts the relevant values from external systems operated by other government agencies.

This solution implies that data collected or processed for one purpose, is utilized for another purpose. The matching of government files is a major issue in current data protection policies. Practices like data base surveillance (or "Rasterfahndung") are of growing concern[15], and the use of or plans for the introduction of PINs, which are seen as a facilitation of the matching of files, are general political issues in many countries[16].

Data protection is concerned with the individual, the interest of the data subject to control personal information relating to himself or herself. Issues like data base surveillance, or the computerization of governmental files, may perhaps better be perceived in a broader perspective, where the interest of groups, or the interest of an individual as a member of a group, is emphasized. This is often named *"group privacy"*, and makes it easier to concentrate on the systematic properties of a solution, rather than the often incidental consequences with respect to an individual. The perspective of group privacy will be taken in this section, while the problems of the conventional data protection will not be further pursued. This does not, of course, imply a priority of the issues, but rather an emphasis of that perspective which most adequately brings out some of the impacts computerization will have on the legal decision process, and explicate the relation to the traditional ideals of the rule of law.

When accessing an external system for retrieving values for a certain criterion, the first issue will be to determine whether the two criteria are *identical* for all purposes within the context of the systems. It is a trivial observation that criteria indicated with identical natural language phrases in two statutory texts may, when interpreted according to legal meta-rules, turn out to have significant differences. In exactly the same way, two variables with identical tags may in significant details differ, making a match between the two systems inappropriate.

One typical example is the variable "income". Under the tax legislation, several income concepts are defined - taxable income with respect to state and local taxes, income relevant for the calculation of a certain social benefit, etc. In an infamous Swedish case, systems were matched to identify possible evasion of value added tax. During the trials, it became evident that different income concepts had been matched, making a large number of inappropriate indications of possible evasions. Swedish law does actually define more than 25 different income concepts[17].

But even when identification is appropriate, other features of the data stored in an external system must be examined. Brief mention will be made of two features like this.

The values of criteria will change over time. Annual income will obviously rarely be identical for two different years. When matching systems, one must therefore pay attention to whether the values refer to *the same period in time,* otherwise anomalies may arise.

The system for housing aid gives a typical example of this situation. To be entitled to this type of aid, both the housing unit and the income of the household has to meet certain tests. The address, retrieved from the central population register, should be current within 8 weeks, while the income figures are current within 10-15 months. When major changes in the household take place, these will be reflected differently in the two systems: A student graduating and moving into a qualified housing unit with a very high salary in his or her new job, will be given housing aid until the lagging income figures catch up with the change; a household reducing its income due to job layoff, child birth etc, will have to wait for the income figures to catch up before qualified as entitled to aid[18].

In the system for housing aid these anomalies are seen as part of the price to be paid for a simplified administration of this type of social benefit. But it offers, nevertheless, a clear illustration of the consequences of matching data referring to different periods of time.

Another issue is the *verification level* of the data in different systems. Verification implies costs, consequently the data will be verified only to the extent appropriate for the objective of the system. When systems with different objectives are matched, one may import data which have been subject to verification routines of a lower standard than appropriate for the importing system.

This leads to concern for the *data quality* in the systems maintained by governmental agencies. This concern is acute, as little is known of the data quality of such systems.

There are indications that give cause for alarm. The Office of Technology Assessment of the US Congress organized a check of samples from criminal history records. In North Carolina, only 12.2 % of the summaries were found to be complete, accurate and unambiguous. The corresponding figures for California and Minnesota were 18.9 % and 49.5 %[19].

One may, of course, hope or believe that the data quality of the government agencies in one's own country exceeds what was disclosed in the US study. It is difficult, however, to escape the notion that as long as confidence is based on hopes, it does not satisfy the requirements implied by the ideals of the rule of law. There should be procedures, for instance routine sampling, to ensure that the data quality satisfies the standards necessary for basing a computerized system on the matching of files.

4 Supervising computerized systems

An important element of the legal decision in public administration, is the procedure for review of the decisions. Traditionally this has been initiated by the applicant, who may appeal a decision to a higher level within the administration, and who also may take a decision for review to the courts.

In principle such procedures may also be applied to decisions produced by a computerized system. But in practice it may be less than satisfactory.

Obviously, a computerized system always will decide a case according to its program. Omitting the rare incident of a system failure, the case will be decided according to the rules as represented by the programs governing the system. The values of the variables may be subject to review in the individual case. They may, of course, be incorrect for some reason or the other. But if the variables are correct, it is less than meaningful to apply the system once more: The result must necessarily be identical.

With respect to the system of housing aid, this has resulted in abolishing the traditional procedure of review, replacing it with a limited review of the values of the criteria to secure that these are correct. If they are correct, the appeal is dismissed.

There are additional problems when values are retrieved from external systems. In such a case, there may be doubts as to which agency has the authority to decide whether the value is correct; the agency operating the system resulting in the appealed decision, or the agency operating the external system.

Without taking the discussion further, it would seem obvious that a case can be made for the thesis that the current procedures for review are unsatisfactory when applied to computerized systems. There would seem to be a need for some sort of system audit, in which the elements discussed above are taken into consideration, and where the auditing authority looks into whether the system is adequately designed for the task it is doing. Such an audit may be caused by an appeal from an individual, but cannot be limited to an individual case: It must embrace many aspects of the system: The way in which the legal rules have been represented in the system, the way in which decision makers are presented with the issues, the documentation accompanying the system, etc.

Today, there has not emerged a general solution for the review of such systems. Partly this is due to the simple fact that we have not sufficiently researched the changes in the decision situation caused by the introduction of computerized systems, the relation between such changes and the ideals of due process and the rule of law. Partly it is due to a lack of appropriate authorities and traditions within public administration itself. It has been suggested that a parliamentary Ombudsman may be the appropriate agency[20]. It has also been pointed out that the data protection authorities to some extent have the necessary authority and expertise - and there certainly are examples of data protection authorities exercising such control over the computerized systems[21]. But - as mentioned above - the perspective of individual data protection is insufficient to deal with many aspects of computerized systems within public administration.

Today, we see a change in the types of systems employed by public administration. Roughly, one may see the centralized solutions of the late 1960's and mid 1970's as the first generation of systems for public administrations; the distributed solutions relying on terminal networks and soft copies as the second. Currently, systems based on knowledge technology are being introduced: The Alvey project in UK has developed a demonstrator project based on the social security regulations for the Department of Health and Social Services[22], in Sweden prototypes of expert systems for the welfare services have been developed, in Norway expert systems for local tax authorities are being designed, etc. The knowledge engineering will include all the aspects of computerized systems mentioned above, but will include new possibilities and novel problems.

It is obvious that this is a challenge to lawyers, working to maintain and improve the standards of the legal system and the public administrations measured in the terms of due process and the rule of law.

References

Beyond 1984: The Law and Information Technology in Tomorrow's Society (1985) *Proceedings of the Fourteenth Colloquy on European Law, Council of Europe,* Strassbourg. Bench-Capon, TJM/Robinson, GO/Routen, TW/Sergot, MJ (1987)

"Logic programming for large scale applications in law: A formalisation of supplementary benefit legislation" ; ICAIL 1987:190-198.

Bing, Jon (1984) "The Ombudsman and computerized administration"; *Informatica e diritto* pp 83-96.

Bing, Jon (1985a) *"Data protection and social policy" ; Beyond 1984* pp 82-98.

Bing, Jon (1985b) "Modeller av rettslige avveininger, med et eksempel fra norsk interlegal rett"; *Tidsskrift for rettsvitenskap* 395-431.

Bing, Jon (1986a) "Rettslige aspekter ved datamaskinbaserte forvaltningssystemer"; *Nordisk administrativt tidsskrift* pp 9-23.

Bing, Jon (1986b) "Conseguenze degli sviluppi della tecnologia informatica per la legislazione sulla tutela dei dati"; *Notiziario di informatica, Camera dei deputati,* Roma 1/

1986:1-76.

Bing, Jon (1987a) (ed) F*KUS - Knowledge Based Systems for Public Administration, *CompLex* 8/87, Norwegian University Press, Oslo.

Bing, Jon (1987b) *"The F*KUS concept: Knowledge Based Systems for Public Administration"*;

Bing 1987a:11-71, also Law/technology 1st quarter, Washington DC. Burnham, David (1983) The Rise of the Computer State; Weidenfeld and Nicolson, London.

Eckhoff/Torstein/Sundby, Nils Kristian (1976) Rettssystemer, Tanum-Norli, Oslo. Freese, Jan (1987) *Den maktfullkomliga ofan, WahlstrWidstrand,* Stockholm.

Haft, F/Jones, RP/Wetter, Th (1987) *"Natural language based legal expert system for consultation and tutoring"*; ICAIL 1987:75-83.

Hansen, Johs (1986) Simulation and automation of legal decisions, *CompLex* 6/86, Norwegian University Press, Oslo.

ICAIL (1987) *International Conference on Artificial Intelligence and Law;* ACM Press, New York.

Kandeva-Spiridonova, Emilia (1987) "Exercise of administrative discretionary powers under new conditions"; paper offered to the conference on *"New technologies in public administration: Socio- economic aspects from an interdisciplinary viewpoint"*, Zagreb (ms).

Magnusson, Cecilia/Torvund, Olav (eds) (1988) *Myndighetsdata och rkerhet*, Norstedts, Stockholm 1988.

Maartmann, Hanne Plathe (1987) Personvern i sykepengerutinen, *CompLex* 4/87, Norwegian University Press, Oslo.

Malt, Gert-Fredrik (1986) "Svake normer"; *Tidsskrift for rettsvitenskap* pp 167-191.

McCarty, Thorne/Sridhran, NS (1982) *"A computational theory of legal argument"*; Technical Report, Rutgers University, New York.

Schartum, Dag Wiese (1987) The Introduction of Computers in the Norwegian Local Insurance Offices, *CompLex* 9/87, Norwegian University Press, Oslo.

Schartum, Dag Wise (1988) *"'Forutsatt at EDB-programmet er riktig' - En rettslig gjennomgang av et saksbehandlingssystem i offentlig forvaltning"*; Magnusson/Torvund 1988:127-139.

Sundby, Nils Kristian (1974) *Om normer,* Universitetsforlaget, Oslo.

Notes

1. This chapter is based on a paper for the conference on "New Technologies in Public Administration: Socio-Economic Aspects from an Interdisciplinary Viewpoint" (Zagreb, November, 13-15 1987), but has been revised for this anthology.
2. Much of this paper is based on reports of the Norwegian Research Center for Computers and Law, which has looked into aspects of "deontic systems" (computerized systems representing legal norms in their programs) since 1975, and which since 1978 has been concerned with developing systems, including expert systems, within legal domains. Reports are only cited when relevant for a point made in the text.
3. It is a point of interest to note that this system of supplementary welfare benefits is not based on a statute, but on a plenary decision. The Norwegian constitution does not require the form of statutes unless the rules introduced restricts the personal freedom of the citizen. As these rules in principle only give the citizens additional benefits, the constitutional principle of legality is not applicable. Nevertheless, it is rather unique to

find this type of legal instrument as the basis for a welfare benefit scheme.

4. Norway is one of the few countries which has adopted universal personal identifiers. This was introduced in 1964, mainly to simplify reporting routines from employers to governmental agencies. It has survived survived the data protection debate and legislation, but has been subject of numerous political discussions.
5. In many earlier reports, the term "discretionary decision" has been used. Cf also Kandeva-Spiridonova 1987. This term may give incorrect implication in English, and the term "expert judgement" will be preferred in this paper. It will be further explained below.
6. By "rule" or "norm" in this chapter is meant the content based on one or more representations of the rules in statutory texts, regulations etc. It is convenient to make a clear distinction between the representation of the rules, be it in natural or formal languages, and the rule itself. This will roughly correspond to the distinction between content and form, data and information, syntax and semantics, etc.
7. One may actually from word frequencies for Norwegian language observe that the relative rank of "AND" and "OR" is reversed in newspaper and statutory texts.
8. This example is more fully explored in Bing 1987b, which is part of the current effort at the Norwegian Research Center for Computers and Law to develop alternative designs for knowledge based systems in public administration, the F*KUS concept.
9. Concepts related like "tree" and "forest" may invite to analogous reasoning. McCarty (for instance 1982) has developed a representation of such concepts, using prototypes and deformations, where the different concepts are nodes in a structured space. His example takes the relation between the legal concepts of "cash", "promissory notes", "bonds", "preferred stock" and "general stock", whose distribution by a company takes you from a taxable to a non-taxable situation, based on the well known case of Einsner v Macomber 252 US 189 (1920).
10. The "basic amount" is a figure decided annually by parliament, and on which the calculations of all welfare benefits are based.
11. The theory of expert judgement is mainly based on Sundby 1974 and Eckhoff/Sundby 1976. The Norwegian Research Center for Computers and Law has made this the basis of a computer program modelling binary expert judgement (like "negligence"), known as SARA. This is discussed in several publications, for instance Bing 1985b. Hansen 1986 discusses the possibility of incorporating such elements in legal, knowledge based systems. Similar problems are approached in the LEX project at the University of Tübingen, see for instance Haft/Jones/Wetter 1987, especially p 82
12. In this chapter a discussion of this theory will not be included. Malt 1986 gives a more extensive discussion, attempting to place this theory in a larger context of what he terms "weak norms".
13. One should mention the possibility of a system through robotic devices itself collecting information on a case and utilizing this for a decision. A trivial example would be system for measuring the speed of a vehicle and for scanning the licence plates, which would make it possible to make a decision on speeding. But this type of system does not have an important role in current legal computerized systems.
14. Cf Maartmann 1987:40, Schartum 1987:233. Schartum's more recent research concentrating on computer programs in a selection of public agencies, contain several similar examples. CF for instance Schartum 1988 for some preliminary results.
15. Cf Bing 1985a and 1985b for a discussion of social policies and current issues of data protection.
16. A recent and most interesting example is the politics related to the introduction and defeat of the Autralia Card Legislation.

17. For a critical discussion of the case cf Freese 1987:96.
18. There are manual routines to handle the gravest of these anomalies in the system.
19. Cf Burnham 1983:74. The research was conducted bij Dr Kenneth C. Laudon. The source does not specify what is understood by the phrase "complete, accurate and unambiguous", a phrase commonly used in data protection legislation. It has been suggested to the author that most cases are instances of lagging updating, making the data in the system incomplete.
20. Cf Bing 1984:1986a.
21. Cf the "social acceptance principle" as applied by the New South Wales data protection committee, Bing 1986b:39.
22. Cf for instance Bench-Capon/Robinson/Routen/Sergot 1987.

Expert Systems in Public Administration
I. Th.M. Snellen, W.B.H.J. van de Donk, J.-P. Baquiast (Eds.)
© Elsevier Science Publishers B.V. (North-Holland), 1989

Chapter 9

Expert Systems: Bias and Control

*John Rae**

Abstract
Increasingly expert system technology is being employed in decisions that involve resource allocation. This chapter argues that there is an urgent need to consider security issues with respect to expert system development and maintenance. In particular it is important to establish an independent audit function to ensure the integrity of expert systems in the public domain.

1 Introduction

This chapter offers a conceptual framework in which to view the problems of bias and control in expert systems. It will be argued that these problems are not new regardless of whether the system in question is manual or computerised in the form of a knowledge-based system (KBS). Similar problems have a long history in the accountancy profession and there are lessons to be learned from established accounting practices. In fact, given adequate controls, the development of KBS's will afford public administrators a greater opportunity to constructively enhance the degree of control over the behaviour of administrative systems.

---

* Information Technology Instutute, University of Salford,
Salford M5 4WT, England

In the first section we shall consider the role of the knowledge engineer in the system development process and in particular consider the necessity to widen and separate the knowledge engineer's functions to include a system auditor.

Next we shall consider the recent case of St George's Hospital Medical School where the Commission for Racial Equality (CRE) found that, via a computer programme, the School had discriminated between applicants on racial grounds contrary to the Race Relations Act of 1976.

Finally we propose a framework in which to place the development and maintenance of KBS's with a view to preventing the inclusion of bias, howsoever it arises, in public administration systems.

2 The role of the knowledge engineer

"If all knowledge is explicit, then to search for a solution is an absurdity,
For either you know what you are looking for and then there is no problem
Or you don't know and then you cannot expect to find anything."
Plato - The Republic.

The impetus for the development of expert systems clearly rests upon the fact that all knowledge is not explicit, and this implies that the application of this knowledge is limited to those who possess it - the experts. There can be significant advantages gained if such knowledge can be made more explicit and more widely available to those who require it.

There are now many examples of the use of expert system technology where commercial organisations have gained a competitive advantage via the process of making scarce knowledge more widely available [for several such examples see Leonard-Barton and Svolka (1988)]. In the sphere of public administration there is also significant potential to improve both the quality of service and the productivity of staff if KBSs are developed as decision support tools. However, there is also a danger: KBSs are complex rule-based (usually) systems encoding expert knowledge; the combination of program structure and a knowledge base can serve to obscure the overall behaviour of the system. This places a responsibility on both the programmer and the commissioner to provide adequate means to investigate the behaviour of the system.

Traditionally, though admittedly it is a rather short tradition, the programmer or Knowledge Engineer (KE) has played a neutral (even amoral?) role in the construction of Expert Systems (ES). The primary function of the task has been to replicate, with a high degree of accuracy, the decision process of the human expert. This decision process may include elements of bias which contravene the norms (legal and customary) of society. However, strictly speaking this is not the concern of the KE who of necessity acts as an impartial observer and translator.

The role has been viewed much as a newsreel photographer, they are not responsible for that which they observe they merely photograph and reproduce. Unfortunately, the two are dissimilar. Looking at a photograph does not recreate the actuality of the event but using an expert system does, including the possibly highly undesirable consequences.

Without the introduction at an early stage of a voluntary system of KBS controls the domain of public administration will undoubtedly face a greatly increased probability of a major scandal at some point in the near future. In all likelihood the consequence of this will be the rapid introduction of legislative based, probably restrictive and possibly ill-conceived controls.

The issues of bias/error or abuse of KBSs is closely related to the issues of information security and privacy in general [see for example, Canning (1986)]. The overall subject of computer security is concerned with three main issues:

- Availability, the extent to which a computer system is operational at the times required of it. Thus critical parts of the system need adequate precautions against disasters such as fire and flood,
- Integrity, this relates to the accuracy of the programs and data held in the system. It is in this area that this contribution falls. Issues here relate to the extent to which control mechanisms exist to prevent and recognise human error and deliberate attempts to corrupt the system, and
- Confidentiality, which is concerned with the control of access to data held in computer systems.

The growth in computer usage, the legal pressures on management to take responsibility for data security, and greater public awareness all add weight to the argument for KBS controls.

These circumstances are by no means new nor unique: accountants have dealt with similar problems for some years in the area of computer-based accounting information systems and, of course, for very much longer in the case of manual accounting systems. The answer was to introduce a set of standards, a system of controls, and a policeman - the auditor. In the UK, as with other countries, there is a legal requirement for a company to have their accounts periodically audited, that is, an independent accountant must examine the company 'books' to attest the credibility of financial statements and to detect possible fraud and error.

When KBSs are constructed that determine, in part or whole, who gets what, when and how there is a need for accountability. It is not sufficient to leave the safeguarding of assets to the expert and the KE. There is a need to have evidence that the expert system is indeed a true and fair system. This means that the role of the KE must in future system development explicitly accommodate the audit process. The more complex programs become the greater the difficulty to demonstrate their correctness. This implies that there is a great responsibility placed upon the KE to make provision for an independent audit process. We shall return to this in more detail in a later section.

3 The case of medical school admissions

The CRE report "Medical School Admissions" (1988) highlights the problems of replicating administrative practices which may unwittingly or otherwise incorporate an automatic bias. The admissions program was a relatively simple 'algorithm' and its bias was not difficult to observe, nevertheless, it was some time (1982-1986) before the matter came to public attention. How very much more difficult it will be to highlight possible bias or errors of 'judgement' in large and complex rule structures that exist in the domains of social security, taxation, insurance or banking and finance.

The admissions system was accurately replicating (90-95% correlation) the candidate gradings of the selection panel and the report states:

> "The fact that Dr. F's program so closely correlated with the actual decisions made by the academic selectors indicates that the factors he included were an accurate replication of those employed by the selectors." (page 9)

The system assessed candidates on two main sets of factors - academic and personal. Academic factors included examination results - actual and expected, and these accounted for 75% of the final selection score. The personal factors included: headteacher's report, age, hobbies, sports, handwriting, connection with St George's, the candidates type of school and parental occupation. Additional factors in this section were race (Caucasian or non-Caucasian) and gender.

The candidate, after being processed by the system was given a ranking number; the lower the number the 'better' the candidate and the greater the likelihood of being offered an interview and subsequent place at the school. In fact only candidates with a rank number (ultimately expressed in percentiles) of less than or equal to 40 (and in one year less than or equal to 26) were interviewed.

The factors "non-Caucasian" and "female" carried 'negative' weightings:
non-Caucasian = 1.05
female = 1.33
non-Caucasian female = 1.3965

Using these weights the candidate's score from the other factors was multiplied by the appropriate number. In this way approximately 60 applicants per year were affected adversely by this race and gender weighting bias.

Dr. F was in this instance the knowledge engineer and the purpose of producing this KBS type admissions program was to reduce inconsistencies in the selection of candidates and he did so by

> "... observing the decisions of the selectors over a number of years and adjusting the program accordingly. In short the program aimed to mimic the judgement of the selectors." (page 8)

This process of adjustment, via feedback, is concerned with control over the accuracy of replication and is clearly of itself insufficient to ensure a true and fair system. The KE was merely ensuring the accurate replication of the discrimination that already existed in the academic staff selecting candidates.

The school failed to introduce effective control measures to ensure the fairness and accuracy of the system. There were on four occasions an opportunity to amend the system:

1. In 1982 a working party to review admissions procedure was set up and actually considered the program - no amendments were made.
2. The admissions officer informed the Academic Registrar in 1984 of the discriminatory elements in the system - no amendments were made.
3. In 1985 another working party was set up to explore the program further, the sub-group charged with this task never met.
4. During 1985 it was discovered by a new Academic Registrar that the data on racial origins were stored in the computer. This arose out of the Data

Protection Act registration procedure. The School Secretary assumed that this was for information purposes only and was not a selection criterion and thus no action was taken.

The St. George's system no longer operates but it is almost certain that similar systems will come into being and in general KBS's that determine the right of access of the public to resources will increase. The inadequate procedures currently applied to the development of such systems will produce further examples of bias and or system error. In the next section we describe a framework of control based upon three levels of feedback and the introduction of an auditing process.

4 Establishing control: The feedback framework

In this section we employ a systems theory framework to highlight the points at which controls need to be established via the use of standards, practices and independent audit. The independent auditor, having conducted an audit, will provide an opinion, open to public inspection, on the truth and fairness of the particular KBS employed in the public domain.

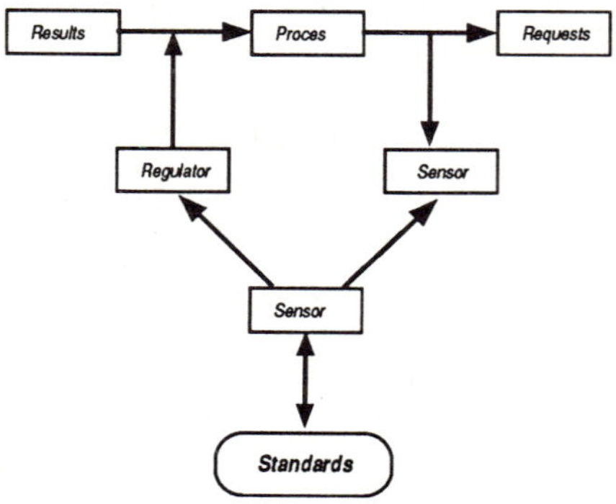

Figure 1: The basic control system

4.1 The basic control system

Figure 1 shows the basic systems theory approach to self-regulation with the main process being monitored and adjusted via a feedback loop which periodically samples the output of the system and checks it against preset standards and if necessary adjusts the process to produce the desired outputs. In order to make clear the proposed KBS feedback control mechanisms we first need to examine the process of knowledge acquisition.

4.2 Knowledge Acquisition

Knowledge acquisition by the KE is still an art that is mostly shrouded in mystery. For example, the now classic MYCIN system as described by Shortliffe (1976), has in total some three sentences devoted to the subject of knowledge acquisition. Of course, there are more extensive discussions of knowledge acquisition methodology [see for example Attarwala and Basden (1985)] but it is still true to say that much of the focus of published ES description is on system performance and not knowledge acquisition methods.

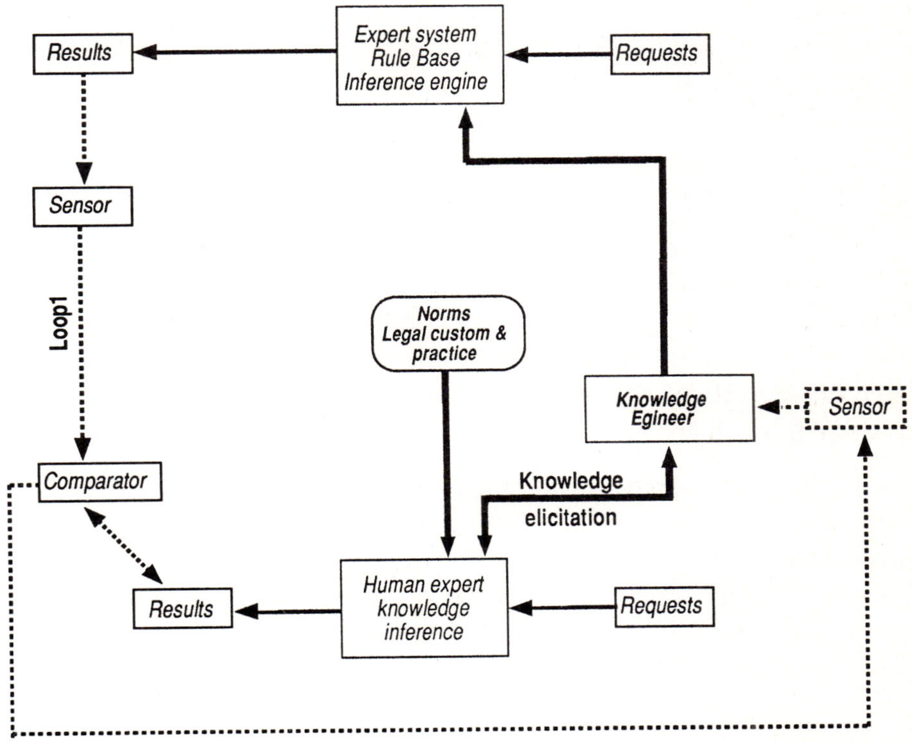

Figure 2: The existing feedback loop

Usually knowledge acquisition is considered to occur in stages. The number and description of stages differ according to the author; Waterman (1981) has three stages

1 structure the initial domain,
2 first working model, and
3 debugging and refining;

whilst Duda et al (1979) have four stages

1 initial domain structure,
2 first working model,
3 debug, and
4 testing.

However, in practice such stages are not clearly defined because iterations to achieve agreement on output between the system and the expert quickly blur the stage boundaries.

The basic activity involved in KE entails encoding expertise which has, by some method, been extracted from the human expert. Once sufficient expertise has been encoded the model is checked for accuracy via test data to see if the results are in agreement with those of the expert. This is the first feedback mechanism discussed below.

4.3 The First Feedback Loop

Currently we have in position for most KBS's only one feedback loop, this is shown in figure 2. This feedback loop consists of the KE sampling output (sensing) and comparing it with the desired output that resulted from the original human expert. The system is adjusted to produce an acceptable degree of correlation. This was exactly the process in operation at St. George's and described above.

Of course, St. George's is not alone in establishing only one control loop this is quite common at present. In fact this corresponds to the state of financial auditing in the UK up until 1900, except as it happens for banks and railway companies whose previous record of honesty was already shown to be dubious! It was soon apparent, however, that this was not a good practice and that the audit function must be impartial and independent.

4.4 Audit Provisions

The KE should provide an adequate means for an auditor to check the historic performance of the system. Essentially this means a complete recording of events as computer files on the system. Such a record might be quite large but given the development in optical storage methods, and in particular Write-Once-Read-Many (WORM) disks for tamper-proof records, this should not be a major problem.

KBSs do currently provide one important audit feature - the ability to show/explain the rule used in a particular stage of a transaction and thus one major feature of an audit trail is already in place, that is, the ability to trace a transaction through the system to highlight suspect code.

It is normal in accounting systems to have a segregation of duties, such controls should also exist for KBSs. In particular there should be a clear distinction made between the users of the system and those responsible for updating and amending the rule-base. Only run-time versions of the system should be available to users the uncompiled code version must be in a secure area.

It is the responsibility of management to ensure the KE makes these provisions, and others, such as adhering to documentation standards and proper validation tests, are a normal part of system construction. It would be entirely improper to rush into KBS construction in the belief that they are exempt from normal software development constraints. KBSs are in fact just a software mechanism for handling fuzzy problems.

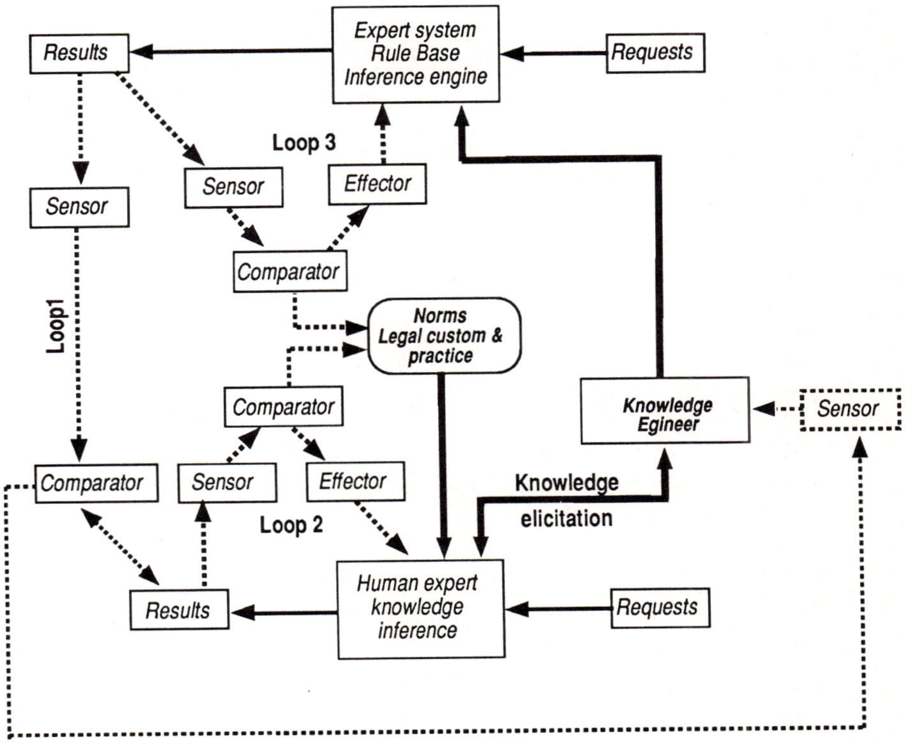

Figure 3: The three feedback loops

4.5 More Control Loops

Figure 3 shows all the control loops in position. Loop 1 leaves the KE as the conventional observer and translator plus the duty to provide adequate security and audit mechanisms.

The independent auditor appointed by the owners of the system must review periodically during the construction of the system the internal controls which includes documentation, access rights and the provision made to safely update the system.

Loop 2, describes what should already exist by way of an internal management review of the decisions made by human administrators. If such a practice does not already exist then it should be part of the function of the independent auditor to conduct a preliminary survey to satisfy himself or herself of the validity of the present system. Should such internal controls already exist then it is up to the auditor to be satisfied that such controls are adequate.

Finally loop 3. Here it is envisaged that the KBS is up and running and is largely if not totally independent of the previous manual system. At this stage the internal controls should function to safeguard the validity of the KBS, but the system and all its controls are periodically reviewed by the external auditor and receive a statement of worthiness.

Such control measures would certainly have prevented the admissions system bias and in general they would promote the status and reliability of KBS's.

5 Conclusion

Clearly there is much work to be done before an independent audit function could exist. There are many issues that need to be considered including the following questions:

- Who are the auditors?
- What professional body represents such a group?
- Which KBS's should be audited?
- Should legislation be required to make auditing a legal requirement?

Not surprisingly such questions were being asked at the turn of last century about accounting information systems (for example see T. Lee (1982)); it was not until 1948 in the UK that it became a legal requirement for an auditor to attach a statement of reliability to both the company balance sheet and the profit statement. Even so it took until 1967 to make it compulsory for all companies to be audited by a qualified professional accountant!

Public administrators will not have such an extended period of grace, the development of systems in this domain are too much subject to the public gaze and the glare of publicity. At the very least there needs to be an establishment of the practice of a good system of internal controls that will diminish the probability of irregularities occurring. Such controls are a minimum but for large KBS that are visible and used by administrators on behalf of the general public they are insufficient. Such systems are vulnerable both to irregularity and to crises of confidence thus controls at this level must include an independent audit.

References

Shortliffe,E. H. *Computer-Based Medical Consultations: MYCIN,* Elsevier New York. 1976

Duda J, J. Gashnig and P. Hart, *Model Design in the Prospector Consultant System for Mineral Exploration,* in D. Michie (ed) Expert Systems in the Microelectronics Age, Edinburgh University Press. 1979

Waterman,D.A., *Rule-Based Expert Systems,* in Machine Intelligence, Infotech State of the Art Report, Series 9 No. 3, Pergamon Infotech Ltd. 1981

Lee, L.: *Company Auditing,* Gee & Co Ltd. 1982

Attarwala,T. and A. Basden, *A Methodology for Constructing Expert Systems,* R&D Management Vol. 15 No. 2. 1985

Canning, R.G. *Information Security and Privacy,* EDP Analyzer, February , Vol.24 No. 2. 1986

Commission for Racial Equality: *Report of a Formal Investigation into St. Georges Hospital Medical School.* 1988

Leonard-Barton, D. and J. J. Svolka, *Putting Expert Systems To Work,* Harvard Business Review, March-April. 1988

Expert Systems in Public Administration
I.Th.M. Snellen, W.B.H.J. van de Donk, J.-P. Baquiast (Eds.)
© Elsevier Science Publishers B.V. (North-Holland), 1989

Chapter 10

An application for admission in public school systems

*Manuel Olave**
*Vladislav Rajkovic**
*Marko Bohanec**

Abstract

An application of expert systems for admission procedures in public school systems is presented in this chapter. The specific problem under consideration is selection of applicants for public nursery schools. The selection is supported by an expert system which evaluates, classifies and ranks applications. The main emphasis is on explanation of the underlying knowledge and solutions, suggested by the system. The system has been developed using DECMAK, an expert system shell for multi-attribute decision making. This chapter presents: the background of the selection problem, a brief overview of the DECMAK shell, description of the expert system and its development, practical results, and the impact of normativity to the results.

1 Introduction

The objectives of this chapter are to present the results of applying an expert system to a multi-attribute decision making process in a public school system which evaluates, classifies and ranks options to accept students, and to qualitatively assess the sensitivity of the results to changes in the administrative normativity.

---

* Institut Jozef Stefan,
Jamova 39, Ljubljana, Yougoslavia

The specific problem under consideration, common in excess demand public service agencies, is to select 300 out of 600 applicants for a nursery school in a closely populated young family neighborhood in Ljubljana, Yugoslavia.

Considering that 300 rejected families would not be happy with the decision, and particularly since this problem was being confronted by other school districts too, the school authorities established a pilot project at this particular school with the aim to develop a methodology for selecting applicants. To this effect a task force team was established consisting of 13 experts from diverse disciplines.

The expert team encountered formidable problems facing the Acceptance Committee, among them their own heterogeneous composition and the different levels of knowledge that each member possessed about the specific problem. Another problem was that the existing procedure for selection was not very helpful in decision making and required data not available in the application forms. Furthermore, there was a high degree of unreliable and in some cases missing information in these forms.

Given the challenges posed by the situation the expert team included two consultants which led the development of a computer-based decision support system. The consultants used an expert system shell DECMAK which is a system of computer programs intended to help the decision-maker cope with multi-attribute decisions (Bohanec & Rajkovic 1987). The theory which underlines this system is based on a new approach to multi-attribute decision making, which combines the traditional (numerical and analytical-oriented) methods with artificial intelligence, mainly expert systems and techniques of machine learning.

The results of the two years of development and testing indicate the following:

a A simple survey of parents of accepted and rejected children shows that they accepted the decisions made with the help of the expert system.
b The work of the Acceptance Committee in nursery schools has been considerably reduced and they feel relieved of the burden of personal explanations by the explanatory power of the methodology.

The results of this application seem sensitive to the following norms:

a The norms guiding the selection and structure of the expert team;
b The norms defining the role of the expert team leader and the system consultants;

c The norms establishing the relationship among the public school authorities, the Acceptance Committee and the expert team.
d The norms establishing the approval process of the decision making criteria (the semantic tree) and the decision rules.

2 Background

Recent socio-economic trends in the Socialist Federative Republic of Yugoslavia indicate that most young families' income is generated by both parents. In Ljubljana, capital of the northern republic of Slovenia where unemployment is almost negligible (below 1%) and with a burgeoning of new housing developments populated by young families, the demand for children's admission in nursery schools outstrips supply, notwithstanding the fast growth rate of new schools.

This general problem was exemplified in a particular Ljubljana district where there were approximately 600 applicants for 300 spaces to be considered by the Acceptance Committee in the local nursery school each year. This expert team found formidable obstacles, some of them inherent in the group approach to multi-attribute decision making. Among these problems the following ones can be highlighted:

a Knowledge heterogeneity: The Acceptance Committee consisted of people with different backgrounds and with varied perceptions about the child-family context. The result was a complex array of approaches to solve the problem and few parameters to serve as the basis for consensus.
b Lack of unifying evaluation methodology: The methodology used by the Committee was borne out of expediency and as such the criteria chosen kept changing as a function of time and of the subjective whims of the members. As a consequence the results were inconsistent.
c Inadequate information: Because the methodology was never unambiguously stated and accepted the data requirements were also loosely specified. Therefore the gathered data did not provide adequate information to help decision-makers.

Facing such powerful obstacles it was not surprising that the Acceptance Committee members felt frustrated and had a general feeling of guilt for not performing fairly in the decision process and not providing the school authorities with a clear answer to the question asked by at least 300 parents: Why was my child not accepted?

To solve the problem a project was initiated to design, develop, test and implement a methodology to support the Committee and consequently the school authorities in their acceptance procedures utilizing a computer-based decision support system.

The project called for establishment of an expert task force team consisting of 13 members including two decision theory experts, one of them selected as chairman of the group and both given the technical responsibility of the project.

The team faced a ranking and selection problem with multiple criteria and a lack of accurate and reliable information to make the pertinent decisions.

To develop the decision support system they recommended the use of an expert system shell named DECMAK that would enable to arrive at a selection methodology which would aggregate qualitative assessments for each criterion and would provide answers whose inner logic would be transparent for the clients.

3 Expert system shell DECMAK

The main tool used in developing the decision support system to rank nursery school applications was DECMAK (Bohanec & Rajkovic 1987). This is an expert system shell specialized for multi-attribute decision problems, i.e. problems where several alternatives (also called options) are to be ranked according to their quality. The quality depends on a particular set of attributes.

DECMAK is an expert system shell. Its main purpose is to help the user to build a problem-specific knowledge base. The system offers a number of tools for this purpose (Bohanec & Rajkovic 1987). The knowledge base is then utilized in solving the problem, i.e. ranking alternatives.

The structure of the knowledge base closely corresponds to the common multi-attribute decision making schema (Keeney & Raiffa 1976) consisting of two major elements:

1 Attributes structured in the form of a semantic tree, and
2 Decision rules that define the quality of alternatives as a function of the given attributes.

The process of building an expert system using DECMAK has two phases: first, the knowledge about a particular decision problem (i.e. attributes and decision rules) is acquired from the decision-maker(s) and encoded into a knowledge base, and second, the knowledge base is utilized to evaluate and rank options.

Decision rules are entered into the knowledge base in the If-Then form, for example:

IF Social conditions of the family are problematic,
AND Health conditions of the family allow acceptance of a child,
THEN a priority acceptance of the child is recommended.

Such rules are accomplished by a mixed-initiative dialogue between the user and DECMAK (Bohanec & Rajkovic 1988). Mainly, DECMAK suggests conditional parts of rules to be assessed, and the decision-maker just gives their "THEN" values which are immediately checked for consistency by DECMAK. For verification and justification of the knowledge, DECMAK is also able to translate the rule representation into other representations such as decision trees, aggregate rules and graphics that show the same knowledge from different viewpoints and at different levels of detail.

In the evaluation and ranking stage, the explanation and analysis of the results are specially emphasized. To this effect, DECMAK incorporates the following capabilities (Bohanec & Rajkovic 1987):

- An interactive evaluator for what-if analysis;
- Automatic explanation of the evaluation process;
- Selective explanation of advantages and disadvantages of each alternative;
- Selective comparison of alternatives;
- Sensitivity analysis;
- Option generation.

The DECMAK system has been successfully applied in about thirty practical decision making situations such as:

- Evaluation of computer systems for an enterprise;
- Selection of computer hardware and/or software for schools;
- Evaluation of production control and data base management software;
- Trading partner selection;
- Feasibility evaluation of a project;
- Selection of applicants for a given job;
- Performance evaluation of public enterprises.

4 Development of the expert system

The development of the expert system to rank nursery school applications was divided into two stages:

a building the knowledge base, and
b evaluating and ranking of the alternatives.

The first stage included two activities: assessing and structuring attributes into the form of a semantic tree, and definition of decision rules for classifying alternatives as a function of the attributes. The second stage was a practical test of the system. The knowledge base was utilized to rank the applications according to their acceptance priority.

4.1 Building the knowledge base

4.1.1 Structuring the attributes

The decision-making problem domain is represented in the form of a semantic tree which consists of the most relevant attributes that could describe the conditions of the child's family. There are three main categories of attributes:

1 Occupation of parents and characteristics of the nursery,
2 Family structure and financial standing, and
3 Social and health status of the family.

These categories are represented by internal nodes in the tree. They are aggregates of eight elementary attributes or tree "leaves". For instance, the category "Family structure and financial standing" is an aggregate of

a Form of the family,
b Number of children,
c Housing conditions, and
d Financial standing of the family.

The complete structure of the tree is shown in table 1 where the root (least indented line labeled U) represents the final evaluation of the application. The internal nodes of the tree are labeled A, B, C and D, and the leaves are represented by K1 to K8. The application for each child can then be described in terms of the values of each of the eight elementary attributes which were obtained from the application forms.

(U)	FINAL EVALUATION VALUE OF THE APPLICATION
(A)	OCCUPATION OF PARENTS AND CHILD'S NURSERY
(K1)	Parents' occupation
(K2)	Child's nursery
(B)	FAMILY STRUCTURE AND FINANCIAL STANDING
(D)	FAMILY STRUCTURE
(K3)	Form of the family
(K4)	Number of children
(K5)	Housing conditions
(K6)	Financial standing of the family
(C)	SOCIAL AND HEALTH PICTURE OF THE FAMILY
(K7)	Social conditions
(K8)	Health conditions

Table 1: Tree structure of the attributes

(U) FINAL EVALUATION VALUE OF THE APPLICATION:
- (1) acceptance is not recommended,
- (2) acceptance is recommended,
- (3) acceptance is very much recommended,
- (4) priority acceptance is recommended,
- (5) special priority acceptance is recommended.

(A) OCCUPATION OF PARENTS AND CHILD'S NURSERY:
- (1) convenient,
- (2) less convenient,
- (3) inconvenient,
- (4) critical.

(K1) Parents' occupation:
- (1) usual,
- (2) pretentious,
- (3) of great pretension.

(K2) Child's nursery:
- (1) proper,
- (2) less proper,
- (3) improper,
- (4) critical,
- (5) very critical.

(B) FAMILY STRUCTURE AND FINANCIAL STANDING:
- (1) convenient,
- (2) inconvenient,
- (3) critical.

(D) FAMILY STRUCTURE:
- (1) less critical,
- (2) critical,
- (3) very critical.

(K3) Form of the family:
- (1) complete family,
- (2) completed family,
- (3) incomplete family,
- (4) foster family.

(K4) Number of children:
number of preschool and school-age children.

(K5) Housing conditions:
- (1) convenient,
- (2) less convenient,
- (3) critical.

(K6) Financial standing of the family:
- (1) convenient,
- (2) inconvenient.

(C) SOCIAL AND HEALTH PICTURE OF THE FAMILY:
- (1) acceptance is not recommended,
- (2) acceptance is recommended,
- (3) priority acceptance is recommended.

(K7) Social conditions:
- (1) non-problematic,
- (2) slightly problematic,
- (3) problematic.

(K8) Health conditions:
- (1) acceptance is not recommended,
- (2) acceptance is recommended,
- (3) priority acceptance is recommended.

Table 2. Attribute values

The specific value of each attribute belongs to a previously defined discrete set of values. For example, the attribute "Social conditions" can take one of the following three descriptive values:

(1) Non-problematic

(2) Slightly problematic:
When education ability of parents is low (unequal, inconsistent education, exaggerated pretentiousness or indulgence, neurotic reactions of parents), or there are improper relations in family (easier forms of parental personality disturbances, privileged or ignored children, conflicts in the family), and

(3) Problematic:
When there exist improper educational ability of parents, improper rela-

tions in the family, social and antisocial forms of restraint behavior of parents or other members of the family.

A summary of the values for the remaining attributes is given in table 2. The values for each of the elementary attributes (tree leaves) were obtained from the child's parents and, in particular cases, from professional institutions such as the Centre for Social Affairs. An application form was carefully designed in order to obtain:

- relevant data containing a complete picture of the child's family status, and
- data which could be:
  - expressed with the leaf-attribute values,
  - obtained with a certain reliability,
  - verified and examined.

The appropriateness of the attributes and application forms was tested in practice, critically analyzed and changed. For instance, the initial design of the tree was complex. It consisted of about 30 attributes. The tree was later reduced to the form shown in table 1. Some attributes were omitted because they either had relatively small influence to the final evaluation results or could not reach the required reliability levels.

4.1.2 Decision rules

Data from the application forms provided individual attribute values for the leaves of the tree (table 1). Each application could then be described with coded values. For instance, the coded value for "Child One" was represented as follows:

"Child One": 2 3 1 1 3 1 2 2

were the codes drawn from table 2 signify:

(leaf K1) Parents' occupation:	pretentious (2)
(leaf K2) Child's nursery:	improper (3)
(leaf K3) Form of the family:	complete family (1)
(leaf K4) Number of children:	(1)
(leaf K5) Housing conditions:	critical (3)
(leaf K6) Financial standing of the family:	convenient (1)
(leaf K7) Social conditions:	slightly problematic (2)
(leaf K8) Health conditions:	acceptance is recommended (2)

A numerical coding of descriptive values was chosen in order to simplify data manipulation due to the large number of applications.

Probably the most crucial task to build the knowledge base was to identify and define a mapping of partial leaf values into the final evaluation value. The expert team proposed aggregation of lower-level values utilizing decision rules.

An example of such rules for the social and health picture of the family (attribute C in table 2) is the following: "priority acceptance" is recommended (value 3) regardless of the value of social conditions (K7) if health conditions (K8) say that priority acceptance is recommended (value 3). On the other hand, "acceptance" is recommended (value 2) if health conditions (K8) are recommended (value 2), even if social conditions (K7) are slightly problematic (value 2).

Table 3 shows the complete set of rules for the social and health picture of the family. In the whole knowledge base, there are five such tables, one for each aggregate attribute (node) in the tree. Each table can be considered as a one-level aggregation function.

According to these rules the applications are finally classified into 5 classes. To refine the ranking within a class an aggregation formula was used, tested and proved quite useful in practice.

Social conditions (K7)	*Health conditions (K8)*	*Social and health picture of the family (C)*
	Acceptance is not recommended (1)	Acceptance is not recommended (1)
<= Slightly problematic (2)	Acceptance is recommended (2)	Acceptance is recommended (2)
	A priority acceptance is recommended (3)	A priority acceptance is recommended (3)
Problematic (3)	Acceptance is recommended (2)	A priority acceptance is recommended (3)

Table 3: Decision rules

The formula was the weighted average of the values of the attributes:

$$\underline{F} = \sum_{\underline{x} \in A} (\underline{w}(\underline{X}) * \underline{x})$$

where:

$\underline{F}$ evaluation value
A set of all attributes, i.e. leaves and aggregate attributes
$\underline{X}$ an attribute
$\underline{w}(\underline{X})$ weight of attribute $\underline{X}$
$\underline{x}$ value of attribute $\underline{X}$.

Weights were chosen such that the evaluation value $\underline{F}$ would lie in the interval from 1 to 5. As rules also classify applications into 5 classes, a comparison of both kinds of evaluation results was made possible.

The values of the attributes, denoted $\underline{x}$ in the formula, represent numerical codes of descriptive values. These results were not influenced by the number of values of a certain attribute, but only by its importance. In this particular case, lower-level attributes had lower weights.

The knowledge base, consisting of a set of tables of decision rules and the formula, was proposed by the expert team, but the Acceptance Committee could change it according to their own judgment. However, they could not change the semantic tree (tables 1 and 2) or the application form as they were the common basis (dictionary, language) for the comparison of data and results.

4.2 Evaluation and ranking of applications

After the nursery school collected the applications and examined the data and the subsequent Acceptance Committee's review of these data as well as of the knowledge base, the evaluation was performed using DECMAK. The result was presented as a list of children's names arranged according to priorities as depicted in table 4. The codes correspond to table 2 and the evaluation classes are shown near the evaluation results which were obtained by the formula for intra-class ranking.

	Name	Evaluation attributes (leave values) K1	K2	K3	K4	K5	K6	K7	K8	Evaluation result (formula)	Priority class (rules)
1.	Child One	1	4	1	4	3	2	3	2	(4.48)	5
2.	Child Two	2	3	3	2	3	2	3	1	(4.46)	5
3.	Child Three	1	3	3	3	1	2	2	2	(4.08)	4
4.	Child Four	2	3	3	1	3	2	2	1	(3.81)	4
...											
27.	Child Twenty-seven	2	3	1	1	3	1	2	1	(3.11)	4
...											
38.	Child Thirty-eight	2	3	1	1	1	1	1	1	(2.61)	4
39.	Child Thirty-nine	2	3	1	1	1	1	1	1	(2.61)	4
40.	Child Forty	1	3	1	3	1	1	1	1	(3.11)	3
41.	Child Forty-one	2	1	3	1	2	1	1	1	(2.95)	3
...											

Table 4: Applications, ranked according to the acceptance priority

If we compare the applications 27 and 40 in table 4 we can see that the formula evaluation result is equal in both cases (3.11). Yet we must not equalize them or even compare because they belong to different priority classes (4 and 3, respectively).

As a first approximation, the Acceptance Committee could have cut-off the list at the point where the number of applications corresponded to the number of free places in the nursery school. But in practice, there were marginal cases around the cut-off line which required some further consideration.

In spite of the two level approach (rules and the formula) some applications obtained equal or only slightly different final evaluation values (e.g. applications numbered 38 and 39 in table 4). The reason is that the data did not allow to make further differentiation among such applications. In those cases the Acceptance Committee decided to give additional treatment to these applications. Nevertheless, the work of the Acceptance Committee was reduced from several days to approximately one day.

This process allowed to explain the evaluation results to the parents since once they were acquainted with the list (table 4) they could compare their children's positions with the others on the basis of real data which influenced the priority. The decision rules, for which the Acceptance Committee was responsible, were also easily explained.

5 Results

The expert team implemented and tested the expert-system-based methodology with the involvement of school authorities and of the members of the Acceptance Committee. The school authorities adopted the approach and endorsed it to higher authorities in the city of Ljubljana and the Republic of Slovenia. They are presently considering the application of the methodology developed for the pilot project, on a larger scale.

At the beginning of the project some members of the Acceptance Committee thought that the system was an additional burden for them that would require more work and learning a new, unproven technology. But later on they almost unanimously agreed that possessing an explicit methodology and the reduction of the dependence on subjective valuations simplified their work, reduced the time of deliberations and allowed them to explain without ambiguities the results to the school authorities. Consequently, it was also easy for the authorities to explain the results to the parents of the applicants.

Nursery schools and other professionals involved in the problem have immediately adopted the approach. The amount of work became smaller and consistency of decisions higher. As a consequence, the number of conflict situations between parents and nursery schools decreased.

The critical evaluation of the system results indicated the following:

a The children that needed nursery the most were accepted. This was proved by an analysis of accepted and rejected children, based on questioning some chosen families (Rajkovic et al. 1985). This was also shown by the fact that the complaints on the Acceptance Committee decisions were rare.
b The data available in the decision making process gives school authorities the possibility to organize children in an optimal manner for their educational requirements.
c The work of the Acceptance Committee has been shortened from 4 to 5 days to 1 to 2 days. Considering that the Committee is composed of 10 to 15 members this implies a considerable savings of time.
d Legal security of people has increased since it became easy to give reasons for individual applications being accepted or rejected. The proposal of a new regulation on accepting children to nursery schools is based on methods used in our work.

6 Sensitivity of the results to normativity

For this admissions system to be implemented on a larger scale than the pilot project it is clear that certain norms must be defined. The design of these norms should take into consideration the sensitivity of the results to their characteristics. The experience of the pilot project indicates that the following norms appear to affect the outputs of the system:

a Norms guiding the selection and structure of the expert team.
b Norms defining the role of the expert team leader and the system consultants.
c Norms that establish the relationship among the public school authorities, the Acceptance Committee and the expert team.
d Norms establishing the approval process of the decision making criteria (semantic tree) and the decision rules.

6.1 Selection and structure of the expert team

Perhaps the most important decision to be taken by school authorities is the definition of who will constitute the expert team. In the pilot study the fact that one member of the Acceptance Committee was an expert on decision theory and was eventually made chairman of the expert group contributed greatly to the success of the project.

Diversity of the backgrounds of the expert team had a dual effect: positive since it enriched the knowledge sources but also negative since it was difficult to achieve consensus. It also appears that the number should be reduced from the 13 used in the pilot study to 5 or 7.

6.2 The role of the expert team leader and system consultants

The expert team leader in this case was acknowledged as an authority in decision theory and that facilitated his work. Since the project has important technical inputs, it appears that the chairman should have the capability to be a "knowledge engineer" to transfer the expertise of the group to the knowledge base of the expert system. If this is not possible this role could be played by a specialized expert system's consultant.

6.3 Relationships

The relationship among authorities, Acceptance Committee and the expert team must be clearly defined: The expert provides the methodological support, the Acceptance Committee recommends and the authorities decide. It became very important in the pilot study that any overlaps should be avoided, particularly the expert team should avoid at all costs the "temptation" to decide on behalf of the authorities.

On the other hand, the Acceptance Committee is a heterogeneous group of nonprofessionals gathered together for a short time. Consequently, there should be a person (decision moderator) who acts as an "interface" between the expert system and the members of the Committee, thus allowing the members to concentrate on essential elements of decision making, e.g. on rules and critical cases.

6.4 Approval of the semantic tree and decision rules

The building of the expert system knowledge base requires that the semantic tree is clearly defined. Since the methodology is based on the application of the semantic tree, its structure will determine the outcome. It is therefore very important for the decision-makers to approve the form of the tree and its logical implications.

The same thing can be said about the decision rules that permit the aggregation of attributes. They should be clearly explained to the decision-makers and their approval should be obtained before proceeding with the project. In the pilot project particular care was placed in this procedure and it can be said that it was instrumental in the successful final acceptance of the system by the school authorities.

Ackowledgements

We would like to thank the Research Community of Ljubljana, the Nursing Communities of Ljubljana-Moste and Ljubljana-Vic, and the Nursery Schools Vic, Oton Zupancic and Koseze that financially and professionally supported this project.

References

Bohanec, M., Rajkovic, V. (1987). *An Expert System Approach to Multi-Attribute Decision Making*. Proceedings of IASTED International Conference "Expert Systems" (ed. M.H. Hamza), Acta Press.

Bohanec, M., Rajkovic, V. (1988). *Knowledge Acquisition and Explanation for Multi-Attribute Decision Making*. Avignon: 8th International Workshop "Expert Systems and Their Applications".

Keeney, L.R., Raiffa, H. (1976). *Decisions with Multiple Objectives: Preferences and Value Tradeoffs*. John Willey & Sons.

Rajkovic, V., et al. (1985). *Computer-Based Decision Support System for Nursery Schools* (in Slovene language). Ljubljana: "Jozef Stefan Institute" Report IJS DP-3920.

Expert Systems in Public Administration
I.Th.M. Snellen, W.B.H.J. van de Donk, J.-P. Baquiast (Eds.)
© Elsevier Science Publishers B.V. (North-Holland), 1989

Chapter 11

SEMAPI: An expert system for public administration procurement

*Noël Aucagne**
*Isabelle de Lamberterie**
*Dominique Quelenec**
*Michel Rocfort**

Abstract

SEMAPI, an expert system for public administration procurement operations in the data processing market, is the result of a collaborative effort involving five experts from the CCM and two knowledge engineers from the company Framentec. The system runs on PC type microcomputers. It requires a 20 Mbyte hard disk and 640 Kbytes of RAM.

SEMAPI is continually updated as french regulations are modified thus ensuring legal conformity at all times. SEMAPI is therefore an effective means of communicating regulatory evolution.

1 Introduction

In the French legal system, "public contracts" (by which a corporate body governed by public law buys goods or services) are a specific category of contracts, governed not only by the general principles of contractual law (Code of Civil Law), but also by a body of specific texts : the "Code on Government Procurement". These texts apply equally well to the operations of national government, bodies (the State and its public establishments of an administrative character, "établissements publics à caractère administratif",

* National Center for Scientific Research,
Institute for Comparative Research on Law and Institutions,
27 Rue Paul-Bert, 94204 Ivry sur Seine CEDEX, France

or EPA), as, with a few variations, to the operations of local authorities such as departments and communes.

Furthermore, the fact that France belongs to the European Economic Community (EEC) and GATT obliges the persons in charge of public procurement to also conform to the rules laid down by these bodies in the field of "public contracts". However, these rules do not either exactly or completely cover those of national law. They must accordingly be applied sometimes instead of national regulations and sometimes in combination with the latter.

Correct implementation of this complex set of rules can thus in practice raise quite difficult questions.

However, the organizational system of the French government does not comprise a central body in charge of executing, on behalf of the other administrative authorities, all the procurement function tasks. These tasks come under responsibility of and are executed by the authorities of each ministry, EPA or local authority. There are thus a large number of authorities in charge of correctly applying all the rules described above.

Only at the Ministry of the Economy and Finance is there a collegial body: the "Central Commission for Procurement", (Commission Centrale des Marchés - CCM), whose role it is to develop specific rules for public contracts and to supervise their application. At this Commission a prior consultative control system is installed with respect to the formal conformity to rules of each contract, but only for contracts concerning state bodies or EPA.

The results of these controls led the CCM to believe that it could be useful to make available to buyers, in the form of an expert system, the means of ensuring more easily that procurement operations always, and at each of their stages, comply with all the rules applicable to each specific case. But it was also considered that it is conceptually very difficult to realize straightaway and in a reasonable length of time an expert system covering all procurement activities, no matter what their subject is. It was thus decided to address in a first stage only one type of contract involving high expenditure and concerning all buyer departments. This explains the choice of contracts relating to procurement of data processing equipment (computers) by a corporate body governed by public law.

This equipment is indeed universally used and already widespread at all levels of administrative bodies. Furthermore, it is most frequently produced by transnational firms which all have well defined technical and commercial stragegies. Opposite these firms it is important for public buyers to reinforce their negotiation capacity by sufficiently harmonized, albeit not always identical attitudes and requirements.

Finaly, when it is a matter of State purchases, there is also the obligation of complying which specific budgetary directives concerning the planning and financing methods of data processing equipment.

These are the reasons which led to the decision to begin by realizing an "Expert System for Data Processing Public Contracts" (Système Expert pour les Marchés Publics d'Informatique") whose acronym is : "SEMAPI".

2 The prospect's context

2.1 Different types of situations

The very broad distribution of data processing equipment means that a great number of bodies are involved in preparing, negotiating and concluding contracts concerning this equipment, and as was previously stated they are fairly highly autonomous.

Some of these bodies have high and frequent activity in the data processing field. They have a sufficiently large personnel to have been able to specialize a few persons in their procurement departments and divide tasks among them in an organized manner. Their problem is then to ensure good communication, both between the various specialists who intervene and among all the latter and top management in charge of strategic choices.

Other bodies, on the contrary, only occasionally realize data processing operations. Their level of resources (human and financial) does not enable them, in general, to have specialists of these operations in their procurement unit. These units officials thus need to be guided step by step as to how to conduct procedures and apply rules. There are evidently very many intermediary situations between these two extremes.

2.2 What difficulties are involved in public administration procurement operations ?

The preparation and writing of an invitation to tender, its associated legal and contractual documents and the analysis of tenders received calls on highly specialized knowledge of three sorts.

- Technical expertise : to state technical specifications accurately (usually

taking an existing computational environment into account). The integration of new data processing systems into existing context must be carefully planned and their evolution must be foreseen.
- Legal expertise to ensure conformity with all aplicable laws
- Financial expertise: to develop a sound financial proposal given the budgetary constraints to be met.

The signing of a major contract is usually subject to verification by one or more legal bodies. Any omission may result in delays in the final signing or even its cancellation.

The preparation of public procurement operations requires a delicate balance of legal, technical, practical, and strategic factors. Given such a complex formula, it was only natural that a computerized solution be considered. And of the conceivable computational techniqes available, only that of an expert system is designed to handle the enormously varied types of knowledge, both theoretical and experimental, required to provide satisfactory solutions.

In addition, since most users of such a system are not computer specialists, natural language-type communication with the system had to be used (with the additional condition that expression be clear, concise, and accurate).

The result of a concerted effort by members of the Commission Centrale des Marchés (CCM) and specialized knowledge engineers, SEMAPI has proven that such a computerized solution is viable.

2.3 SEMAPI : The constraints

This is why SEMAPI was designed from the outset of its preparation as a tool capable of several types of use and therefore necessarily modular. It was also planned that the production of each module should lead to the formation of a set of results which would be both memorized to be directly accessible for other modules and which could also be printed out on paper whenever necessary for communication between specialized officials or for the purpose of accounts to top management or control bodies.

The successive treatment of these intermediary results should lead to :

- a proposal of a control reports outline and a list of contractual clauses complying with rules and the best practice of specialists.

- the provision of methodological assistance to evaluate and grade consulted offers of suppliers.

Another constraint imposed is open-endedness and adptation capacity of the computer. In the first instance, indeed, SEMAPI must be able to be kept uptodate permanently with regulations that are not stable in the medium term either at national or Community level. In the second place, it should be possible to graft, as it were, on to SEMAPI a complementary element providing users with the means of complying efficiently and without any errors with European directives concerning data processing standardization. In the last instance, finally, and at a more distant date, SEMAPI must contain enough common elements to serve as a core for expert systems that are similar but adapted to contracts having another subject than data processing epuipment.

2.4 SEMAPI : Realization method

The nature of the project and the constraints imposed on it of course do not enable administrative bodies, and in particular the project developer (CCM), to take charge of its realization alone. They above all lack the artificial intelligence knowledge and logical computation skills. An invitation to tender was thus launched to begin with, following which a realization contract was signed with the company Framentec.

But it is also clear that this company's knowledge engineers could not alone gather and put into utilizable form the necessary knowledge and rules to completely develop the system. The contract signed with Framentec has thus been a cooperation contract to a large extent. Framentec has been authorized to question, in many government sectors, people specialized in the preparation of data processing contracts. In addition, a small group of experts, specialized jurists and confirmed practicians, has worked throughout the project (for around sixteen months) with the knowledge engineers to provide them with information and ratify at each stage the direction given to the reasoning and the system's progression.

This organization was efficient since most of the concatenation between modules was correct as of the first assembly attempt, and since it only once appeared necessary to reorganize the project's module structure.

3 Description of the system

3.1 Overview

SEMAPI is an expert system designed to assist public administrations in the elaboration and writing of invitations to tender and facilitate the analysis and selection of tenders received.

It may be used in any context which involves procurement of data processing products such as hardware, catalog software packages, and associated services (installation, training, maintenance, documentation, etc).

SEMAPI offers purchasers and their collaborators (data processing and legal consultants) active support for all of the following tasks.

- writing of an accurate description of functional and technical specifications
- choice and application of procedures to be used when announcing invitations to tender
- choice of financing options which correspond to the resources available and the budgetary rules to be respected by the administration in question
- preparation of documents required for the invitation to tender and of the principal clauses of the contract
- evaluation and classification of tenders received in response to the invitation to tender
- preparation of reports required for various controlling bodies.

SEMAPI's easy-to-use natural language user interface makes it possible for the user to verify each step of the process leading to the automatic generation of the various contractual documents required.

SEMAPI is a stand-alone software package which runs on PC-type microcomputers.It has already attracted the attention of numerous french public administrations, from local to national level (indication of number?). SEMAPI is also a powerful educational tool which might play a very useful role when the time comes to deal with European-level regulations.

3.2 SEMAPI, an active solution

3.2.1 The knowledge base

The hub of the expert system, SEMAPI's knowledge base, contains all of the knowledge and experience gathered from the numerous experts consulted in the following fields.

- regulations, all applicable portions of the legal code concerning the french administration and in particular those sections dealing with contractual law
- common practice, a compilation of strategies and know-how used by administrative purchasing officers who write and oversee contracts on a daily basis
- the recommendations of french interministerial advisory committees dealing with public procurement operations and the data processing market
- technical constraints imposed by the current state of technology.

3.2.2 A modular, didactic approach

SEMAPI is designed to provide support for both full-time professional purchasers as well as those for whom public procurement is only an occasional task.

For the full-time professional, SEMAPI serves as a design support system. It verifies that all necessary information has been provided before proceeding to automatic generation of contractual documents.

On the other hand, SEMAPI offers the occasional user a complete and rigourous step ty step method for the preparation of contracts and the management of tenders as well as a full range of suggestions, recommendations, and explanations. SEMAPI is thus an educational tool as well. The method used (which reflects the practice of the experts) is embodied in a logical sequence of modules each of which is composed of groups of questions formulated in terms which are familiar to the user.

Each of the four modules used to create contractual documents is entirely independent of the others. SEMAPI recommends, however, that they be used in the following order :

- analysis of data processing needs
- choice of financing options
- choice of type of contract
- choice of consultation mode.

Thanks to its four independent modules, SEMAPI simplifies the allocation of tasks to the appropriate persons the data processing expert can enter the technical specifications while the legal consultant prepares the contractual portions of the dossier. SEMAPI can also generate several versions of a given contract based on different sets of hypotheses.

SEMAPI also ensures the overall coherence of the dossier a critical task when a large number of people work together in public procurement operations in a field as complex as that of data processing.

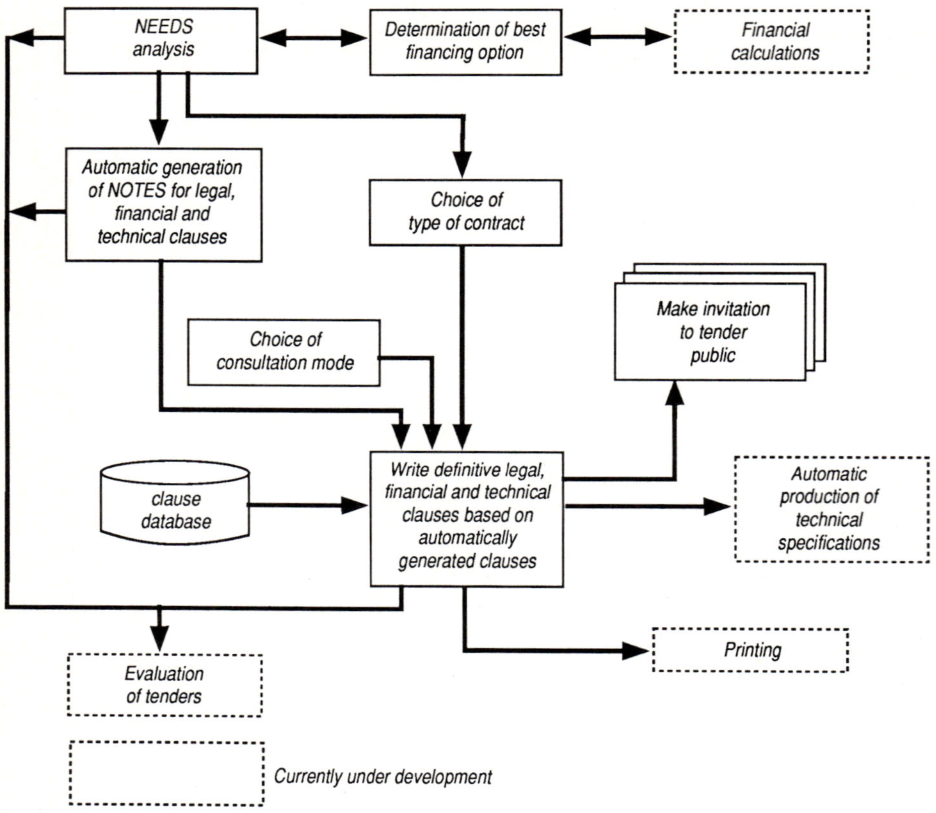

Figure 1: Functional diagram of SEMAPI

3.3 Step by step expertise

Each user operation corresponds to a module in the expert system. An operation consists of validating one or more of the assertions proposed by the system. Examples are found in the following pages.

Analysis of date processing needs

This phase is critical. The analysis of data processing needs is necessary in order to determine the object of the contract. SEMAPI uses the following procedure.

a define the context. The procedure which one wishes to computerize is currently executed by hand. No data processing equipment is currently available in the department.

b provide motives and justify need for data processing systems
The volume of data to be processed may have become too great to be handled manually.

c provide a functional description of the need
The system will process confidential data coming from outside the department.

Choice of financing options

This module is used to make the choice of the best type of financial plan form among.

- purchase
- leasing
- rental
- long-term rental

The procedure used is as follows.

a consider the object of the contract
I need hardware and a software package

b take into consideration other pertinent criteria such as
- unit price of hardware being considered
- total estimated value of the contract
- available budget
- degree of flexibility of rental terms
- etc.

This module also suggest payment terms for services included in the contract using as a basis.

- type of services
- type of contract
- financing options selected

Assistance in the choice of the type of contract

The aim of this module is to help the user select the legal form of the contract. The factors taken into account are:

- knowledge of the quantities and/or values of the services to be provided
- the object of the contract
- the dates on which different services are required
- the budget.

Assistance in the choice of consultation mode

This module helps the user to determine by what means the market is to be consulted.

Notes for the writing of contractual documents

This module is the intermediate step between the preparatory phases described above and the writing of the final draft of the various documents used in the invitation to tender. If describes the user's functional and technical needs in contractual form. If the user wants the supplier to install the equipment, this fact will be indicated in a technical clause.

Assistance in writing of the various legal and financial documents

SEMAPI automatically generates proposed technical, financial, and legal clauses for the contracts as well as legal documents necessary for the invitation to tender.

Assistance in the selection of tenders

This module helps the user to classify replies based on the choice criteria selected during use of the "analysis of data processing needs" ans "notes for technical, financial, and legal clauses" modules. The following procedure is used.

a make a selection based on technical criteria
b classify the proposals which are technically valid
c make a second selection based on financial criteria
d make a definitive classification of the proposals satisfying steps atoc
e justify the choice made.

4 Conclusion

The CCM made it policy to first deal with french public administration procurement operations in the field of data processing (covering both hardware and catalog software products). The positive results of the SEMAPI project make it possible to hypothesize several possible extensions to the project :

- inclusion of contracts for preliminary studies
- inclusion of data processing procurement operations involving countries having economic ties with France.

In addition, it may soon be possible to study the possibility of adapting SEMAPI to the broader context of the European market.

Expert Systems in Public Administration
I. Th.M. Snellen, W.B.H.J. van de Donk, J.-P. Baquiast (Eds.)
© Elsevier Science Publishers B.V. (North-Holland), 1989

Chapter 12

Knowledge-based systems in complex administrative work: Job placement at employment offices in the Federal Republic of Germany (FRG)

*Anne Höhmann**

Abstract

Computer-based decision support systems in public administration are instruments to achieve goals inadministrative work. As such, they exert a considerable influence on the carrying out of a specific task. There is thus, a reaction to the underlying normative conditions of administrative work. Conventional decision-support systems will tend to take into consideration an easily formalized knowledge rather than informal aspects of individual experience. The quality of service and the scope of manageable tasks change according to technical and organizational features. The use of data bases fed from various sources requires a new set of rules. Expert systems seem to provide at least the technological potential to introduce knowledge not yet formalized in problem solving. Possible positive effects of advanced technologies can be used only under favourable organizational conditions.

1 Problem Outline

Information and communication technology has become an increasingly important feature of public administration. Not only the formalized and structured tasks have been taken over but also administrative tasks which up to now had not been handled in this way are given access to technology-based

---

* Research Group on Informatisation in Public Administration, Kassel University, Mönchebergstrasse 17, D3500 Kassel, Germany

support systems. Of particular interest are those fields which - like the job placement process - have little or no effect on structured tasks. The support of qualitative decision-making by conventional technological processes has resulted in a number of changes in the execution of a particular job. These changes are dependent on - among other factors - the informational basis on which a decision is made.

With more advanced, efficient information and communication technologies, in particular expert systems, such areas of administrative work which have little or no structure will be affected and thus a number of difficulties will disappear.This applies above all to those difficulties which arise from a lack in flexibility and insufficient storage capacity in the system. Here, obviously, there is a reduction of information on which to base a decision.

Certain difficulties have already been observed in the field of supporting qualitative decision-making processes. These will surface again and will then be more significant. For this reason, empirical data and observations based on the application of information and communication technology in the field of computer-supported job placement will be presented here.

This chapter is based on the result of a research project carried out by the Forschungsgruppe Verwaltungsautomation (Research Group on Automation in Public Administration) at the University of Kassel. It involves the Federal Employment Institute (FEI)(Bundesanstalt für Arbeit)[1] and its pilot project "Computer-Based Job Placement (coArb) at Employment Offices in Hesse" (Trost, 1983:321 pp).

This pilot project was carried out by the FEI between 1979 and 1985. The research group was responsible for the analysis and additional research (financed by the Federal Ministry of Research and Technology as part of the programme "The Humanization of Labour") (Höhmann 1984 and Grimmer 1986).

Computer-supported job placement is an interactive method applied in the research period on the basis of decentralized office computer systems (Grimmer 1986 a: 25 pp and 71 pp).This method enables the employment service official to trace job seekers and job vacancies in one data body and according to various criteria of selection.

Thus, job placement has no underlying expert system technology. In the course of the job placement procedures, however, the research showed up the risks and possibilities of using expert systems in the future.

First, the legal provisions for "Job Placement" and the objectives of computer-supported job placement will be described. How the automated decision support performs in the finding of mediative solutions and what bearing this has on the administrative service will follow. The computer-supported job placement will then be confronted with the risks and possibilities of expert system technology.

2 Computer-supported job placement

2.1 Objectives and Tasks of Job Placement

In Germany, objectives and tasks of job placement are regulated by the Job Assistance Law (Arbeitsförderungsgesetz, AFG). According to Article 14 of this law, it is the responsibility of the Federal Employment Institute to create adequate conditions in order to match job seekers and job vacancies leading to satisfaction for both employers and job seekers. The Federal Employment Institute has to take into account the details of the vacancies, the skills of the job seekers and their personal circumstances.

The employment service officials therefore need information which enables them to give equal attention both to the particular circumstances of vacancies and to the qualification and personal circumstances of the job seekers.

Job placement depends on the situation of the labour market.The Federal Employment Institute has only a limited influence on supply and demand of labour. To ensure successful jobplacement, it is essential that details of job vacancies are circulated to the employment offices (the employer is,however, not obliged to file the vacancies). Employment service officials are only authorized to make proposals for job placement; an employer is by no means obliged to comply with these suggestions.

Job placement goes beyond the mere display of vacancies. It comprises an advisory service regarding personnel requirements and job opportunities (15 AFG) and includes social aspects in particular (provided that applicants are equally qualified).

It is the task of the employment service official to provide the most qualified preselection of applicants. The employment service official's preselection has to meet all the explicit requirements given by the employer and take presupposed requirements into consideration. Simultaneously he has to consider the job seeker's personality. For example, would a particular job seeker, with his specific skills, fit into the employer's company? The decision will finally be made by the future employer appointing that person who seems most qualified.

Collection, storage and processing of data on vacancies and applications are characteristic of the employment serviceofficial's work. The information necessary for a successful job placement, particulary for the submittal of qualified placement proposals, is initially gathered from written documents (reports, applications) and from interviews with clients.

As a service, job placement is an information and communication process between employers offering positions and employees seeking work. There is also an informationsystem available within and between the various placement departments of the different employment offices.

In the course of the job placement procedure, considerable importance is attached to the individual attention given to job seekers. From the start the employment service official should attempt to realize the particular characteristics of his clients and to take them into account in the placement proposal. In doing so, he should avoid routine service or preplanned conclusions (according to the guide lines for jobplacement, edited by the State Employment Office, Hesse, April 1, 1981, No. 28, p.25). It is clear that employment service officials need a broad information basis in respect to both the individuality of the applicant and of the jobvacancy in order to complete their task effectively.

2.2 Support of decision-making in job placement

The Federal Employment Institute developed the method of computer-supported job placement with the intention of supporting the employment service official's work. The efficiency of job placement should be maintained and, if possible, be improved, particularly in order to achieve a speedy matching of job seekers and vacancies. The object is to relieve employment service officials of routine work. Another purpose is the creation of a transparent labourmarket.

As a result of the introduction of information technology there is a new priority: the transparency of the labourmarket gains a new rank. This means that proposals to fill a particular vacancy are no longer the sole responsibility of the employment service official dealing with that vacancy(i.e. the official who received the details of the vacancy in the first place) Instead, the vacancies are taken into consideration by other service officials submitting proposals for job placement. To a certain degree, the details of the job seekers also receive more attention.

With the introduction of information technology, the collection, storage, processing and distribution of information receives partial support on a technological basis and partial automation. The registration of these data, however, brings about a reduction of the overall available information. The use of information technology requires the registration of formalized and standardized data according to a given scheme(Grimmer 1986 b: 221 pp) (see below). Information in databases is made available to the employment service officials throughout the commuter area (the area in which reasonable offers for vacancies can be submitted to a job seeker). It follows that each employment service official has access to his colleagues' information.

2.3 Diverging Interests in the decision-making process

Complex decision-making processes in job placement are supported by the help which in formation technology provides.

Complex decision-making in this context means the decision an employment service official has to arrive at in a given situation. It is not strictly regulated but the employment service official must employ discretion in the evaluation of different kinds of decisions.

The data base and information provided have to enable the employment service official to reach a decision in his placement suggestion that meets different, or even diverging, interests.

The employment service official

- has to comply with the rules, particularly those of the AFG, as well as with subordinate legal guide-lines and administrative regulations;
- must meet the employers' wishes regarding the requirements of the vacancy to be filled;
- should take into account the interests of the jobseekers in respect to skill and qualification;
- has to satisfy the interests of all those in contributory social security schemes by trying to match vacancies and job seekers both quickly and inexpensively;

- is entitled to expect a degree of personal jobsatisfaction. He should, for example, be allowed to institute his empirical knowledge - the criteria which he has acquired over the years should be included and activated in his proposal for job placement.

3 Support of the employment officer's decision-making process through computer-supported job placement

3.1 Increasing importance of formalized data

It will now be explained specifically to which areas of jobplacement the decision-making process is applicable. In the course of job placement the data on vacancies and applicants, initially recorded manually on file-cards, will be further formalized and standardized, beyond the degree of manual formalization. This is due to the fact that the use of information technology requires a highly structured body of data (Brinckmann et al. 1986 in this context the importance of forms regarding the collection of relevant data for the decision-making process within the administration). The outlined technological procedure features a limited storagecapacity. Which data will be fed into the system of automated processing will be decided predominantly by given norms.

A job description cannot violate the anti-discrimination laws- the description cannot discriminate on the grounds of sex or nationality. This is the case even if the employer wishes otherwise (Höhmann 1984: 128). If the employment service official does not take into consideration the criteria desired by the employer in his selection of applicants, the employer on his part may not accept the placement proposal, since he is not obliged to comply with the suggestions of the employment office.

Data storage in job placement, strongly oriented towards given norms, has both positive and negative effects. One of the positive effects is that in certain cases a higher degree of the applicants' equal status can be guaranteed. There will be negative consequences, however, if the quality of the placement proposals diminishes. This could lead to the advertising of fewer vacancies, due to the decreasing influence of job placement.

The conventional, non-computerized job placement was also carried out according to the legal provisions. However, there was more space on the file-card for hand-written (informal)entries (Höhmann 1984: 148). Furthermore, restricted propagation of vacancies by employment service officials led in most cases to placement suggestions by that employment officer who had also received the advertisement of this vacancy. As a result of his personal contact with the employer, this official had invariably more information on the vacancy than was recorded on his conventional, hand-written file-card. This information was personally memorized. He could include the information in his decision on whether or not to make a placement proposal. The emphasis in the placement procedure therefore lay in the individual attention given to the clients.

The computer-supported job placement provides for the distribution of a vacancy description to various employment offices. Thus, in the case of an employment service official not filing a vacancy himself, the chance of incorporating information not entered in the system is reduced. This means that the employment service official will have to rely more on information provided by the computer-supported job placement system.

3.2 Importance of non-formalized data and data difficult to formalize

It is only under certain circumstances that the computer-aided job placement can provide support for thedecision-making process. For instance, the information made available must be adaptable to the particular, individual tasks of the employment service officials.

As a rule, the decision of employment service officials as to whether or not a placement proposal can be made, need not depend entirely on the mere matching of job seekers and vacancies.

The decisions of the employment service official are based on 'hard' data (formalized) and 'soft' data (non-formalized).'Hard' data include, for example, the formal qualification requirements of an employer, as well as professional degrees and proof of experience which a job seeker will need to provide if he wants to be placed in a position. As shown above, these 'hard' data will be stored in the course of jobplacement with the support of knowledge-based systems and form the basis of the search criteria for data base queries.

The particular environment of the working place and the character traits of an applicant can be regarded as 'soft'data. 'Soft' data are written down only to a very small extent. They are written "between the lines" and/or represent the empirical knowledge of the employment service official.The settlement of an employment contract on the basis of a job placement proposal depends to a great extent on the evaluation which the employment service official gives to the 'hard' and 'soft' data.

The employment service official needs not only differentiated professional knowledge, but also a degree of insight into the structure and variation of the labour market. Knowledge insight alone, however, is not sufficient for the daily placement tasks. The employment service official requires further skills - the capacity to associate, intuition, creativity and empathy. Those traits aid the successful placement of the client and ensure a degree of job satisfaction on the part of the official.

In computer-based job placement, it is mainly 'hard' data which is provided as basic information. The employment service officials are dealing more and more with this kind of data. They themselves also work under unsatisfactory conditions, for example, stressful work hours (Grimmer 1986b: 249). These factors together lead to a negative imbalance in the desired solution of this problem - namely the appropriate evaluation of 'hard' and 'soft' data - and thus contradict the qualitative aspect of the solution.

3.3 Decision-makingsupport within the framework of job placement

Computer support of job placement aims at qualitative improvement. The employment service official should have easier access to a larger number of vacancies. This improvement can be achieved by automated data processing which allows selective placement proposals. The decisive factor when considering the aptitude of a particular candidate for a job vacancy is the information which is available on the individual job offer.

A qualitative improvement in job placement and consequently better solutions will not only be accomplished by access to a larger number of vacancies. The vacancies must be formulated in such a way as to enable employment service officials who have no extra knowledge about particular vacancies to make placement proposals on the basis of retrievable information. Even if the descriptive capacities of the system are insufficient as a result of technological deficiencies, methods must be provided to enable the user to retrieve information in order to exercise a more problem-oriented approach. Plenty of time must be available for this important issue.

Decision-making, like the submittal of placement proposals, is based on communication and interaction. Job placement thus depends on various sources which are fed from a common database. This means that the job placing officials must have access to certain information from job offer officials even if the information does not belong to the retrievable data.

Computer-supported job placement increases the transparency of the job vacancies, a factor recognized by the Federal Employment Institute. Additional information can be obtained which puts retrievable data into the right context. With the introduction of the computer-support system, the FEI also facilitated telephone contact between the various officials (Höhmann 1984: 155).

An increase in data maintenance is necessary and simultaneously a greater period of time for data processing and analysis, when employment service officials actually want to utilize given information in the carrying out of their tasks. They will need more time, and most certainly thenecessary qualifications. They will need, for example, more information on profession profiles in order to be able to accurately evaluate information on vacancies from such professional areas with which they were up to now not acquainted.

A qualitative improvement in job placement cannot be achieved solely with the introduction of technology. Compulsory regulations pertaining to the entry and processing of information as well as to access are a necessary addition.

Part of the problems resulting from the use of computer-based decision support systems can be solved by conventions and normative regulations.

3.4 Improved decisions through improved technology?

It has been demonstrated that the use of conventional computer-supported systems often requires extra effort in order to accurately evaluate and classify information retrieved by data processing. Assuming that the employment service official has associative capacities, intuition,creativity and empathy, it remains uncertain whether it is feasible to continue to support the employment officials' activity through advanced technology, e.g. expert systems.

Does the introduction of additional technological means of procuring and evaluating information actually improve the possibilities of qualitative support in decision making? A refinement of the "raw material" information, for example through the use of friendlier user interface or expert system technology, is necessary.

Expert systems promise new potentials for decision support. With the help of expert system technology it should be possible in the future, for instance, to show the data in its context and to find reasonable solutions through communication with the user.

Expert systems are presently being developed as software programs. They will, in all probability, support the decision-making process and facilitate the problem-oriented processing of information by dividing entered data into context- and significance-oriented categories. They contain knowledge reduced to rules, the so-called knowledge base, i.e. expert knowledge. Expert systems also include facts relevant to decision-making (these data can also be stored in an external data base) and processing schemata responsible for the correct linkage of rules in the knowledge base (Fiedler 1987).

Such systems will probably increase the possibility of an improvement in the quality of service in public administration. Basically the support systems render a service to decision making in that they combine non-formalized knowledge and individual experience.

It is important to request knowledge which has not yet be enformalized, and together with the experts prepare and establish new rules. In the job placement procedure and in other areas of public administration as well, we will have to take into account difficulties in the use of expert system technology: only those rules and empirical knowledge should be stored which are easy to generalize and which can sustain legal examination. However, a very large part of empirical knowledge is to be found in the grey area between, on the one hand unauthorized and, on the other, authorized evaluation of information. It is not by chance that these evaluations have not yet been published or standardized. In particular, empirically based subjective evaluations of certain clients- both employers and employees - which are decisive for the placement success must not be stored for reasons of data and personal privacy.

A whole range of new rules will probably be necessary as a result of the introduction of this new technology. Pilot projects on a small administrative scale are necessary to establish to what degree as yet unpublished rules are adequate for analysis in expert systems. Further, these rules must be scrutinized to ascertain how far they can stand up to legal examination.

3.5 Conditions for the development and use of expert systems

The method of job placement itself brings with it the problem of considering 'hard', formalized data in the problem solving process. Using expert system technology, this problem will reappear, possibly even more decisively.

If expert system technology cannot adequately process and generalize knowledge that has not yet been formalized, we run the risk of continuously guiding decision-making along fixed rules of the system. This could be the case if

- a divergence from given decisions must be accounted for;
- technological norms get out of control and lose touch with reality (Göbel/ Schmalz 1986);
- the qualifications of the employment service officials are not sufficient to evaluate the decisions produced with the help of the support systems on the basis of their own knowledge.

These dangers can only be avoided if expert system applications are developed slowly and are participation-oriented. There must be sufficient time and qualified personnel available for the decision-making as well as for the maintenance of expert systems (cf. Karl/Ohm1988). The dilemma that public administration has always been faced with - that of taking varying interests into account when it comes to carrying out a specific task - will certainly not be solved solely by the introduction of advanced technology.

The decisive factor in the adequate solving of problems in administrative work will be advantageous organizational and personnel conditions. For this reason a humane, well-founded scientific assistance must formulate and test the respective standards and to press for their realization.

References

Brinckmann, Hans; Grimmer, Klaus; Höhmann, Anne; Kuhlmann,Stefan; Schäfer, Wolfgang (1986) *Formulare imVerwaltungsverfahren. Wegbereiter standardisierter Kommunikation* (Beiträge zur juristischen Informatik, 12) Darmstadt

Fiedler, Herbert (1987) Grundlagen und Anwendungsmöglichkeiten von Expertensystemen fur die Justiz. in: *Informatik und Recht,* Heft 3, S.101 - 107

Grimmer, Klaus (Hg.) (1986 a: b: c) *Arbeit derArbeitsvermittler und ihre Veränderung durch Informationstechnologie, Arbeitspapiere der Forschungsgruppe Verwaltungsautomation,* Heft 39: Band 1:Technisch-organisatorische Rahmenbedingungen, Heft 40: Band 2: Auswirkungen auf die Arbeit und Heft 41: Band 3:Dienstleistungsqualität und Informationsverbund, Kassel

Goebel, Jürgen W.; Schmalz, Reinhard (1986) Probleme beim Einsatz juristischer Expertensysteme in der Rechtspraxis. In:*Computer und Recht,* Heft 8, S. 510 - 515

Höhmann, Anne (1984) Erfahrungen mit der Einfhrung der computerunterstützten Arbeitsvermittlung in Arbeitsämtern. Fallstudien zur Arbeit der Arbeitsvermittler und ihrer Veränderung durch Informationstechnologie, *Arbeitspapiere der Forschungsgruppe Verwaltungsautomation,* Heft 38, Kassel

Karl, Helga; Ohm, Christof (1988) Expertensysteme im Widerspruch - Umbruch des Wissens und gegensätzliche Berufskulturen. In: *Projektgruppe Automation und Qualifikation* (Hrsg.)

Frigga Haug, Helga Karl, Christof Ohm, Werner van Treeck, Thomas Waldhubel und Gerhard Zimmer: *Politik um die Arbeit*. (Argument-Sonderband AS 167)Berlin/Hamburg 1988

Schaper, Hans-Heinrich (1988) *Informationsverarbeitung in der Bundesanstalt für Arbeit*. Stuttgart, Berlin, Köln, Mainz

Trost, Renate (1983) Datenverarbeitung in der Bundesanstalt für Arbeit. In: *Arbeit und Beruf*, S. 321 ff.

Notes

1 The Federal Employment Institute is a corporation of public law (Körperschapt des Öffentlichen Rechts). Its main function is job placement, vocational guidance and the allotting of unemployment insurance. The FEI is the only corporate body to authorize job placement.

Expert Systems in Public Administration
I. Th.M. Snellen, W.B.H.J. van de Donk, J.-P. Baquiast (Eds.)
© Elsevier Science Publishers B.V. (North-Holland), 1989

Chapter 13

A development tool for expert systems in the field of regulations

*Pierre Levine**
*Jean-Luc Minel**

1 Needs

An expert system for processing regulation dossiers must incorporate a number of management modes for handling data and knowledge. The descriptive details of the dossiers to be processed are represented by data values comparable to a database management system. The exploration strategy employed by the liquidator or investigator of the dossier depends on a strategy management module; this must be capable of dynamically examining the hypotheses formulated by the liquidator and of calling expert modules specialised in evaluating regulation conditions. Finally, the results of the expertise and its justification must be expressable in the form of a detailed report. Figure 1 shows the architecture of a development tool suited to these tasks.

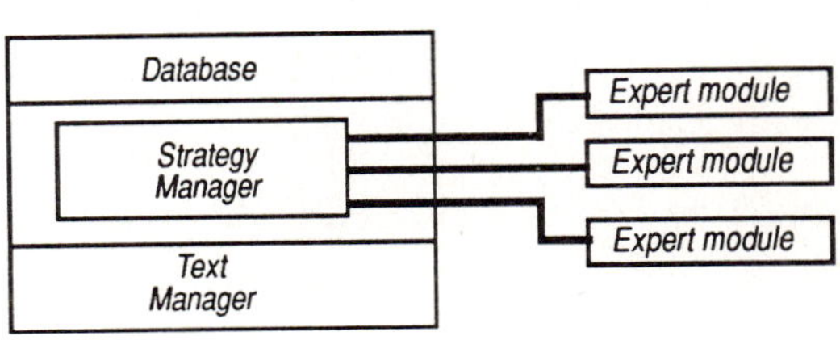

Figure 1: Architecture of the development tool

* Informatics Service, National School for Public Administration (E.N.A.), 13 rue de l'Université, 75007, Paris, France

While the construction of the data base poses few problems, the same cannot be said of the knowledge base which is the foundation of the strategy management and evaluation modules. To this end we have devised the methodology and the development tools briefly described below.

2 Methodology for the construction of a knowledge base

2.1 Mastering the strategy of exploration

The construction of a knowledge base initially requires the definition of the exploration strategy to be used.

The first generation of expert systems were designed with knowledge bases in which the rules were stored as the expert defined them, leaving the inference engine free to choose which rules to apply.

This option rapidly ran up against the real life conditions of use of an expert system, to wit:

- the person using the system, who must answer the questions it generates, usually has to consult a paper, administrative dossier, company balance sheet, etc. This implies a continual coming and going among his papers as he follows the engine's questioning strategy.
- the user may have knowledge of elements which, for the case in question, would enable him to get a diagnosis more rapidly.
- the engine's strategy may theoretically be optimal, but in fact it can only correspond completely to a marginal number of real situations.

Here is an example to illustrate the problem:

An expert system is required to examine dossiers of candidates for an institute for advanced studies. During the procedure it has to check that the candidate satisfies the age requirements:

- the candidate must be less than 30 years old on October 31 of the year of the entry exam. But the candidate can benefit from an age limit extension depending on different criteria which can be combined:
- the length of his military service;
- the number of dependent children;
- civil status (married, divorced, single);

For these criteria to be taken into account, the candidate has to provide documentation. We have shown the conditions and documents necessary in figure 2.

Conditions to verify	Documents required
Age < 30	*Birth certificate*
Age < 30 *+ length of military service*	*Birth certificate* *service record*
Age < 30 *+ length of military service* *+ number of childern*	*Birth certificate* *service record* *relevant documents*
Single woman *E,mployed* *At least one child*	*Relevant documents* *employers declaration* *attestation of child*
Handicapped applicant	*attestation of handicap*

Figure 2: Required conditions and documents

On examining this table, several strategies are apparent:

a A strategy based on minimising the number of question asked, which will initially seek to establish whether the candidate is handicapped, since this condition results in the minimum amount of calculation and document checking. This situation is nevertheless rarely met in the dossiers processed.

b A strategy based on statistical analysis of dossiers from preceding years, which will begin by exploring the most frequently encountered conditions and will have the opposite inconveniences.

To express these strategies requires a suitable formal framework, simple enough for specialists unfamiliar with data processing concepts.

For this reason we have introduced the idea of exploration schemata. Each exploration schema is of the form:

```
IF        OBJECT A    PREMISSES
IF        OBJECT B    OF STRUCTURE

THEN      OBJECT C    ACTIONS
                      OBJECT D  OF STRUCTURE
```

Such a diagram signifies:

IF object A
AND object B have been evaluated, whatever their values,
THEN begin evaluating object C and object D.

No object values are expressed in a schema (the rules of the schema will reveal them).

We must stress the interest of such an approach, which to begin with frees the designers of the knowledge base from the wearisome task of writing out all the possible combinations for the rules.

In addition, the subsequent actions of the schema can include:

- calls to resolution procedures outside the expert system;
- calls to a database;
- calls to an expert system to evaluate a given object.

These exploration schemata will enable us to check that the strategic paths are truly exhaustive.

They also help us to consider which objects should be simultaneously proposed to the user at each stage of the system's analysis.

All these objects should be grouped together as *actions* in a single exploration structure, allowing the user to choose his strategic path in the light of the information available to him at the moment of consultation.

We shall use graphics to illustrate these scenarios. For example, the schemata:

IF DATE OF ENQUIRY
AGE OF APPLICANT

THEN STATE OF HEALTH
LEVEL OF RESOURCES
CONDITIONS OF RESIDENCE
REQUEST VALIDATED

will be represented by figure 3.

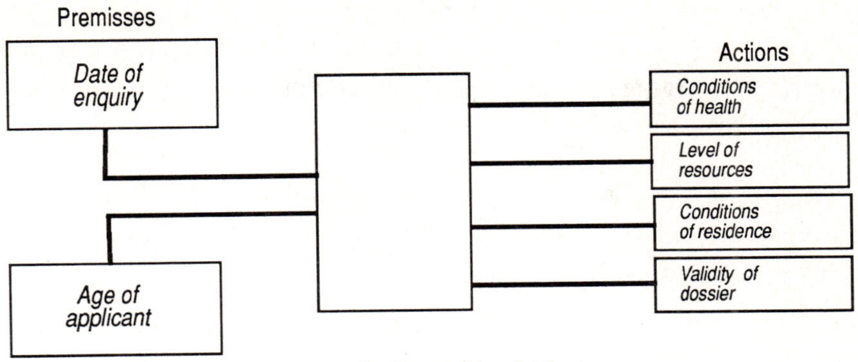

Figure 3: Examples of schemata

2.2 Managing the hypotheses generated

Processing a dossier generally requires the formulation of one of more working hypotheses.

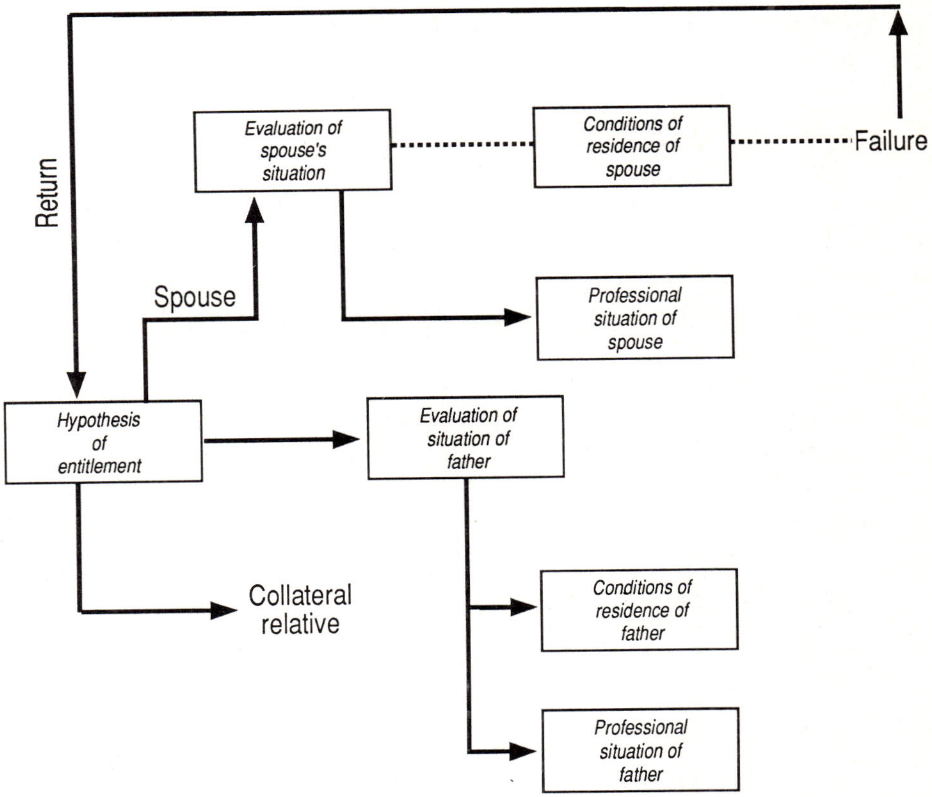

Figure 4: Managing hypotheses

For example, in the field of legislation covering social assistance, a person who has not contributed sufficiently to a social security organisation can nevertheless be attributed benefits inherited from the rights of his spouse, parent, etc. This means that an individual has several sources of entitlement that satisfy the regulations. If there is an obstacle to one source of entitlement, from the spouse for example, it will be necessary to go back and explore the possibilities offered by a parent. This notion of hypothesis and return in case of a failure is illustrated by figure 4.

Furthermore, during the design of the knowledge base for the strategy manager, it is important to distinguish concepts which are hypotheses from those which are only choices. To sum up, the strategy manager must provide the various functions shown in figure 5.

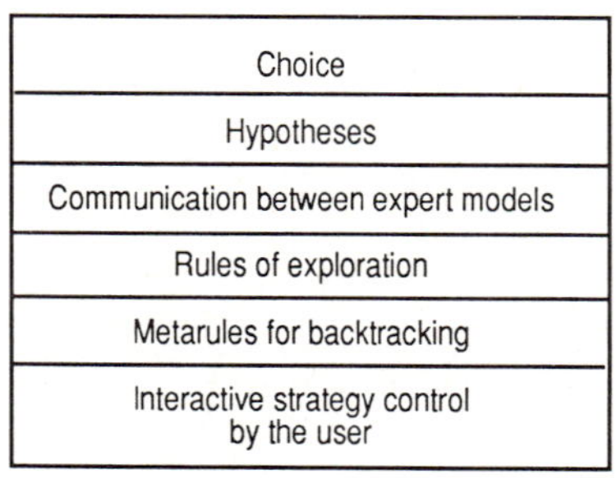

Figure 5: Main features of a strategy manager

3 Building knowledge bases for use in evaluation

Each identified concept in the knowledge base used to manage exploration strategy can contribute to a finer evaluation by the expert. (This refers to a local or specific expertise which must be developed in accordance with the previously mentioned constraints. For example, it is important to evaluate the conditions of residence of the applicant for social assistance).

The creation of a knowledge base for evaluation purposes requires a specific formal schema because:

- the concepts must be hierarchised to express their respective importance;
- the structured model must be able to serve as reference for discussion between experts.

This conceptual representation (and physical, if based on adequate software) will be a most useful aid to managing knowledge bases over time. In effect, while the declaration mode enables important gains to be made in the conception of expert systems, these gains can be obliterated by the workload necessitated by the introduction of new rules or new concepts.

The representation of structured models of knowledge requires the use of a means of formalisation, the evaluation structure.

3.1 Representation of knowledge in an evaluation structure

An evaluation schema expresses the dependance which exists between an explained concept and explanatory concepts.

Each element of dependence between concepts is called an evaluation structure. These schemata are then organised in a non-cyclic graph which takes into account the relative importance of the concepts through appropriate use of hierarchies.

These hierarchies can be the result of the conditions of intervention of an object rather than the weight accorded an object. For example in the field of administrative regulations a legislation on the conditions of nationality will be expressed as follows:

The conditions of nationality are satisfied if:

a the applicant is of French nationality;
b the applicant belongs to the EEC;
  b1 the applicant has been resident in France for more than two years and has a professional activity;
  b2 the applicant has been resident in France for more than two years and has more than two dependent children;
c the applicant does not belong to the EEC;
  c1 the applicant has been resident in France for more than two years and has a professional activity;
  c2 the applicant has lost his French nationality by marriage.

This is represented in the form of evaluation schemata in figure 6.

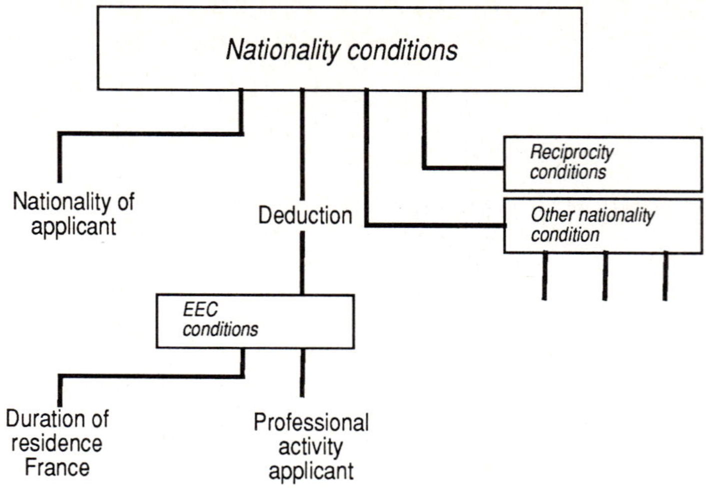

Figure 6: Diagram of deductive evaluation

This form of representation has been expanded to include methods of calculation. For example, figure 7 shows an evaluation with regard to age limit, where "diff-date" is a pre-existing function in the development tool.

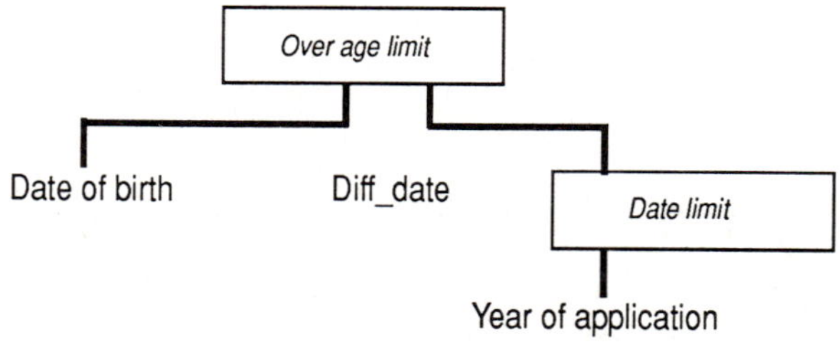

Figure 7: Calculation schema

4 The contribution of methodology and software to maintenance of regulations

The modification of the text defining a regulation can be carried out at several levels. Firstly, the introduction of a new value to an existing concept and a new rule, which is the equivalent of inserting a rule of inference in the knowledge base. Secondly, the structural modification of a text, which means that a new concept must be included. The position of this concept can be rapidly discovered using the modular tree architecture of the existing knowledge bases, and appropriately inserted in the corresponding exploration structure. The knowledge base management tool verifies the structural coherence of the modification by checking that no juridical loops are introduced (e.g. "to decide A you must know B, and to decide B you must know A"), and also by checking the existing rules against the new legislation. This guarantees the legislator against the creation of non-communicating or contradictory levels of regulations.

Figure 8 shows the question put to an expert who has just introduced new conditions for reducing social assistance.

Rules concerning the schema CONDITIONS FOR REDUCTION
IF 1) Reason for reduction = Specialised accomodation *IF 2) Level of hospitalisation reduction = indifferent* *IF 3) Conditions reduction specialised accomodation = Satisfactory* *IF 4) Conditions reduction incarceration + ???* *THEN Conditions for reduction = Satified*

Figure 8: Conditions for reduction

5 Impact of the use of a declarative methodology on the conception and control of regulations

From the point of view of normativity the use of an expert system in a number of French administrations has enabled the following points to be brought out:

a Insofar as concerns the conception of regulations, the methodology enables a new text to be considered as a juridical module complementary to the existing knowledge bases, with the possibility for the jurist of testing hypotheses and measuring their impact both in the domain of global coherence of the various regulations and at the level of in-depth modification of their legal foundations.
Another little explored potential is the development of systems using the inspector's expertise, approach and the rules he applies to formalise qualitative judgements.In this respect, certain systems currently being developed will without doubt be of great interest in their approach to the clarification of criteria and exploration schemata, leading to a better assessment of administrative organisations.

b Procedures for checking administrative regulations.
The increasing complexity of the organisations controlled and the multiplicity of regulations and techniques relevant to an in-depth control today

present the inspector, a generalist rather than a specialist, with a further problem.

In practice this development is marked as much by the growing time taken by controls and the use of expanded teams to perform them, as by the diversity of requests for controls.

The very broad definition of the powers of a general inspector can lead him to intervene to settle conflicts between individuals, to uncover frauds, to pass judgement on the operation of organisations or procedures, to evaluate policies.

This intervention can concern fields as different as medical activities, personnel management and data processing.

The use of an expert system as an approach to checking both security and conformity to regulations provides easy access and easier and more exhaustive control of complex procedures or regulations.
The possibility of demonstrating the reasoning of an expert system facilitates explanation of the differences between the inspector's results and those obtained by the organisation being controlled, thus favouring dialogue.

6 Conclusion

This methodology and its associated development tools have been used by the DRASS Aquitaine (Direction Régionale de l'Action Sanitaire et Sociale de l'Aquitaine) to control the allowance for handicapped adults, thanks to financing by the Ministry of Health and the CIIBA (Comité Interministeriel pour l'Informatique et la Bureautique dans l'Administration). The knowledge bases have been created by three DRASS inspectors without data processing experience, with knowledge engineering assistance from the ENA (Ecole Nationale d'Administration).

Begining in October 1986, the development phase and the test phase each required two months work. Today all 22 regions of France use this expert system, enabling them to carry out systematic controls with important results both financially and in the field of administrative regulations.

The legislation on French nationality has twice been modified in depth, enabling us to verify the validity and performance of the exploration schema format; the time necessary to modify the knowledge bases did not exceed 3 or 4 days' work by inspectors.

Expert Systems in Public Administration
I. Th.M. Snellen, W.B.H.J. van de Donk, J.-P. Baquiast (Eds.)
© Elsevier Science Publishers B.V. (North-Holland), 1989

Chapter 14

Some reflections on the economic viability of an expert system

*Marcel Aucoin**

1 Introduction

The design and implementation of expert systems in an administrative environment is necessarily subject to special conditions.

As van de Donk and Snellen (cf. Chapter 1) have demonstrated, several spheres of rationality need to be taken into account - political, legal, technical, administrative, economic. I am further prepared to acknowledge that the sociological features of the environment cannot be overlooked either.

These different types of rationality can (cf. Chapter 1) serve as positive pointers and create conditions conducive to the development of an expert system; also, however, they may put up constraints and may even prohibit certain things.

All this is generally unclear in reality, and we can only gain by making more explicit what is barely so at present.

I shall be seeking, in this study, to shed light on the debate with reference to an actual case, namely the construction by the Banque de France of a business diagnosis expert system entitled COSIE* (better known in France by the acronym A.I.D.E.- Assistance Informatique au diagnostic d'Entreprise).

---

* French National Bank (Banque de France),
39 rue Croix-des-Petits-Champs, 75001 Paris, France

In emphasizing the notion of economic rationality, we may state the problem thus: what gains, over de medium run, might jusitify the expences necessary to build and implement an expert system? The question obviously refers to the paramount criterion of all economic activity, namely that it must earn more than it costs.

But one may object that administrative activities are not subject to this type of criterion, for the simple reason that they do not always end in monetary revenues.

One answer to that might be that, while administrative activities frequently have no monetary value, they always have costs and the need to justify them remains: the fact of having no monetary means of evaluation is a primarily technical obstacle.

Acknowledging the appropriateness of investigating the economic viability of an expert system, the next question is: could our analysis serve to identify norms capable of guiding the builders of expert systems or the decision-makers called upon to provide the necessary resources (intrinsic norms relating to the knowledge base; and extrinsic norms concerning the implementation of the expert system by different users (van de Donk en Snellen, chapter 1).

Before offering a tentative answer to these major questions, it is worth reviewing the three key elements conditioning the long-term economy of an expert system, namely:

- the expenditure stream,
- the revenue stream,
- the expenditure/revenue equilibrium.

For the purpose of this analysis, I shall draw chiefly on our experience in building COSIE (Aucoin, Micha and Pham-Hi, 1989).

2 The expenditure stream

Costs incurred in the construction of COSIE fall into three categories:

- knowledge base (rules, facts)
- computerization
- management.

In one respect, COSIE embodied little that was innovative in comparison with conventional computer applications; consequently, the traditional criteria in this sphere ought to apply to the implementation of expert systems.

However, leaving aside the fact that these criteria are relatively vague, an experience such as COSIE presents a number of original features in economic terms. We are dealing here with a particular dynamic in that, from the time of construction of the initial breadboard to the current version, the system has grown constantly over the years and, as in any birth, the process has been accompanied by modifications affecting every part of the system. Its highly systemic, evolving character does not facilitate the proposed analysis in terms of separate fragments.

2.1 The knowledge base

The knowledge base concerns first the facts, and then the logical rules used to formulate a diagnosis, by means of formal and deductive reasoning.

2.1.1. Facts

The COSIE system depends on the Banque de France Balance Sheet Data Centre's data base, which has approximately 23.000 members, including 12.000 industrial firms. Only the latter are currently concerned by COSIE, many of them having been monitored over five years at least (approximately 50% of them).

With more than fifteen year's experience behind it, with a richer and more reliable (in terms of quality) body of information than other comparable bases, the value of this base lies also in:

- the wide range of statistical analyses carried out by the Balance Sheet Data Centre,
- and the aggregation of data by sector into about 500 references which serves to shed light on the individual diagnoses, by comparison with equivalent firms in terms of activity or size.

Data are gathered and processed in keeping with three norms that shape the effectiveness with which they are used:

- *a contractual norm*
  When it receives accounting data, data significantly broader in scope than that communicated to the French tax authorities, the Banque de France has no statutory powers to compel disclosure of the said data.
  It relies solely on the good will of the companies participating and on the notion of partnership.

- *an ethical norm*
  In return, the Bank guarantees to treat individual data in strict confidence. Under no circumstances may they be communicated to a third party without prior consent of the firm concerned.

- *a scientific norm*
  A crucial factor in the value of any scientific experiment is the thorougness with which it is prepared. Similarly, all data utilized by the Balance Sheet Data Centre are carefully checked for consistency and, where necessary, restated with the consent of the firm concerned.
  One cannot overstress the importance of this norm in all expert systems. Admittedly it is expensive, but the high cost of managing the Balance Sheet Data Centre's data rigorously ought to be an incentive to extract the maximum amount of useful lessons from it.

2.1.2 The rule base

From the outset, when constructing the first breadboard of COSIE in 1984, it was clear that the experts at the Balance Sheet Data Centre were already thinking spontaneously in terms of production rules of the type: if H, then C.... All that was required then was to extend the knowledge base (currently it contains 1.000 rules), specifying their analytical domains.

All this occurred through a complex dynamic process involving a proliferation of feedbacks with a great many parties, both inside and outside the Banque de France. Between 1987 and 1988, the COSIE system was validated on more than 2.000 cases, resulting in extensive revision of the rule base.

In addition to this utterly indespensable *validation norm,* there was the difficulty of keeping the rule base consistent.
In theory, it is often said, rules can be formulated in bulk, their order being immaterial to the proper working of the inference engine.

That is not how things are in real life, simply because producing a full and global diagnosis of a company's evolution over four consecutive years (with five series of accounting data to be analysed), is more complex than detecting the cause of a breakdown in some piece of machinery.
The rule base must be consistent with the AIM of the expert system, and with the FORM of the results one wishes to obtain. This too is a norm that needs to be complied with, though that is not easy to achieve as it calls for a good deal of thought.

Lastly, the rule base may be enriched considerably. I am not thinking here of the coefficients of plausibility used in EMYCIN-type medical diagnosis models, as their determination is too subjective.

What we have done in the case of COSIE amounts to measuring, for the selected rule of the type; if H, then C, the percentage of cases p (H) for which the conclusion has been verified on the Balance Sheet Data Centre population, counting the number of cases for which hypothesis H has been found to be true. For example, let the rule be:

If H,
then company X is competitive (C).

Observation may show us, for example, that in the reference sample selection, H is true for 25% of firms, therefore (C). That would strenghten us in our conviction, for we are in the presence of a relatively rare occurence. The contrary would have been the case had the percentage p (H) of the rule been 75%, thus reflecting a widespread occurrence.

This leads us to recommend a *statistical calibration* of all rules utilized, to make it easier to select hypotheses and ultimately to ensure the credibility of the conclusions.

Validation and consistency norms, and a statistical calibration norm - all these cost money. In the case of COSIE, however, these costs were relatively modest thanks to a series of factors, i.e.:

- The considerable accumulated knowledge of the Balance Sheet Data Centre's "Methodology" unit,
- Recourse to resevoirs of outside knowledge, used chiefly for expert evaluation purposes (e.g. the agreement with the French Agency for the Exploitation of Research - ANVAR),
- The use of doctoral level academics, encouraging them to contribute their knowledge and research capabilities in a stimulating new field.
- Large-scale utilization of young managerial grade personnel undergoing initial training at the Banque de France Training College: their curriculum includes 8 weeks of work on practical subjects, so it was possible to assign more than 40 trainees to the COSIE project in 1986 - 1987 - 1988,
- Very widespread use of managerial staff in the branches to validate the knowledge base with reference to real-life case studies.

In economic terms, the moderate monetary outlay - which greatly favoured the development of the COSIE project - ought not to blind us to the scale of the human investment in man-months spent on designing and assembling the rule base.

2.2 Computerization

An expert system can only yield its full economic potential if full allowance has been made for technical norms and constraints regarding data base access, calculation of indicators, control of user access, security of data transmission, and lastly continuity of service and "user friendliness".

An essential norm is the need to think of the overall information system right from the outset; many expert systems, whether or not designed for use in an agency network, never got outside the laboratory door for failure to respect this. It has surely been underestimated in COSIE's case.

The decisive factor, in this respect is, on the one hand, the number, and on the other the dispersal of users, these two factors being liable to push up distribution costs considerably.

For complex problems such as those that the COSIE expert system is supposed to resolve, experience has led to selection of a handful of basic principles:

- *custom design,*
  to ensure the closest possible match between the goals sought, the knowledge utilized, the degree of dissemination of the system, intended use and required performance - i.e. the possibility of being distributed among a large number of users.
  This principle holds also for simpler applications than COSIE.
  Even if development tools are available on the market, there is always one that is better-suited to the problem in hand. The idea of a universal engine is still utopian.
- *avoid total dependence on outside suppliers*
  With the aid of a small in-house team under Mr. Pham-Hi, the Bank judiciously selected outside components.
  Not only did this choice foster emulation, it also permitted the gradual accumulation of a substantial body of know how.
- *do not cut off system engineers from specialists in the field of expertise concerned*
  While it is true that marriages between rather different cultures are fraught with communication problems, experience shows that team work is more

productive than bringing in knowledge experts to establish a bridge between the two. That greatly facilitated the development of production rules on the one hand, and properly matching the inference engine and its functionalities with the desiderata of the financial experts at the Balance Sheet Data Centre, on the other.

- *be pragmatic and realistic*
  This may seem to be something of a contradiction in terms. On the one hand, one needs to adapt very flexibly, being ready to modify the form of the rules and the rules themselves, if the end goal so requires.
  That may call for great strenght of character on the part of the players involved, particularly when one thinks of the efforts and uncertainties that any change entails where computers are concerned. In 1985 - 1986, at an intermediate stage in the project, the engine, which had been written in APL language, had to be totally rewritten in C, as the original one proved unsuitable for regular utilization, even though it has been extremely useful in developing the knowledge base. Meanwhile, the transition to an "object-oriented" conception of the rule base required the latter to be totally redesigned.

On the other hand, one must resist the temptations of perfectionism. If not, one faces the prospect of proliferating rules to deal with a host of special cases, or constant revision of these rules with no likelihood of stabilizing them.

That is when one comes up against the consequences of Gödel's theorem: for fifty years now we have known that the more one increases the complexity of a formal system, the greater the risk of destroying it (J.C. Perez, 1988: p. 57). This is because any formal system of representation of knowledge is liable to encounter cases not capable of being represented within this system, or cases revealing inconsistencies or contradictions even.

Similarly, we may find that different paths of reasoning flowing from the same facts do not necessarily yield consistent conclusions: in that case, there is said to be an inconsistency. Attempts to rectify the rule base could shift the anomalies observed elsewhere, with the risk that they may emerge later on in some unexpected place.

Bearing in mind these practical difficulties, the wise course is to resist the proliferation of rules, and to interpret the results with a pinch of salt.

In the case of COSIE, these considerations led the Balance Sheet Data Centre's experts to adopt a universalist approach in their choice of rules: this consists in accepting rules borrowed from different schools of thought concurrently, on the assumption that a single conclusion arrived at by several distinct paths will be all the more valid for that.

In all, experience shows that the costs of computerizing the COSIE expert system increase with time. Initially, starting from a ready made fact base that needed marginal adaptation only, development of the inference engine did not require a very great many man-months.

In 1987, therefore, a team of four engineers and technicians under Mr. Pham-Hi, working in close symbiosis with experts in micro-economics, succeeded, in under 9 months:

- in developing an engine that was thrifty in machine time, capable of running on a desktop computer with 640K RAM, and extremely user-friendly.
- in porting the engine onto a large mainframe, accessible from Banque de France branches via the Transpac data link.

This time frame is debatable, however, insofar as the quality of the computer solution demands a very high level of technical competence on the part of the experts; they must in addition be capable of devising solutions of their own rather than trying to adapt ready made methods.

But computerization costs rise relatively as the expert system moves into its "commercial" phase, which means making COSIE available to a large number of users spread among widely scattered sites. That in turn means gradually converting to an industrial-type system of maintenance in order to keep the service running at all times.

2.3 Management

Developing an expert system designed to operate at a large number of sites and in contact with thousands of businessmen calls for time and determination. One should leave sufficient time between commencement of initial studies for the first breadboard and the moment the finished product is made available to end-users.

In COSIE's case this was necessary:

- to allow ideas to ripen,
- to adjust course in response to different viewpoints,
- to allay the fears of habit-bound practitioners and staff representative organizations,

- to convince the ultimate decisionmakers - the branch managers, bankers, chartered accountants , businessmen, personnel, etc. - that the project was worthwhile.

That implies the need for a determined and well-structured managerial force to push the project through to its conclusion: that is what happened in the case of COSIE, with the setting up of a project task force answerable directly to the Authorities of the Banque de France at the end of 1986 (three years after the commencement of preliminary studies at my initiative).

This is by no means a negligible cost, nor can it be dispensed with. One might call this a *sociological norm*: one must leave time for things to work themselves out, secure maximum support - especially at the top, and reduce resistance to a minimum.

More specifically, managing the project entails:

- communication,
- organization,
- market research,
- training,
- maintenance.

Communication in both directions with the various interested parties is vitally important: without it, any ambitious project is doomed to failure.

Builders of expert systems often overlook the question of organization, because most ventures remain inside the laboratory. Yet, as one seeks to progress, problems or organization and coordination become ever weigthtier, particularly as they require extensive consultation, owing to the systemic nature of artificial intelligence (AI) projects of any consequence.

One criterion of succes for an expert system is that other people than its builders use it willingly. To achieve this, it is vital to approach the project from a commercial standpoint, in order to determine and capture the market of potential users.

Training is obviously vital to the economic succes of a project such as COSIE, e.g.:

- training practitioners to use the system and, above all, to understand its underlying philosophy. One does however need to avoid the following pitfall, which is that the practitioner is liable to sit back and allow himself to be run by the expert system. On the contrary, the expert system should serve to make the most of the practitioner's knowledge, helping him to reason like a true expert.

Among COSIE's functions included for this purpose are extensive self-training possibilities, backed by a library of case histories,

- training for its "sales force", because markets are not won by spontaneous generation. In an ancient institution such as the Banque de France, with its strongly-rooted administrative traditions, this represents a considerable psychological wrench.

Another vital aspect is to sustain the project, because it is important to keep it alive and healthy. The problem is that in a good deal of research work, personnel turnover is high. So it is necessary to manage the project on a basis similar to the one used in large-scale conventional computer applications.

For that, one needs to solve the problem of finding technically competent people capable of handling the problem. The best solution is to call in specialist firms, while gradually developing the necessary inhouse capabilities.

3 Revenues

Many kinds of revenue are anticipated from an expert system like COSIE. These are powerfully conditioned by a handful of features, some of which have been mentioned already, e.g. its dynamic and systemic aspects, and frailties associated with the consequences of Gödel's theorem.

Others flow from the *qualitative* nature of the ramifications of this kind of project. However, as in the field of education or training, the absence of direct monetary returns in no way diminishes the value of the qualitative payoff.

Correlatively, it is worth pointing out that, when dealing with the emergence of a technique as new as expert systems, still only in its infancy, one needs to take a long-term view. For if the short-term monetary returns are minimal in comparison with the scale of the investment, the long-term gains for the economy as a whole could be substantial.

3.1 For individual firms

Set against the not insignificant cost of supplying accounting data to the Banque de France (fiscal plus additional data), the diagnosis, written entirely in everyday French and in a perfectly individualized form, represents a substantial *plus*.

Extensive experience (2.000 cases) over the past two years show that this does meet a need, and that it can greatly help to:

- improve management,
- develop understanding of financial realities,
- disseminate inside the firm (executives, works committee, senior management) the results of an outside audit performed by an independent body.

One particularly motivating factor inside the firm is the fact that it is expected to *play an active role* in the expert audit process. The notion of an *automatic* system should be rejected: an expert system should not have the last word under any circumstances.

But it may have the first word, to guarantee a comprehensive sweep of the data, via a standardized approach, and with calibrated references. In that way, the diagnosis serves as a basis for a thoroughgoing expert audit.

Another important point: a diagnosis that presupposes a triangular dialogue between the expert system, the Banque de France official and the businessman must be performed at the request from the firm. Naturally, that does not rule out the possibility of other people or bodies contributing, if the firm wishes to consult them, or at the request of e.g. the auditors, chartered accountants, chambers of commerce, trade associations or even the authorities.

All in all, the development of COSIE has helped generate awareness of the fact that each firm's relationship with de Banque de France improves if treated as a whole, involving reciprocal contributions, and whose quality can be assessed globally, by both parties, each with regard to its own desiderata.

Within this contractual framework, the service provided by the Banque de France ought not to be considered as a "one-off" affair, but rather as a *stream of services,* which may for example comprise several types of diagnosis (provisional but quick, definitive but lenghtier, with a variety of sectoral references, e.g. similar lines of business, firms of a given size, etc.).

This stream of services - and the supply is due to expand very rapidly, especially with respect to forecast-based management - can be sold for cash.

That is why market research is now in progress to determine the appropriate price for it, on the understanding that the goal is not to earn a net profit but to cover costs.

3.2 For de Banque de France

The Banque de France is involved in a wide range of activities, spanning:

- it's statutory Central Bank of public service functions,
- and functions useful to the community, and even commercial functions.

In actual fact, these functions are not as clear cut as the distinction may suggest. For example, the Balance Sheet Data Centre was designed to perform macro economic and sectoral studies rather than to perform services for business. Initially, these services were conceived as a means to encourage businessmen to join the Balance Sheet Data Centre.

COSIE may serve to modify this outlook, with a shift of emphasis to the performance of services for companies while earning as much as possible in order to fund general research required by the authorities.

Among benefits accruing to the Bank from COSIE it is worth mentioning:

- a facelift for its image, which now looks a little more modern,
- a significant strengthening of its data bases (in quantity and in quality) and a very powerful boost to their commercial exploitation,
- a considerable increase in its level of expertise: the development of a knowledge base is a genuinely creative act, for there is no comparison between things as they were before and the existing base,
- the existence of this base serves as an excellent source of reference for practitioners, who are largely helping to improve it,
- this thereby serves to limit arbitrary individual judgments in assessing firms, and to introduce nationwide standardization of analytical methods. This does not imply a drop in quality; rather, on the contrary, a serious strengthening. Nor indeed does it rule out the possibility of additional personal contributions by local Banque de France officials,
- the introduction of new ways of perceiving and conceiving computer systems should be a source of change, thanks to the involvement of a number of young managerial grade officers in the construction of COSIE,
- the sense of having developed a service that is useful to the community at large,
- last, but not least, as a training tool, the expert system possesses remarkable educational virtues. The Banque de France's Training College was moreover closely associated with the project and was in fact its initiator.

3.3 For the banks

Though currently confined to the individual use of members of the Balance Sheet Data Centre, the COSIE expert system will in the coming years be adapted to the balance sheets as disclosed by firms to the tax authorities.

While less rich in data, these accounting documents are far more numerous and, to all intents and purposes, belong within the public domain. They will serve as a basis for the construction of an expert system for assessing bank risks, which should greatly facilitate everyday bank operations where lending decisions are concerned.

4 The cost-revenue equilibrium

Having reviewed costs and revenue streams, it is legitimate to ask what are the gains generated by the COSIE operation, i.e. whether it is economically or socially viable, and on what terms.

4.1 Is there any chance of its being profitable?

Overal costs entailed in an expert system such as COSIE concern:

- the costs of the fact base,
- the costs of the knowledge base,
- the costs of computerization and computerized distribution.

Without being in a position to quote any absolute figures, it does look as if the fact base accounts for more than 70% of costs per member firm, the remainder being spread in equal parts between the other two items, leaving aside management costs.

The scale of these costs is due to the need mentioned earlier in paragraph 2 for high quality information, which in turn calls for high calibre personnel in both the financial sphere and computer science, in the central departments and the branches alike.

It would be interesting to know what the breakeven point would be in order to cover overall costs by setting a market price for the AIDE diagnosis.

On closer examination it appears that at a Frf 10.000 threshold, a perfectly reasonable price, the breakeven point would be unattainable at present. That means that if we take as our criterion the overall cost of the service, that that burden can only be shouldered by the community as a whole, i.e. by an institution such as the Banque de France for example. The excess cost would be justified by non-monetary and qualitative returns discussed above.

If we consider only the marginal cost engendered by the expert system, foreseeable revenues ought to reach breakeven point, and well beyond, very quickly. It would be perfectly justifiable to charge on the basis of this marginal cost, insofar as revenues would serve to fund research, development and innovation, and also relieve pressure on net expences.

The most likely hypothesis then would be a steadily rising volume of activity to somewhere between the two breakeven points (in terms of overall cost and marginal cost respectively).

4.2 Learning to think like a business

In order to come close to the ideal situation, an administrative-type institution like the Central Bank would certainly gain by learning from some of the lessons provided by private firms:

- adopt a customer-oriented outlook - which presupposes market research, a capacity to supply the services that are most in demand, and to do so with a high regard for quality - and to train people with this end in view,
- be capable of investing, which means spending first and reaping the benefits later. That implies thorough economic research in a multi-year perspective; but the time is not quite yet ripe for that.

4.3. Changing administrative habits

The transition to the supply of fee-paying services (which are by no means incompatible with the notion of public service) ought to pave the way for more far-reaching changes. If the Bank truly is concerned to change things and attitudes, it will probably need to set up project-management units enjoying some degree of independence from the traditional chain of command.

In return, particular attention would have to be paid to monitoring the management of these projects, whose costs and revenues would be subject to precise, thorough and detailed analytic accounting procedures.

The reason for this last stipulation is that where expenses systematically outrun revenues, the cost is ultimately borne by the community at large. It is only reasonable, therefore, that an executive committee with responsibility for the project should scrutinize the collective utility of non-monetary, qualitative "revenues", and should arrive at a judgment concerning the balance between the latter and the recorded deficit. This "general interest" norm is absolutely essential.

The change is possible, but it will take time. To hasten the process, institutions such as the Banque de France (where this is now happening) will need to develop a plan to supplement their annual budgets (which are merely a means of allocating expenses).

The plan offers a means of comparing expenses with the activities they are designed to fund, measured in appropriate units. It therefore provides a basis for systematic scrutiny of the grounds for each expense, which is a step along the road to economic rationality.

5 Conclusion

To conclude, we believe that it is possible to assess the social utility of, and even earn a return on (at least at the margin), expert systems introduced into an administrative institution. However, this presupposes a delicate process of learning about the specific mechanisms of private firms. But the process is not an automatic one. Indeed, the same conclusion applies to all projects - EDP - or otherwise - of any consequence.

So it is worthwhile encompassing these within a cogent, multi-year, overall framework capable of providing a basis for a *plan*.

The Authorities of the Banque de France have recently established just such a *corporate plan*.

In technical terms, this will lead to the supplementing of annual budgets (which are simply an exercise in allocating expenses) by more refined management methods, e.g.:

- careful and systematic measurement of results obtained, be they qualitative, quantitative or monetary,
- carefully reconciling "expenses" and "revenues" as defined above,
- systematically questioning the grounds for expenses.

In that sense, supplementing the notion of budget with that of a plan would represent an important step towards ecnomomic rationality, provided the people concerned gradually steep themselves in what we call the "spirit of enterprise".

In the final analysis, I believe that the essential contribution of a business-service oriented expert system such as COSIE is to establish a mutually beneficial pairing of the parties : for businesses in this particular instance, and for the Banque de France also, as it is gradually brought into greater symbiosis with its environment.

The lesson may well be valid for all administrative institutions.

References

Aucoin M., Micha B., Pham-Hi D.*An expert system for Corporate Check-up at the Banque de France,* 1989 .

Van de Donk, W.B.H.J., Proceedings of the Leuven Meeting on "Expert Systems and Normativity", in: *International Review of Administrative Sciences,* 1989, Vol. 55, nr. 2, June 1989.

Van de Donk, W.B.H.J., Snellen I.Th.M., *Knowledge Based Systems in Public Administration . Evolving practices and Norms* (in this volume).

Perez, J.C., *De nouvelles voies vers l'Intelligence Artificielle - Pluridisciplinarité - Auto-Organisation - Réseaux neuronaux.* Paris, Masson, 1988

Expert Systems in Public Administration
I. Th.M. Snellen, W.B.H.J. van de Donk, J.-P. Baquiast (Eds.)
© Elsevier Science Publishers B.V. (North-Holland), 1989

Chapter 15

An expert system for corporate checkup at the Banque de France

*Marcel Aucoin**
*Bernard Micha**
*Duc Pham-Hi**

Abstract

This chapter[1] will briefly describe the expert system that we have developed at the Banque de France analyzing the history of the project in the context of the evolution of Artificial Intelligence technology, then, describing the main aspects of corporate check-ups and drawing tentative conclusions on axes of future development. Finally, lessons will be drawn from past experience to feed some reflections on decision making and its system support.

1 The why's and the hows...

The traditional role of the Banque de France, as the Bank of banks has given it a privileged place in the fabric of the french Economy. In the past, its provincial branches acting as liquidity suppliers to local commercial banks, which discounted on the paper market for credit seeking firms, necessarily acquired profound acquaintance with the businesses within their operating radius, which justify their informal, de facto role of "rating agencies". Nowadays, our 233 provincial agencies collect yearly about 25000 sets of business reports plus additional, qualitative data, from industrial firms in each of every branch of activity and send them to our central services where all the data are analyzed and merged into sectorial statistics.

---

* French National Bank (Banque de France),
39 rue Croix-des-Petits-Champs, 75001 Paris, France

One of these central departments in charge of sectorial studies is the Balance Sheet Data Centre where French companies can freely apply for membership in exchange of extended information on their businesses. In return, they receive each year an individual diagnosis as well as brochures presenting the state and evolution of those sector averages concerning their activity. The match of a firm's set of report figures against its branch of activity's median statistics would show its relative strenght and weaknesses, as compared with competition. Business managers can infer from those documents their position and their trend relative to the sector's general performance, as well as the relevance of their individual strategies.

Thus appeared the need for an exhaustive, fast, efficient way of analyzing and generating litterary business audit commentaries in standard, everyday language, automatically from the 500 or so figures, characterizing any firm.

The capture and codification of business analyst' know-how by expert system techniques seemed to be a promising solution since it would

- preserve and amplify scarce and/or costly human expertise,
- increase productivity, as far as interpreting and commenting purely numerical reports for 25.000 firms is a long and tedious task,
- distribute this know how to 233 remote sites, which would render analyses exhaustive and uniform in quality.
- take into account qualitative factors: indeed, even though many concepts have been added, for instance functional and analytical balance sheets, goods flow or cash flow analyses, discriminating factor analyses, what came out of the Balance Sheet Data Centre remained till now essentially based on financial reports figures.
  Up to now it did not keep score of non quantitative factors, therefore did not reflect the real risks and opportunities of a situation,
- finally, act as an on-the-spot, continuous training program since the explanatory function of the Expert System and its interactive mode of dialogue with the user would make it an excellent tutorial support.

2 Project history

We started during winter 1983 with a small group consisting of two engineers in training and Pham-Hi, and we tried to adapt a very simple forward chaining inference engine of the EMYCIN type without probability factors to a small rule base of about 40 rules of financial analysis in use at the Balance Sheet Data Base.

The language used was Interlisp, a version of LISP developed by the Upssala University in Sweden. We had a terminal linked to a non-bank computer on the Paris XI Saclay Research Center.

In summer 1984, a rough prototype showed that some interesting results could be obtained and drew the attention of the Balance Sheet Data Base. Because the bill for external computer use was high, we decided to switch to APL, a scientific interpreted command language we had long installed on our IBM machines. That year, a forward chaining engine was built, using boolean algebra to calculate True/False values on a set of rules which were basically boolean equations with interconnecting variables. Each variable had a string of alphanumeric characters associated to it, so that whenever a "true" value was reached the system printed the associated text.

This system was judged satisfactory if not by end users - there were none at this point -, at least by knowledge base developers, who added more and more rules, and at the same time, asked for some self explanatory function in the Expert System. The knowledge base grew to 600 rules by June 85, and the grouping of rules into packets did optimize the working of the inference cycles. A form of explanation was achieved through backward-chaining mechanism: at core was a logical formula expander which substituted each of the individual conditions on the "IF", or left hand, side of the boolean equation, with its own conditions of fulfillment, and so on until the primary conditions - sets of figures coming from balance sheets or profit reports - could be found. The leaves of the "tree" thus obtained by expansion were next "trimmed", eliminating identical terms and "already dead" branches. A forward chaining cycle would start again on the remaining tree to find the paths that could lead to the sought-after conclusions.

At the end of 1986, with over 1000 rules, it went into a test operating phase, after laboratory runs, in several branches of the Banque de France from different regions of the Country. The introduction of Expert System proved then to be a well accepted innovation, and users wore mostly in favour of its development.

At this point, some conclusions could be drawn:

- The expert system approach had very strongly motivated the domain experts.
- The choice of APL as a fast prototyping language was most fortunate; it helped:
    * grow a 1000-rule knowledge base in a short period of time,

  * introduce financial experts who were laymen in EDP fields to logic processing,
  * give a clear view of the type of knowledge and rules being captured, and the type of inference engine that must be built, in the end project,

- The use of this prototype in APL was a strong vector in promoting expert system approach to end-users: it gave them first-hand experience, and demystified (somewhat) the esoteric world of Artificial Intelligence. Two mayor inhibiting set-backs, however, had to be solved on this product version:

  a Too much host computer resources consumption.
  b Long and tedious deduction phase before arriving to the point on each topic, and each synthesis of diagnosis contains just a set of sentences listed in the order of rule-firing, therefore giving a "patchwork" appearance which dit nog read like flowing, everyday language.

Without going into Knowledge engineering details, it can also be pointed out that there was no compilation of rules and no control possible on global consistency since the set of boolean variables had no semantic depth. Some logical loops were present in the system and went on undetected until run into.

Therefore, in 1987 we set out to build another inference engine with a totally different architecture, based on object-oriented-programming methods, and drawing some inspiration from the semantic network model of linguistics, written in C, a language which can be compiled to run efficiently. It was time to put into practice what Pham-Hi had long preached for, as far as this Expert System was concerned: Object oriented programming. Much stress is put upon the user friendly interface, allowing the expert system user to read every day, natural language. At the same time, we developed a Compiler and an Optimizer for the rule base, which permitted mathematical study of the network of rules and objects with standard Operations Research methods.

Naturally enough the old rule base had to be entirely re-written which reduced considerably its size (about a third less), some meta-rules having been identified and relocated in the upper level of text generation.

3 Corporate checkup

3.1 The scope of the checkup

The purpose of this checkup is to identify the strengths and weaknesses in the behaviour of the enterprise, via a multi-year review of its general situation, and by measuring the degree of consistency of its strategy, or where it is going wrong, if at all.

The checkup scrutinizes economic and financial aspects, taking into account the interaction of phenomena, and thus first identifies symptoms, then seeks the causes and effects of any particular trend identified.

The proposed checkup is established by exploring twenty or so economic and financial themes, culminating in a set of partial syntheses and a general report:

MENU

Economic aspects :

- production policy (productivity)
- the products-markets relationship (competitiveness)
- investment policy and relevance
- industrial strategy
- growth policy
- economic dependance
- managerial policy
- commercial policy
- Syntheses : Growth and efficiency
Performance and strategy
Potential and management

Financial aspects :

- profitability
- working capital requirements
- funding
- financial structures
- financial strategy
- Syntheses : Profitabilty
Funding
Financial structures

Checkup report

The checkup involves processing accounting data contained in a computer file, and qualitative data supplied by the firm's managers in the course of the diagnosis itself.

The firm's participation is required in the first place in order to provide answers to questions asked by the expert system, and secondly in order to interpret the phenomena observed correctly.

The diagnosis is in no way a standard product generated by some automated process. On the contrary, each one is personalized by the presence of the firm's manager and authentified by the local Banque de France official, who will add his own comments.

3.2 An original methodological approach

The expert audit contained in the rule base draws its inspiration from the diagnosis design selected by the Balance Sheet Data Centre.

But the logic of the Expert System, its rigorous reasoning processes and ability to go on enriching its knowledge base continually, represent a new vision of business analyses, providing a far more comprehensive and coherent picture of the firm.

3.2.1 Field of investigation

This encompasses the economic and financial aspects that express the global and dynamic vision of the firm, as focused on by the Balance Sheet Data Centre. A degree of balance has been sought between the "horizontal" field of the expert audit (19 themes are dealt with) and the degree of detailed analysis of each topic, so that it is always possible to gauge the consistency of the firm's behaviour.

The diagnosis does not grow out of summation of juxtaposition of facts, but rather out of their combination.

3.2.2 A global analytical method

Through the initial expert audit rules and their gradual enrichment, the diagnosis leads to establishment of a series of behavioral profiles.

This is not the mechanistic outcome of algorithms capable of being illustrated in terms of symmetrical decision trees, for example reflecting a systematic cross-sorting of accounting ratios presenting two or three positional values.

The constituent factors of the profiles have been introduced into the rules by means of logical and pragmatic reasoning.

This approach has highlighted three fundamental features:

- The mode of representation and formalization of knowledge, associated with a text editor, reveals a great variety of profiles. It thus corresponds to a multiplier process that tends to reconstitute reality's complexity via a conceptualized approach.
- The need to break down human reasoning in order to reconstruct it in the form of rules within a formal structure makes it necessary to visualize the expert audit so as to show how the concepts used are closely interlinked, and to illustrate the need for globality in the logical process.
- The design of the expert audit shows how complex analysis is, and the poverty of the vocabulary capable of identifying the "diseases" to which the firm is prone in the light of the symptoms observed.

3.2.3 A pluralist approach to analysis

The COSIE2 system's expert audit also incorporates different methodological approaches from the ones in use at the Balance Sheet Data Centre when focusing on the same aspect of the firm.

The expert system is consequently universalist in character, which places it at the crossroads of current analytical methods.

Needless to say, divergences may appear where different methods used to validate a conclusion yield different results.

These divergences do not necessarily imply that the experts made a mistake in formulating their rules. It is conceivable that the utilization of more than one approach may yield different intermediate conclusions. Generally, these apparent contradictions reflect the complexity of the problem, indicating the need to pursue the analysis in greater detail or to request additional data or explanations from the firm. In all cases, they serve to attenuate the scope of the crude findings produced by the initial expert audit and to moderate their plausibility.

Where conflicting intermediate conclusions are arrived at, the system proposes a trade-off representing the experts' preference, or else confines itself to noting the absence of convergence.

Risk analysis, for instance, which examines risk from a variety of standpoints (manager, banker, Central Bank or shareholders) thus eliminates the element of arbitrariness that would be entailed if only one standpoint was adopted. In this type of situation, the system explores all the indicators and, depending on the case, either pronounces an unambiguous conclusion, qualifies its appraisal, or highlights the conflicts.

This makes the system more like a "reasoning machine" than a conclusion-generating tool.

3.2.4 *A presentation of relativity and uncertainty*

The expert opinion that emerges is based as much on rules of internal logic, and even normative rules, as on judgments resulting from comparison of the firm's behaviour with that of its professional environment, or with standard behaviour patterns of company populations, as in Balance Sheet Data Centre practice.

Together with the regular position, with references to the mean, quartiles and deciles of a set, coefficients measuring the relevance of the rules have been introduced in order to quantify the probabilistic nature of the conclusion.

For example, a statement concluding that a firm is competitive is completed by the rider: "results verified for 25% of firms in the sample".

Similarly, the "financial situation, examined in accordance with the customary criteria of the banking industry, must be qualified", is completed by the rider: results verified for 40% of firms in the sample".

3.2.5 *An accumulating process*

The deepening of the rule base, which is a permanent process thanks to the knowledge acquisition and formalization procedures, incorporates the experience of the system's users.

Confrontation of behaviour as conceptualized by the Expert System with observed patterns, as evidenced by the firm in the course of the interview, may lead to modification of certain rules.

For example, the existence of firms that were undoubtedly competitive, but which did not meet the criteria of the general rule laid down on competitiveness[3], resulted in the production of complementary rules of the type:

> "Competitive firm despite a moderate drop in gross operating margin, on condition that this margin is kept at a very comfortable level and that sales volumes grow".

In this process of constant adaption, the expert audit system gains in relevance through the addition, modification or elimination of certain rules.

In its present state, it is the outcome of progressive enrichment through continuing research and experiments on more than 2000 company case histories over the past six months in several of the Banque de France's branches and sub-offices.

4 COSIE functioning: checkup production

4.1 Checkup report

For each topic - such as, for example, growth policy, - a literary text, written in every day language - except, of course, for financial vocabulary, - is generated by the system step by step, as more qualitative data is acquired through a conversational mode with the user, in one of the many pop-up windows opened for dialogue. In fact, before this dialogue begins, some 500 figures from central data bases belonging to Balance Sheet Data Centre. Data Base have been sent to the Expert System by a servicing virtual machine. From these original figures, the system computes ratios and makes a secondary level of aggregates of accounting items. Basic elements like Sales evolution or Working Capital Requirements level are determined. They then allow the meta-knowledge coded in the system to prune out some parts of the Knowledge base, kill rules and orient text generation with more relevance to the case being studied. This in turn results in intelligent user dialogue.

- *Semi-natural language is provided both in diagnostic text and explanations given by the system.*

In fact, to explain a precise word the user has designated with his cursor in a full screen mode, a translation module refers to both the Rule-skeletons dictionary (where rules are stored as more groups of pointers) an the lexical dictionary it built during compilation phase. As a result, users read rules in plain French whereas the system itself works only with pointers. There are 2 advantages to this system:

* faster access is achieved through pointer sequences leading down to the final conclusions.
* the use of shared pointers reflects closely-related concepts. Indeed, the network of pointers reproduces in the workspace of the machine the closest "semantic" network to the model in the financial expert's mind that could be designed from the Knowledge base. Rules with premisses and conclusions written in plain every day language could never be able to represent this Second level relationship.

4.2 Components of the Expert System

We now move on to the components of the Expert System on which this check-up is based.

- First comes the Rules and Text-frames Compiler. This component does the work every time something changes in the Knowledge base, but for each Expert System session it is not activated.
  Its purpose is to "dismember" the expertise knowledge into computer-stored fragments, analyze each word encountered to separate elementary vocabulary terms, put them in different dictionaries, set up pointers to each new word it learned. This is reserved for domain expert use only.
- Secondly, each time a user session starts, a fact-propagator sub-program computes the value of about 200 boolean variables from the figures available from balance sheets or profit reports, then injects them through the network of pointers, validating or inhibiting each node as they pass. The network of objects representing basic facts about the 19 topics is this way prepared to meet queries.
- Finally, for each user query a backward chaining-like mechanism is activated, not between the rules, but between the objects forming the nodes of the causal chain. These nodes know each other since they have ad-hoc pointers, so that each question asked is answered rapidly and to the point.

The architecture of our system is thus a hybrid mixture of forward propagating mechanisme with backtracking mechanism working on a fundamentally object-oriented data organization.

Indeed the whole network can be viewed, from the Connectionist point of view as multiple layers of parallel structures where different levels of pointers stored in objects allow multi-directional propagation of facts.

For instance, the object "Competitivity" is structured thus :

Competitivity
- attached aspect No. 1 : = "3 year evolution"
  * value : (e.g. above average)
  * nature of validation mode : (by rule, by direct answer, ...),
  * list of rules concluding on this object-notion
    + rule A
    + rule B
  * list of Object-aspects influenced by this one:
    + Object X, attached-aspects X1, X2, X3, ...
    + Object Y, attached-aspects Y1, Y2, Y3, ...

   * default value : (average)
- attached aspect no. 2 = "cause of evolution".
- etc.

5 Putting the system to production use

The Banque de France network of branches covers the whole of France with over 230 sites linked to our host computers in Paris. This expert system must be made available even to the remotest corners of the nation.

There are many ways to distribute this service but the operating model will have to take into account the existing environment, procedures and networks.

Two main issues appear:

A.What should the global operation mode be?

We can choose from many installation options, which can be grouped into 3 categories :

a remote use of central host computers through terminals
b local use of micro-computers making temporary online links with host mainframes, only for data extraction and version up grades.
c local use of our network of office automation micro-computers considered only as mailboxes receiving file transfers without having to establish on-line links.

In order to start the validation phase as fast as possible, the bigger 20 to 30 provincial branches have been endowded with the first solution (a) - to get acquainted with the expert system - since winter 1987.

The first phase lasted until winter 1988; during the year 1989, in addition to the first solution which will be extended to more than 50 branches, in June, will be experimented the second solution (b) in 15 branches, mainly for marketing goals.

In the third and last phase probably by the end of 1990, all our 233 sites will have either a link to mainframes where they would use time sharing processing to work on virtual machines hosting the expert system, or micro-computers with a resident local version of the same expert system.

B. How should the expert system approach be generalized to other fields?

The easiest way to pursue the effort to collect knowledge bases and spread the use of expert systems throughout different departments of the Banque de France would be to re-adapt the functions written for this one expert system to other problem domains.

However, it does not seem to be the wisest, or even the safest way, to proceed. Indeed, expert system terminology is fallacious when used indiscriminately: speaking of inference ENGINE, one tends to think by analogy of the portability of a motor ENGINE which can be geared to a lawn mower then later, to a garden water pump.

Skipping technical aspects concerning the global/local characterization of variables used in subprograms or such unavoidable sufferings in recycling a software, on a purely conceptual phase one can point out the following hazards:

- inadequate report output : semi-natural language might be unnecessary or too time-consuming to construct in some domains...
- inadequate input elements or format of data. Information might be lost or irrelevant facts might be added...
- inadequate inferencing process : sometimes induction is more efficient than deduction...

As a matter of fact, one easily understand that performance, being dependent on specificity and complexity, can only vary inversely to versatility. On the purely data processing aspect, one need to be aware of the following setbacks, in case many users independantly customize their own expert system from an existing shell:

- undecipherable source texts due to different layers of program added one on top of the others;
- communicability for small PC based software between themselves or with the host data bases cannot be easily achieved without the help of computer people;
- non conformity to other operating systems or compilers;

Independant programmers will loose time rediscovering old solutions or adopting divergent solutions to the same problems;

Due to all these reasons it is strongly recommended to unify or at least to federate expert system developments.

6 Future AI techniques experimentation

Two domains of research seem of particular strategic importance:

- *A multi expert, multi engine system*
  In the same field of expertise, different parts may concern widely different inferencing modes; the same engine core should not be applied to deductive analysis and inductive synthesis. A Multi-system architecture can be designed with a "blackboard" or a Context manager as a central structure around which are grouped various types of inference engines, controlled by outside meta-knowledge. Prototype building for any field of expertise is simplified to matching adequate inference process with the "global shape" of rules. A delivery process will collect at last only those features of each engine or the central structure that have been called upon in any particular domain of expertise, extract them from the Multi-system and pack them together to compile and link, separately from the rest; thus delivering a neat, adequate, concise execution module.

- *Natural language*
  Collecting expertise is often complicated by the fact that modes of reasoning other than zero order logic rules seem "unnatural" to the domain expert. If the domain is best viewed in an object oriented way, coding the knowledge base first in production rules often leads to loss of information, redundancy and circular reasoning.
  Therefore, a natural language comprehension module should be coupled to an inductive, learning-capable small expert system to help deduce from sample reports written in plain language the most adequate form for knowledge representation.

  At this point it may be relevant to discuss whether with all the efforts we have made and shall be willing to make, we have progressed any inch further toward constructing a worthwhile automated decision making system. Our contention is that, in the end, it is neither the goal nor an achievable task.

Reasoning in business and finance has the following characteristics:

- it's input can never be reduced to a finite set of data; one can even wonder if that set is discrete, even if bound and finite : as you delve deeper and deeper, as your resolution power gets sharper, you can always perceive more details behind the details.
- it's output must convey this feeling of depth and ambiguity, if only just a split second before the final operational decision is reached: a banker may

grant a loan, a trader will buy, but the decision support system must have also transmitted what causes, or should cause uncertainty.
- it must therefore rely more on techniques of composite imagery processing, and global pattern recognition and matching rather than on analytical path exploration.

To put it picturesquely, seeking to reach a decision by following individual reasoning paths would be like appreciating Monet's or Seurat's paintings square inch by square inch. Thus, constructing a decision support system involving not purely physical laws or mathematical facts, but also human subjectivity such as intuition and flair, requires skills similar to those of the painter : in restructuring the knowledge base, or in choosing the reasoning model's architecture, the AI engineer "paints" the state of mind of his subject, the domain expert, with his biases and prejudices all along with his science.

The computer is then not just a computational device, it is the AI engineer/artist's canvas. This paradigm leads us now close to Plato's tale of cave men seeing the outside World only through reflections on cavern walls : Decision making is never directly on the objective real world, when an expert system is involved, but only through the impressionist, subjecti\ve view as rendered by the domain expert, the AI engineer, and the computer.

7. The future of the COSIE expert system

What lies ahead of COSIE rests mainly on its economic worthiness. Built on business and financial expertise concerning manufactures and companies, our expert system's first achievement was to reveal an unexpressed demand :

- More and more companies, be they or not members of the Banque de France Balance Sheet Data Centre's survey population, come in growing numbers to assist to our expert system demonstrations. They all voice the need to foresee trouble and ask the Banque de France for unbiased, objective, counselling in this field. Nextly, the field of study will encompass specific domains such as Trade, Services of Building industries. It will also include Previsional Management and Business forecasting.
- The commercial banks themselves see in this tool a means to appreciate their loan Risks. More specifically, they want to have a better approach for customer rating.
- Officers in most of our branches give an excellent welcome to COSIE, because it helps them establish indepth dialogue with the companies and their bankers.

From a macro-economic standpoint, the spreading use of COSIE should be seen as our contribution to strengthen the French industrial fabric, - especially as regards small and medium firms -, as it upgrades their manager's knowledge and scope in financial matters.

The economic value of COSIE will be determined when we set-up marketable services - at cost price, naturally - based on this expert system, which would render the exploitation of COSIE related products financially autonomous.

On a larger scale, the Banque de France plans to act on the European level through cooperation programs with other Central Banks and EEC Institutions, in the prospect of a single, unified market field in 1993.

Four future axes for development are present in our mind:

1 Firstly, on the Software Engineering side simulation and Forecasting/Planning functionalities should be added to our expert system.

2 Secondly, on the Knowledge Base side, we cannot stop at french sectorial norms to judge french companies performances. We will have from now on, to adopt European standards :

- either through an European Financial Statements Data base or through a linking of existing data bases,
- and through an enlargement of our knowledge base scope to an European scale, and take as input more heterogenous data.

As a whole, data from European and international data bases will be taken into account especially for the large National industries and for companies with much presence in foreign countries.

3 Thirdly, on the Information Management side, we shall develop cooperation to improve COSIE's performances (inference engine, probabilistic rules, Runtime and development versions, legal protection, AI specialists training program for Central Banks etc.....)

4 Fourthly, concerning training courses : Independently from its practical use for companies and analysts, the COSIE expert system can be used as a training tool:

- self-educationally, through its practice
- when used in connection with a library of case histories, which should appeal to many potential users.

Notes

1. This chapter is based on a paper written by M. Aucoin and Duc Pham-Hi and presented par Duc Pham-Hi at the International seminar on expert systems in public administration, Leuven, 6 - 9 september 1988, E.G.P.A. Study Group. The text has been enriched by further developments about the main aspects of Corporate Checkup, written by M. Micha (par. 3.0).
2. COSIE has been better known in France by the acronym A.I.D.E. - Assistance Informatique au Diagnostic d'Entreprise.
3. Three hypotheses to be verified over the past three years :
   a) Expanding sales volume,
   b) Gross operating margin greater than average for the sector of the economy,
   c) Favourable gross operating margin trends.

Expert Systems in Public Administration
I.Th.M. Snellen, W.B.H.J. van de Donk, J.-P. Baquiast (Eds.)
© Elsevier Science Publishers B.V. (North-Holland), 1989

Chapter 16

ESKORT :A toolbox for VAT auditors

*Kurt Vittrup**

Abstract

The Danish Customs Authorities have - together with Axion A/S - developed an integrated toolbox for VAT auditors. The goal has been to supply VAT auditors with an integrated set of tools to support the complex task of auditing VAT accounts. The ESKORT system integrates traditional data processing with a number of expert systems, working on the same set of data.

The ESKORT system was brought into operational use in February, 1988. The system is now in daily use at all district VAT offices.

1 Introduction

1.1 The Danish customs

The Danish Customs Authority is one of the oldest public institutions in Denmark. In 1982, it celebrated its 350 th anniversary. But that does not mean, that it is an old-fashioned organisation.

In fact, today more than ever it is necessary for a public administration to adapt in the best possible way to the technological and other development of society.

---

* Direktorat for Toldvæsenet,
Ameliegade 44, 1256 Copenhagen, Denmark

The Customs Authority's tasks encompass three main areas:

1 Collection of customs duty,
2 Collection of VAT and 21 different excises, for example excise on wine, spirits, tobacco etc, and
3 Various tasks, undertaken on behalf of other ministries, concerning health, safety and quality, connected with the importation or exportation of goods.

The Customs Authority has a total personnel of 5,100. In 1987 the Danish Customs collected a total of 90 billion Danish kroner in VAT. 25 billion kroner was repaid in form of negative VAT. That makes a total cash flow to and from the about 400,000 companies of 115 billion kroner.

The VAT system is dependent upon statements by the individual companies, who have to pay VAT based upon their purchasing and selling of goods etc.. That demands an over all inspection of the companies.

About 40,000 companies are subject to an audit each year. A major part of the auditing procedure takes place at the premises of the company in question.

In 1987 approximately 45 % of the companies made errors, which resulted in additional payments of about 600 million Danish kroner. In approximately 5 % of the companies, the audit resulted in repayment of about 100 million kroner.

1.2 Modernization

One of the goals of a modernization programme, set up by the Danish Government some years ago, is to prevent further growth of the public sector. New needs can therefore only be met by restructuralization of the work in existing areas. That means that quantitative growth must be replaced by qualitative growth within the existing economic framework.

In other words, the public sector is required to renew and improve

- quality,
- efficiency and
- productivity.

It is obvious, that the use of EDP in the Danish Customs is an important criterion for the necessary reconstruction of the Custom's activities. It is therefore, quite specifically, a means of achieving the general targets set for the development of the Danish Customs.

These targets are:

- to improve efficiency in administration as well as control work,
- to reduce the cost and other inconveniences caused by the legislation to citizens and firms to the minimum that is compatible with control considerations, and
- to improve the working climate through decentralization, delegation of competence and responsibility, and greater motivation of the employees.

Besides, as an element of a general tax reform, the Danish Goverment recently decided, that the Customs Authority's control in the companies was to be intensified.

In this connection, the Customs made a plan aiming to accomplish a rise in the additional payments of 50 %. This was to be achieved partly by transferring employees from other tasks, that presently are being automated, partly by efficiency-raise by means of new technology.

1.3 IT strategy

The strategy for using information technology is different for the different tasks:

* The *administration* tasks are characterized by simple manipulation of a lot of data, primarily serving two purposes: to ensure correct collection and to gather information for statistical and control purposes.
  The strategy for this area is to use traditional ADP techniques in a distributed concept, so that the EDP tools become a natural part of daily work.

* The *expedition* tasks - that is mainly the tasks concerning importation and exportation - is characterized by handling a lot of documents.
  Actually, if you put one year's documents together, you could form a "paper-road" from Copenhagen to Cairo.
  Most of these documents are printed out from the company's computer - brought to the Customs Office - and then keyed into the Custom's computer. The obvious solution was then to make this statements by computer to computer communication. And an EDI system for this purpose is beeing developed right now.
  In two years, it is expected, that 60 % of the import statements will be made without paper.

* The *auditing* tasks will in a few years be handled to a great extend by the ESKORT system, described below.

* The real *creative controlling* - that is dealing with economic crimes etc - we think always has to be carried out by the use of human creativity and intuition.

Of course, computerization has no independent value. Its real value lies in the fact, that it is one of the means of achieving the formulated targets.

1.4 VAT Auditing

Today about 800 customs officers are working with auditing of VAT accounts, but the staff is expected to be increased to a total number of 1,300, due to the intensified project.

As mentioned before, VAT auditing normally takes place at the company's premises, and it involves interviews with the person in charge of the business accounts, for instance the proprietor.

The personal visit by a VAT auditor has two purposes. Partly the service aspect in the sense of giving proper advice about VAT Returns, partly because the VAT auditor obtains a better basis for auditing through interviews and observations.

But auditing in the field makes great demands on the auditor. A thorough knowledge of the line of business, keeping of accounts and the laws applicated to the area are essential. Therefore it takes a great deal of experience to become a good VAT auditor.

New members of the staff go through a comprehensive theoretical education combined with a training period.

The young or unexperienced customs officer performing administrative and service tasks usually can rely on older colleagues' advice in case of doubt. But this possibility does not exist during the audit in the field. New members of the staff therefore are accompanied by a colleague before they start auditing on their own.

The main goal for developing the ESKORT system was to create a support system for the VAT officer - an intelligent assistent-helping him to make the right decisions.

The idea is - roughly spoken - that the VAT auditor brings ESKORT with him in the field on a portable computer - instead of VAT regulations, papers on the company and on previous visits, calculators, notebook and pen - and a more experienced colleague.

The basis for VAT auditing are the companies' regular annual accounts. In principle, VAT audition is a full audit of these accounts.

An audit procedure consists of the following tasks:

Collection and compiling of information
The procedure is roughly spoken a comparison of the formal basis, e.g. the companies' VAT Returns, with the real basis e.g. the companies' purchasing and selling of goods and services, to ascertain whether the laws and statutory instruments have been observed. The VAT officer therefore has to collect information concerning the annual accounts and check the formalities. Observations and interviews contribute to throw light on the real basis.

Handling or manipulation of information
Subsequently the VAT officer has to juxtapose and analyse the gathered information to obtain a general view of their coherence.

Evaluation and identification of weak spots
The analysis contains an evaluation of the relevant information. The VAT officer has to identify weak spots, e.g. links in the companies' register and account system where errors may occur.

Control
VAT audit or control in the true sense of the word includes

- a logical audit e.g. the identification of weak spots
- a creative audit where inspection initiatives are generated concurrently with the logical audit
- an intuitive audit where ideas for specific examination spring up spontaneously

Very often the audit leads to gathering of further information.

Advice on VAT matters
The Customs Authorities can - in principle - contribute to increased VAT proceeds in two ways. Partly by examining and discovering errors, partly by advice and instruction on VAT matters so that companies state the correct VAT amounts. Therefore proper service and high quality advice and instruction are important parts of a VAT officers visit.

Documentation

The result of the VAT audit has to be documented in a so-called audit minute.

2 Development

2.1 The developers

ESKORT has been developed by Axion A/S (part of the CRI, inc) and the Danish Customs. Axion A/S is an independent Danish company with the business objective of offering know-how and high quality software solutions, that integrate expert systems and intelligent man-machine interfaces with current software technology to industries, large organizations and government.

The company has become leading in the application of these techniques in the area of public and business administrative systems and financial services. With a total staff of 70 engaged full time, Axion is now one of the largest centers in Europe, working in the expert systems field.

The success is presumably based on three important factors: a highly skilled staff, the application of systematic development methods to expert system technology, and intensive research and experience in developing projects.

2.2 Objectives

The systems development started in 1986 as a research and development project, supported by the Danish government.

The R & D project had the aim of examining, whether it was possible to develop an expert system, which could advice the VAT auditors as to make the right conclusions during the audit. That is concerning where the audit is to be carried out, and how it is done in the best possible way.

The first phase encompassed a pre-analysis, looking closer at the nature of VAT-auditing and digesting existing expert systems' functionality and use.

The original concept aimed at developing an expert system supporting the identification of errors in VAT accounts. The first paper design aimed at a system that - by means of a dialog between the VAT officer and the system - first identified weak spots and afterwards presented a plan containing relevant audit procedures. Without any doubt a system like that would lead to discovering more errors.

At that point of the process the system lived up to the following objectives

- more effective VAT auditing
- more efficient VAT auditing

But were these objectives sufficient? The answer was: NO!

First of all, experiences from the analysed expert systems projects showed, that in practice it is very difficult to make people use "pure" expert systems to a greater extend. In fact, that is very similar to the situation, we all know, that people hesitate to ask for advice at more experienced colleagues.

Especially, it was obvious, that a VAT officer spends a great deal of his time at the company collecting, compiling and analysing information. A system that could assist him only part-time of the procedure might not be used in practice.

The concept was therefore changed radically, and the fundamentally new criterion for success was to develop - *an attractive tool for the VAT officer.*

2.3 Prototypes instead of formal specifications

The second and third phase of the project encompassed developing several generations of prototypes, which could show the functionality of the final system.

Traditional systems development often involves comprehensive functional specifications and user requirement documentation. After having changed the development concept we chose quite a different course of action. Instead of spending a lot of time and energy on further paper work, the efforts were concentrated on fast development of a prototype and thus a fast visualizing of the ideas and the expert system to come.

Thanks to powerful development environments, an early prototype was presented after 1 month.

The prototyping approach proved to be very valuable, and the further development process was sped up. The experts, e.g. the customs officers, could look at and work with the system "live", and this triggered off a lot of comments and suggestions for modification.

The prototyping approach has been continued throughout the developing process. The customs officers worked with the system, commented on it and suggested changes. The computer scientists modified the program, tested it and presented it to the experts. Thus ESKORT took shape in an iterative process and has now reached the state, where it is taken into use at the local VAT offices.

2.4 Knowledge engineering

A very important part of this process was gathering and specifying the accessible knowledge in the area ("knowledge engineering").

State of the art in this area in 1986 was recommending, that the computer scientist through interviews with the expert derives and specify the knowledge and "rule of thumbs" and compile these into rules, that could be implemented in an expert system.

This method was tested here too, but without success. After several discussions and tests with other methods, it was concluded, that gathering and specifying of knowledge was most appropriately done by the domain experts, who have acquired the necessary knowledge to meet the specific demands of expert systems.

2.5 Development tools

ESKORT has been developed by using powerful development tools. After few attempts with PC-based shells for development of expert systems, it was chosen to use KEE(Knowledge Engineering Environment) on a XEROX 1186. KEE is a special tool for supporting the development of knowledge based systems.

The Danish Customs wanted a portable system, a fast system and a reliable system. Therefore ESKORT was going to be transfered from the development environment to a running system.

Although many shells and development environments were tested, the decision was made to choose a conventional programming language. Here, "C" was chosen for two main reasons:

1 Speed of the runtime system.
2 Total freedom in designing the user interface.

The implementation was in MicroSoft C, and ESKORT is performed under MSDOS on an AT compatible PC with 80286 processor.

3 Description of the system

3.1 Context

The Danish Customs' EDP-organization is built up on a distributed concept, based on a 3-level structure:

- Directorate level,
- District custom house level, and
- Work-station level.

The hardware installation contains two main-frames in the directorate, a mini in each of the 31 district custom houses, and a number of terminals and PCs.

ESKORT is implemented on portable PCs, and therefore it is in principle a stand-alone system.

But before an audit visit the auditor downloads all accessible information on the company, the line of business, and on previous visits at the same company. At the company's premise the only requirement is a plug.

During the visit these data is supplemented with accounts data and other information, that is accessible or visible at the premises.

The system is carrying out different analyses (calculation of key figures etc). On this basis and using the rules of the knowledge base, the system gives the auditor advice on where and how, the auditing is done in the most efficient way.

3.2 VAT auditing with ESKORT

In combining expert system technology with traditional data processing ESKORT represents a complete tool box tailored for all phases of a VAT audit:

Collecting and capturing information
Today the different types of information about the companies are registered with paper and pencil. This is a both trivial and time-consuming job.
ESKORT can take charge of information handling - and do it better and faster.

Analysing information
Checking the accounts and performing analysis of numbers is done to day by means of forms and diagrams. Besides being a difficult task it takes a lot of time.

Also here ESKORT will be extremely useful. Even very complicated and comprehensive analyses are done in a few seconds.

Audit suggestions

To separate relevant from irrelevant information, to judge the information, and to reach the right conclusion are true expert tasks.

ESKORT contains knowledge, gathered by and from experts in the field. ESKORT proposes audit suggestions derived from the knowledge base.

Documentation

One of the trivial phases during an audit today is drawing up the documentation. Add to this the difficulty of keeping grasp of the information gathered during the audit.

In ESKORT, all typed-in and generated information is accumulated and can be edited later on by means of a standard word processing system, ending up to be neat audit minutes.

Background information

ESKORT contains law paragraphs from the VAT Law, regulations and rules from the statutory instruments and informations concerning line of business. The VAT officer can look up background information very easily when needed for giving correct advise on VAT matters.

To add up the VAT officer has an electronic notepad at his disposal. Here he can take down notes during the audit.

The system consists of a large number of modules with separate but integrated functions. They are separate in the sense, that the VAT officer can use them independently of each other, and integrated in the sense that the parts work on common data.

ESKORT's different facilities make up a flexible system, and the VAT officer can choose exactly his own procedure.

3.3 User friendliness

User friendliness may be one of the most misused terms in the EDP business. With ESKORT considerable effort has been made in designing a tool that can match today's requirements, and we are convinced that ESKORT deserves the term "user friendly".

The user, for instance, can jump from screen to screen according to the audit procedure that iterates between information compiling and decision making.

User interface

The user interface is the "place" where the user meets the system. He or she has no interest in the program. The user regards the system as a tool and is interested in questions such as - "Is my work going to be easier, faster, more pleasant and efficient?".

User friendliness is closely connected to the design of screens and the design of the dialogue between user and system. The user immediately has to see the connection between the EDP-system and his daily work. This goes for both technical terms, and the procedure into which the system has to fit and deliver support.

ESKORT is built up on well-known terms from real life. Commands and menues are closely connected to the VAT officers' tasks.

Mouse and menues

User friendliness also means minimal efforts remembering commands. ESKORT is based on the "mouse and menu principle". Using menues means that the VAT officer doesn't have to remember commands. He can choose from predefined menues and thus concentrate on auditing, not on EDP.

ESKORT shows coherent menues - from the users point of view -and by means of the mouse one can easily point out the command desired.

4 Introduction of the system

4.1 User test

Late 1987 the final prototype was released. It was found, that the system at that time would live up to the expectations of a valuable tool for VAT auditing. But what would be the users' approach? With regard to getting a provisionally answer to this question, a first user test, comprising 4 VAT auditors, was arranged.

One of the VAT auditors, Karen Tranekær, who participated in this first test phase, stated the following comments to a journalist:

> "I am looking forward to carrying ESKORT with me on audits. The main reason is, that the system will help me to keep the general view. During an audit several things pop up, and one has to remember quite a few things. For instance to compare information, certain aspects concerning

> the line of business, and many other factors. When I am in top form, I do a thorough and proper audit and go home feeling that I have done a good job. But I don't have bright ideas every day.
>
> In these cases I'd like to draw on ESKORT - make use of the expert system part and the audit suggestions. I can check myself and see, if I have overlooked something."

As a whole, the reactions from the test persons was positive, but they also pointed out some conditions, that were not appropriate, e.g. the editing facilities and some of the screenforms. These conditions were - to the possible extend - corrected, and implemented in the final prototype.

On the basis of the total experiences of the project, it was decided to fulfil the systems development at the same time as the prototype was tested at two district offices.

At each district office, a working group was formed, that was placed responsible for gathering experiences and forwarding proposals to the project group, so that the proposals could be implemented in future versions.

4.2 Field test

The system has now been used by 14 VAT auditors since February 1988. The auditors have reported their proposals for improvements, which are implemented in new versions of the system.

In October 1988, the user groups have written a report containing the experiences from the daily use of the system.

The report concludes:

1 ESKORT is a very usefull, valuable and time saving tool for a VAT auditor.
2 ESKORT is a widely usable, motivating and user friendly system, which is easy to learn to use.
3 When ESKORT is implemented all over the country, it will provide a significant increase in the efficiency of the VAT auditing activities.
4 The use of ESKORT on a portable PC at the traders' premises will improve the appearance of the Customs Authorities as a modern and efficient organization.

The report was very positive, and both user groups have made very constructive proposals for improvements. But in both cases some characteristic and general phenominaes was discovered, which could be concluded in the phrase:

"Everyone thinks, he is an expert in his field".

It is a typical feature in some of the comments from the field test, that "the system will probably show the greatest value for those, who are less experienced".

A closer investigation of this statement shows, that it really covers a sort of "professional pride". One does not love to acknowledge, that one have "asked a machine for advice".

This feature is very important, but probably not outstanding. It is maybe more like the dislike of using calculators.

But it is underlining the point, that a system like this must be developed and marketed in a way, that no one can doubt, that the user always is "in charge". With ESKORT a lot have been done to make the use flexible, and by the presentation to the users this flexibility has been attached great importance. In fact, it is in principle optional if and to what extent the auditors will use the system.

5 Evaluation

5.1 Costs

For public institutions as for private companies it is essential to calculate the costs and benefits for a project like this.

Concerning the costs, it is rather easy to calculate the total expenditures.

The systems development, the integration with the existing systems and the hardware makes up a total of about 18 million Dkr over a period of 5 years.

But that itself makes up a considerable problem, getting these development costs financed.

This is mainly because the Danish Customs is very wage-heavy - slightly more than 80 % of the Custom's annual budget goes on salaries. This does not leave enough to cover the investments in hardware and consultancy, that are a vital criterion for achievement of the adp-goals. So far, the needs have been financed in two ways. One of these is some entirely extraordinary appropriations obtained as a result of the political demand for an extra 300 million Dkr in VAT revenue through effectivization of the audit work. The other is government loans made available to promote computerization of the public sector.

Although these loans are interest-free, they do have to be repaid over a certain number of years through savings in operating costs. In practice, that means through personnel reductions, at any rate while the loans are beeing repaid.

Although, in theory, the Customs' staff organizations will not accept cuts of this nature as a consequence of the development of technology, in practice they have come to terms with this necessary "evil", presumably because of the new challenges and thus opportunities, that adp-development offers their members.

5.2 Benefits

But what about the benefits? It is quite obvious, that the system will have effects on

- the productivity of the auditors,
- the efficiency in the auditing area,
- the services, provided to the companies,
- the motivation of the staff, and
- the organisation as a whole.

But how do you measure these effects fair and accurate?
And even if you could do that, how do you sum them up to compare to the costs?

Most likely, you cannot. Instead it might be better to consider this matter in a more pragmatic way by looking at the effects one after one, and by setting up some goals for the expected progress. In other words, you have to consider, "who will be the happy guys, and who will be the sad guys, and to what extend".

5.2.1 Productivity

Based on the field test, where the time spent on each audit visit were carefully registered, the saving of time due to ESKORT was calculated to about 20%. That means, that every auditor by means of the system can carry out 20 % more audits.

5.2.2 Efficiency

It is also expected, that the quality of the work will be both higher and more uniform. Measured by the additional payments, we expect an increase in the efficiency of about 20 % too.

5.2.3 Better services

For the companies, a quicker carrying out of the control means a reduction of the time, in which the ressource of the company is impounded.

Furthermore, especially the less experienced auditor will be able to give the companies better instructions by means of the wording of the act, special decisions etc, which are lying in the system. That means better services, provided to the customers.

In fact that is a rather new approach - at least in Denmark. But it might be one of the most important things for public administrations today - to treat the companies and the citizens as customers, and to think of, what they mean of the level of service, provided.

Especially, in view of the development, that can be expected to result from implementation of the EEC's common market in 1992, the future of the Danish Customs lies in serving Danish trade and industry in the broadest meaning of the word. That is the position to assume, if the Customs are to "stay in business".

Half a year ago, we sent a questionnaire to some 300 representative companies, and asked them about their opinion of the corporate image of the Danish Customs and the level of service in some specific areas, e.g.:

- Do you find the customs authority's visits incriminating?
- Do you find that the customs authority's visits solve many complicated problems?
- Are the visits from the customs authority done in a efficient way?
- Is the character of the customs authority's visits instructive and informing or do they appear like interferences?

We did not love all the answers, but we got a valuable tool for measuring changes in the level of service.

The questionnaire is supposed to be done over again in two years, and we have picked up som specific questions, to which the answers is expected to be different due to the implementation of ESKORT. The goal is an improvement on the scale of at least 10 %.

5.2.4 Motivation

In the same way, we have made a questionnaire to all our employees, concerning motivation and working climate, e.g.:

- Are you satisfied with the quality of the work you execute?
- Do you have sufficient possibilities to organize your own work?
- Do you find it easy to obtain the information that is necessary to execute the daily work?
- Are you often left alone with tasks, which you would like to discuss with others?

It is expected, that the ESKORT system will have a motivating effect on the auditors, as it will both facilitate the daily work and make it more interesting.

Especially the less experienced auditor will probably feel more safe in his work, knowing that he has the "expert" on hand all the time.

Also this questionnaire is supposed to be done over again, and we expect an improvement on the scale for the relevant questions to be over 10 %.

5.2.5 *Spread of competence*

We too expect the implementation of the system to affect the organisation in some ways, especially the aim to decentralise competence and responsability. But it could be a two edged sword.

On the one hand, the system gives the opportunity to spread competence as it makes it possible - in principle - for every auditor to act like an expert.

On the other hand, there is a risk, that the exertise will grow stiff. The development of expertise is dependent upon experiences derived from creativity or intuition.

The Danish Customs are aware of this risk, and try to meet it by introducing the ESKORT system as an expert support system, and by telling the auditors, that it is never enough to do, what the system tells you. They must go further.

Furthermore, a system outside ESKORT is created to pick up the good ideas, new experiences, etc, so that these can be implemented in new versions of the system. In this way, we hope to keep the system dynamic.

5.2.6 *Systems export*

Finally, the Danish Customs have gained considerable knowledge and experience concerning expert systems for audition procedures. It seems obvious to make this expertise available for VAT authorities in other European countries.

Such a cooperation could save time and resources as the danish experiences will be of great use in several fields, as for example:

- knowledge acquisition,
- development tools and methods, and
- establishing and implementation of projects.

So both technological and organizing conditions are present to develop similar systems in other European countries.

As a matter of fact, it is expected, that in a few years this concept of "systems export" will contribute to the economic benefits of the system.

5.3 Conclusions

So far, the experiences from the ESKORT project could derive the following conclusions:

From a political point of view, it seems, that expert systems can transfer knowledge from the best to the poorest and from central government to local offices - and thereby nearer to the customer.

But does that make any sense, if all the rules still are implemented by the central government?

From an "ESKORT" point of view it makes sense in the way, that a proper audit and a good advice always will be in the advantage of those 90 % of the Danish companies, who in fact really want to pay the right amount of VAT.

Besides that, a proper and precise advice on VAT-matters should be pleasing every company.

And when you can transfer the knowledge from central government to the local offices, then you could as well transfer it any further - namely to the companies. There is no law- or control considerations, forbidding that, but of course it is a political question.

From an economic point of view, it is very difficult - as mentioned above - to reach a final conclusion..

It is obvious, that the state income is to arise from the system. However, there is not a set off between state income and state expenditures, and what about the other - "soft" benefits?

Under these circumstances, you might as well act as in a way the Danish Cusoms acted - by saying "The objectives are good - what would it cost us to reach the same by using pure man-power?"

Under these conditions, the ESKORT project turned out to an internal rate of return of about 50 %!

From an administrative point of view, it is worth considering the fact, that in the last decade, society has changed enormously. The catchword “information society” indicates the changes. An increasing number of people are dealing with collection of, handling of, and distribution of information. The information society has great effects on both the companies and the public organizations.

Data, information and knowledge are scarce ressources - knowledge is in short supply, it is unevenly distributed, and it is expensive.

Expert systems, and expert support systems like ESKORT, can make a way of crossing new borders, because they can contribute to

- maintenance and preserving of knowledge
- distribution of knowledge
- quicker decisions
- homogenious decisions.

Expert Systems in Public Administration
I. Th.M. Snellen, W.B.H.J. van de Donk, J.-P. Baquiast (Eds.)
© Elsevier Science Publishers B.V. (North-Holland), 1989

Chapter 17

Knowledge organized: Expert systems in local government

*Jan Chr. van Dalen**

Abstract

In this chapter, two main subjects are dealt with. On the one hand it is clarified that local government organizations (LGO's) can be interpreted in terms of knowledge systems (or more convenient: expert systems). Introducing this way of viewing LGO's, the characteristics and limitations of expert systems, as they are treated in common literature, are described globally. After some discussion about existing knowledge systems in LGO's, a so called Expert System Metaphor is presented.

The second subject is evaluation of expert systems in local government. Especially the economic normativity is mentioned, as a focus on on evaluation. To structure the central concept of effectivity as an evaluation measure, a multi-level analysis scheme is proposed. Some cases on existing or prototype expert systems are presented at last.

1 Introduction

Governmental organizations in general can be studied from a wide variety of perspectives. Traditionally these organizations are seen as bureaucratic structures including specified and formalized tasks and responsibilities. Alternatively they are envisaged by organization analysts as networks of

* Open Universiteit,
P/O box 2960, 6401 DL Heerlen, The Netherlands

different positions, each of them related to some other positions within the same organization. Or, by others, these organizations are seen as a political arena of groups and coalitions bargaining and sometimes fighting with each other. In this chapter local government organizations (in shorthand: LGO's) are envisaged in particular from the viewpoint of knowledge based systems or, as commonly described, expert systems.

One can characterize the variety of different perspectives as metaphors (viz. Morgan, 1986). By the knowledge metaphor, or "expert system metaphor" as I will denote this perspective, the governmental organization is treated as if it in itself were a complex expert system. In a way this idea of envisaging a LGO is based on two reasons. Firstly it is recognized that existing knowledge in an organization can -partly- be formalized in expert systems. Secondly the general characteristics of the expert systems to be designed, can be used as a prescriptive clue to organizational design.

In short it is supposed that a LGO, as an organization, adopts its special place in -local- society from internalized knowledge about acts, regulations, (local) societal customs, population characteristics, social and spatial infrastructure, etc. The knowledge about those several domains is transformed properly into products or services (mainly in the form of policies and decisions) by some decision generating process. Seen from a market oriented point of view, the question about feasible and profitable product-market combinations arises. These combinations explain partly the succes of a governmental organization in its environment. Generally the products and services are connected to recognized problems that are latent or manifest in local society. This way of viewing governmental organizations is of interest since (at least) management of many such organizations nowadays is exploring the boundaries of bureaucracy, is searching for the mission of the LGO and are probing the perspectives of a business-like orientation to service delivery and governmental "production". In this context issues like business strategy, flexible organization and innovation are emergent. The knowledge based (or expert system) focus on these and other issues will contribute to the clarification of the problems and solutions in the every day operation of local government. It may be clear that problem solving and decision making are essential elements in this approach.

2 Local government as it is globally organized

Dutch local government has its place at the lowest level of public administration below national and provincial government. The activities of local government are partly undertaken at an autonomous base as well as at a co-operative base. The latter means that the measures taken by the local government are in concordance with rules and practices of higher level authorities. Sometimes one can see these activities as being delegated. In other cases the activities are complementary to the activities of e.g. regional authorities.

The machinery of local government is globally divided into two parts. One part is the political conglomerate of elected members of the municipal council and the board of mayor and aldermen. The elected members are representing a variety of political parties, each with its own ideology. The council itself is the highest authority in a municipality. The organization of a council is more complex than simply a democratic meeting. The main organization characteristic is the party-wise division of the council (a common organization principle). Furthermore the members of the council participate in committees according to certain policy-sectors of governmental care. Sometimes these committees are covering more than one sector, and are connected to a certain territory within a city.

The members of the political part of the local government machinery (the political management) acquire their knowledge from their party institutions, from newspaper messages, from pressure groups, from civil servants, etc. They collect, interpret and transform information in their own individual, mostly not standardized way. These information activities are colored by individual insights and theories as well as collective party ideology. Information collection strategies (the acquisition of knowledge) in this context can be distinguished in two categories. One is the information seeking strategy. The individual (or group) is deliberatly soliciting information. He or she is performing a planned scanning of the environment for messages about a specific topic. The other category simply exists of information processing strategies. The politician discovers in an unplanned way messages about some topic and processes the information. Such a politician can be characterized as a passive information user, while the former type is his active antipode. The growth of -individual- knowledge is dependent upon these strategies. In some instances knowledge will accumulate along an unplanned path, otherwise the accumulation will happen systematically. These ways of accumulating knowledge can be elucidated by comparing the process with the formation of individual construct systems as described by Kelly and others (viz. Van Dalen, 1987). A construct system can be viewed as an individual theory about the world surrounding the individual. Aggregation of such systems, based on mutual interaction and agreement between individuals, leads to shared group and organizational knowledge "bases", with their own values.

The local government administrative machinery isn't the arena of elected political members only. A second important part is the body of officials, preparing and executing decisions taken by the politicians in office. Especially this part is important for the functioning of government in the long run. Knowledge that is necessary for continuity of the organization, is stored within this part of the organization. Several archives and individual memories support the storage of knowledge. Keeping archives up to date is ideally performed in compliance with given procedures. One can imagine that this way of working doesn't garantee that knowledge is stored in a proper way, nor that all the relevant information is stored. Often, e.g. in the case of a leaving official, it is recognized that with his leave essential knowledge is disappearing. So it may happen that the execution of a certain governmental task does require the generation of knowledge for a second time. That this is an inefficient way of working won't be denied. The proper building of knowledge bases in the organization will help a great deal. The storage of information is not the only way of organizational knowledge accumulation. By making inferences on the basis of some reasoning process, knowledge can be enlarged too.

3 The structure of Local Government

LGO's are mostly treated according to limited number of alternative structural forms. Every form has its own structural and relational characteristics. Moreover every form is based on its own ideology leading to cultural and behavioral features. One of the regularly cited and often actually used forms is the traditional form or hierarchical bureaucratic structure. It is remarkable that when one is speaking about the organization of local government, especially with respect to this structure, mostly the machinery of the officials is meant, and not the organizational form in which the elected politicians are working. It certainly should be preferred to include these individuals and groups into the considerations about the LGO. Traditionally within this structure the town clerk is a pivotal figure. He (or she) is the prime adviser of the board of mayor and aldermen (further referred to as "the board") and of the municipal council. With respect to the administrative machinery he is the senior manager. Next to him are the managers of the several -relative autonomous- departments as schematically visualized in figure 1.

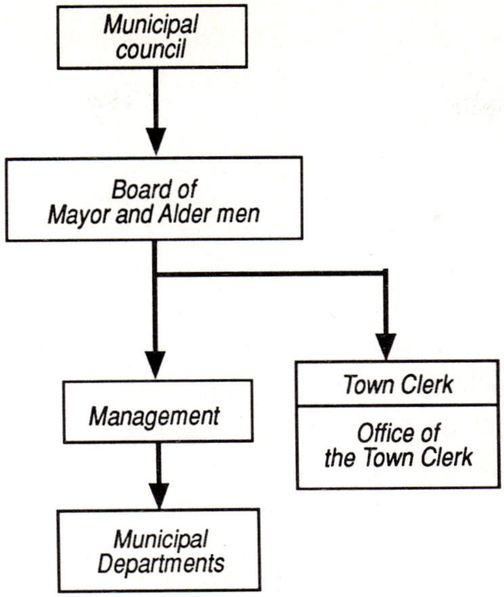

Figure 1: Structure of local government

The autonomy of the departments is relative in the sense that the execution of policies (like the issue of licences, or the design of a roadsection) mostly is performed on their own discretion. Policy proposals on the other hand are first submitted to the office of the town clerk before entering the decision process of the board. So the bureaucratic hierarchy is twofold. With respect to policy execution there is a direct hierarchical line from the board via the department managers to the workers in the departments (eventually with some levels in between). With respect to policy proposals the other hierarchical line includes the town clerk and his office as an intermediary between board and management. One can imagine that this focus on the municipal organization can have far reaching consequences on the flow of information and on the distribution of knowledge in the organization. Even conflicting knowledge bases will be a possible phenomenon, thus disturbing the regular decision process.

The second alternative structural form to be mentioned is the sector structure. One can alternatively call it a market-oriented structure, although the adherents of this form mostly neglect the idea of a market. The design of a municipal organization according to this form leads to some form of a departmental organization (like state level government) subservient to the (political) management of the board. In the pure departmental model every alderman is responsible for his own department. The board is functioning as a management board, where -based on the individual responsibilities- the collective responsibility for the organization at large is taken. In two other variants, the functional model and the open system model, in the board mayor and aldermen are collectively responsible for the organization, without individual responsibility of each of these authorities for their own department. In the functional model all the department managers report to a "director general" (a chief executive officer), who is intermediary between departments and board. Building knowledge bases and information channels takes predominantly place at departmental level. Integrative knowledge, e.g. constituted in a corporate knowledge base is very difficult to design and to implement. Mostly the need for integration is met by some organizational device, like a coordinating bureau, centralizing procedures and the implementation of reporting systems. The open system model explicitly deals with the interaction of the organization with its environment. So much attention is given to boundary spanning relations. The organizational subsystems, each for themselves, are usually dedicated to large clusters of policy fields.

A third alternative has to do with the network structure that is often emergent in LGO's. Sometimes the organization charts are sketched like networks, varying from simple trees to complex networks with interlocking circuits. The attractiveness of a network perspective is the greater freedom the designer has with respect to the operationalization of the elements of the network. One can view the nodes of the network as persons or groups interacting with each other in the context of proposing new policies, or as departments sharing interests, or as committees covering some policy field, etc. So with respect to nearly every aspect of the municipal organization an analysis of the network properties can be made. The networks describing a LGO can be analyzed in a variety of analysis methods. Visual inspection as well as sophisticated statistical analysis are two (apparently opposed) of the analysis modes that are relevant, as long as they are apt to the problems at hand. Two types of networks are to be distinguished in particular. One of them is the formal explicit network as embodied in the formal charts of an organization or in the formal procedures. The other type is the informal emerging network, not formally described, but practically working. Information flows through both types of networks. Some people happen to be thoroughly connected and can rely on a large variety of information, thereby capable to enrich their knowledge base. Other people stay outside the network flows, are pretty isolated and their knowledge about organizational and other affairs is often becoming obsolete at a fast rate.

The last alternative to be mentioned here is the political, or decision making, structure. Every LGO has its own political system, with its own set of key persons, coalitions, ideology, etc. Miles (1980) describes the concept of organization politics in an illuminating way as

> "... the processes whereby differentiated but interdependent individuals or interest groups exercise whatever power they can amass to influence the goals, criteria or processes used in organizational decision making to advance their own interests. "

These "political" behaviors need not be premeditated; many a manager has argued forcefully for his or her departments' point of view, convinced that it is in the best interest of the organization as a whole. The key characteristic of an organization political system is its kind of decision making. Every actor or party (be it e.g. a person, a department, or an ad hoc group of officials) in the organization strives to the realization of its interests by entering the decision process. Sometimes actors seek support of others in the game of organization politics. In other situations actors are powerful enough to act for themselves.

The formal "political" structure of the municipal organization leads to the conclusion that some actors have better (power) positions in the organization than others. They can achieve more than those others with respect to their interests. Nevertheless, bargaining with respect to policy issues is normal practice in a LGO. This bargaining is not always an open and transparent activity. Not every actor is expliciting all the issues and goals he is aiming at. Besides, like many negotiators, actors often try to manipulate time as an instrumental variable in bargaining. Such manipulations create some freedom for the actor to alter his negotiable alternatives. The decision making and bargaining behavior of an actor in this context is strongly influenced by his expectations with respect to his future reputation.

With respect to knowledge base building it is interesting to explore what conditions are manifest when viewing LGO's from a political focus. As remarked earlier, not every actor will make clear all the things he knows about certain issues or problems. Sometimes obviously there is a hidden agenda leading the actions of the actor. On the other hand bargaining asks for some shared knowledge. The choices between transfer of knowledge and witholding knowledge are dependent upon individual factors. The building of knowledge bases will often be practiced in a very dispersed way, mostly leading to sub-optimality of decisions and policies.

A global oversight of the mentioned alternative structural forms may show that different forms each have their own implications for the design of knowledge bases in LGO's. The degree of bureaucracy is obviously one of the factors influencing the design of more or less intelligent information systems that support the characteristic "production"process of Local Government. The orientation on market sectors or policy fields is another. The degree of politization may not be excluded from the set of factors.

It is very essential to consider the structuring of LGO's from the viewpoint of knowledge based and information systems. Lot of complaints about malfunctioning of LGO's can be reduced to the problematic use of knowledge as is manifest in the acquisition of information c.q. the interpretation, the processing, the retrieval, the transfer, etc. The improvement of the functioning of the LGO's can be treated in a proper way along some line of organizational and managerial learning, as will be obvious within a "knowledge environment".

The following paragraphs contain discussions on the knowledge and information aspects of the design and functioning of LGO's. The discussions lead to the design of the so called Expert System Metaphor.

4 Information systems and automation in local government

During this decade automation has gained a prominent position in the field of Dutch local government. Computers were introduced in various work constellations. At first, applications were found in purely administrative taskfields, like bookkeeping and large databases on population. One of the effects of these applications is the growing number of computers installed within governmental organizations. Another effect is the speeding up of administrative procedures. Sometimes this last effect is noticed by people in the public when they are served, sometimes it seems to be only an internal affair. Another -intended- effect is the reduction of personnel, often defined as a goal but hardly met.

As such these developments lead to more efficient and rationalized "production processes" and to a better control of them. However decision processes themselves, being the core of most of the activities of local government, are barely supported by developments in this field of automation.

One of the broadly recognized reasons that decision making itself is so poorly supported by new developments, was the absence of proper information policies in most municipalities. A second reason to be mentioned was the relative lack of commitment of top level administrators in municipal organizations (viz. Hubbeling, 1988).

When time went by new ideas emerged about informatization in governmental organizations. The importance of informatization policies gained ground, giving way to the idea that informatization is a process that developes along certain lines (viz. Van Schaik, 1985). Among others the concept of networking is becoming to be more elaborated, leading to decentralization of work supported by new information technologies. Lately the concept of expert systems within the context of decision making is more and more recognized.

Interest in expert systems is expressed by representatives of governmental organizations as well as academia. The focus on expert systems is clearly different: representatives of governmental organizations mostly emphasize the exploitation of expert systems as -more or less- intelligent information systems. Academic workers have more interest in the challenging problems, like enlarging the power of such systems, or improving the efficiency or reliability.

However, the applications of expert systems are scarce. Examples are found within the field of social services (viz. Van de Donk & Snellen, 1988), and prototypes in the field of the rent act. Mostly these examples cover automated versions of the facts and structure of laws, regulations, etc., as commonly used by civil servants (e.g. social workers). A confounding aspect of the study of expert systems is that the term “expert system” is widely used in a variety of cases with different meanings. As a better term for the collection of interpretations “knowledge based systems” could be proposed, which would do more justice to the wide range of applications and the variety of interpretations. A set of subconcepts can be distinguished in a customary way by three classes:

- data handling systems,
- consultancy systems,
- expert systems.

In daily practice most knowledge-based systems can be classified as data handling systems and very few as expert systems. Notwithstanding the helpfulness of these systems, they constitute a poor representation of the real world expertise in LGO’s.

5 The skeleton of expert systems

Ideally expert systems are seen as simulators of a human reasoning process by applying specific (domain) knowledge and by using inferential knowledge. As such expert systems will be viewed as the creation of artificial intelligence models of some part of the real world, meant to be used as decision support instruments. They can, internally, be characterized by:

- extensive specific knowledge about some domain of interest,
- application of search techniques,
- support for heuristic analysis,
- capacity to infer new knowlwedge from existing knowledge,
- symbolic processing,
- ability to explain its own reasoning.

As stressed before, LGO's may be seen as expert systems themselves. The elements of the systems, the civil servants as well as the political rulers being characterized as such, do have -by training or by experience- specific knowledge about several domains. They rely on certain search techniques with respect to decision making. In a way they obtained the competence to navigate through the organization and through the diverse knowledge based systems. They set certain agenda facilities as a guide, sometimes openly, sometimes hidden. Mainly training supplies them with facilities for heuristic reasoning and with a certain capacity to generate new knowledge from the existing body of knowledge. The symbolic processing that is supposed to be a characteristic of expert systems is often poorly developed in the form of procedures and structures, while new developments in the field of openness and publicity are forcing individuals to improve their capabilities to explain their way of reasoning. So it may be seen as quite natural to make inquiries into the field of expert systems and to develop such systems within governmental organizations.

Schematically the structure (architecture) of an expert system can be visualized as follows:

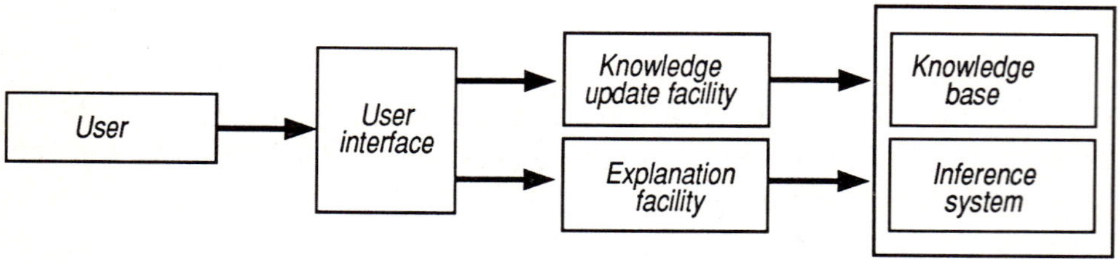

Figure 2: The structure of an expert system

The explanation of the analogy between human expertise embedded in a LGO and artificial expert systems may be clarified with the help of this scheme.

In the traditional day to day practice, civil servants with some expertise are asked for advice (decision support) via some "user interface", which is mostly a simple natural language communication facility. The human expert will manipulate his knowledge base and inference system and then generate an advice. Meanwhile, by this experience, his knowledge base is enriched.

In the case of an artificial expert system things are arranged more formally. E.g. the user interface usually will demand some expertise from the user. In very bureaucratic human expert systems formalization is elaborated too. Citizens will be given access to the governmental system, if they follow some rules, use some forms, etc. The application for and granting of unemployment benefits is a proper example. By experimentation one can try to compare the performance of human vs. artificial expert systems (viz. Turing test) and make inferences about the extent of similarity between the two. But, on a conceptual level too, it is possible to use the scheme of an expert system as a frame of reference to evaluate the functioning of a LGO as a physical expertise exploiting system. Hence, the use of the global structure of expert systems is a proper metaphor with which one can analyse and improve the design and functioning of -parts of- an LGO.

6 Varieties and limitations of expert systems

Expert systems themselves can be distinguished into three categories, dependent on the relative size of the systems:

- assistant: a small knowledge-based system, exploiting a technically limited, but economically interesting, subset of an (human) expert's task;
- colleague: a medium sized knowledge-based system, exploiting a significant subset of an (human) expert's task;
- expert: a large knowledge-based system that approaches the level of a human expert within a given domain.

While these categories are distinguished on the basis of their relative size, one can imagine that the actual operation of such systems require different computer facilities. So, another way of discriminating between them is by required computer facilities. Most assistants are PC-based, colleagues ask for conventional mainframe facilities, while experts normally are implemented on powerful modern computers and require sophisticated development tools. With other writers (viz. Rolston, 1988) and practical users of expert systems one may conclude that most existing expert systems fall into the colleague or assistant category. Very few existing systems can compete with a human expert.

In practice the development and implementation of expert systems is obviously restricted by practical limitations like:

- knowledge being extracted from only a small number of human experts,
- applications limited to a small domain or set of domains,
- applications limited by little need for extensive -temporal or spatial- reasoning,
- the expert task doesn't ask for a large body of general or commonsense knowledge,
- the required knowledge has to be relatively complete, correct and stable.

Notwithstanding the restrictiveness of these limitations, a lot of applications can be developed and implemented. One can think of several applications in the field of social services (calculation of unemployment benefits), taxes (for private persons as well as companies), rent (calculation of subsidies), subsidies in general (e.g. for the establishment of factories or offices), control tasks (e.g. environmental pollution warning systems), etc. These applications belong to the sphere of the execution of policies that are already developed. In the design of new policies expert systems could be supportive too. At least the design of the organizational and work structures in accordance with the knowledge transformation tasks will be usefull. Recent developments in information technology are in favour of this orientation.

A clear benefit of the process of developing an expert system is the implication for human experts to be very explicit and precise about existing knowledge, about their rationalities-in-use and about their own professionality. In this sense learning effects are manifest.

7 Varieties of knowledge bases in Local Government

The execution of tasks in a LGO requires a lot of general and domain specific knowledge (and therefore information). A substantial part of this knowledge is stored in the minds of human experts, be it specialists or generalists, within the LGO. They have been tought during their training several facts and -past- experiences according to their specialities. They develop -so to say- their own paradigm, based upon their training in problem solving with the help of disciplinairy knowledge.

So an official specialized in environmental pollution problems will have sound knowledge about acts, ministerial decisions and regulations, or about technical devices for the control and prevention of pollution. As far as the training background is restricted to law or technical sciences the official will be biased in one or another direction and his knowledge will -generally speaking- be incomplete. During the active workperiod he will acquire for himself domain knowledge about specific environmental problems in specific settings. E.g. some official will specialize in industrial processes, while another will proceed in general citizen generated pollution (waste disposal etc.).

Work experiences will support the personal development of an official, so that he or she can make decisions on problems and solutions without using extensive solution procedures. He or she will learn to make short cuts in problem solving processes, based on experiences in practice. This development in working style is featuring the process of becoming an expert.

Leaving out of consideration the special case of this example, we can imagine that a LGO is crowded with experts. But, who is an expert in one field may turn out to be an apprentice or a layman in another field. Being an expert in a certain field means the possesion of general knowledge and -what is more essential- knowledge of the domain and the capability of solving problems in that domain more efficiently than others. It may be supposed that within a LGO the wide variety of experts corresponds with a comparable variety of knowledge bases.

The organization of the knowledge bases may match with the physical organization, or not. Most LGO's, however, are formally structured in accordance to other principles (alternatives) than the formal or emerging structure of existing or preferred knowledge bases. So nobody will be surprised that it is a common complaint that organizational structures and the structure of data/ knowledge bases are not matching. Often it is concluded that similar databases exist on different places in an organization with different characteristics and for different purposes. Another frequently uttered complaint is about the creation of a wild abundance of personal archives.

When a LGO is attempting to enter the era of informatization, then these complaints emerge in a very manifest and persistent way. Information analysts try to systemize data bases, information flows, etc., and sometimes try to make a start with the design of expert systems. They work along the lines of certain metaphors, that give them a consistent insight into the information and expertise problems that exist. The results of such an approach, however, include a bias in the description of the reality of the LGO. With Stamper et al (1988) we can e.g. distinguish between the following metaphors, expressing the view of information analysts on the phenomenon "organization":

- the conduit metaphor of language, meaning that language is simply a vehicle to transport meanings, ideas, emotions, etc. neglecting the social context;

- the chemical engineering metaphor of data-processing, referring to the translation from natural language to formal language as if "meaning" is fransferred from one container to another.
- the set metaphor of reality, stressing the idea that knowledge and information are "simply" the mathematical concept of sets;
- the correspondance metaphor of meaning, which explains meaning as the link between symbol and what is symbolized;
- the platonic metaphor, regarding reality as an abstract entity, leading to unquestionable, reliable knowledge;
- the information-processing metaphor of mind, expressing the idea that the human mind is quite comparable to a computer (an information processing machine).

These metaphors, as used in practice, lead to an oversimplification of the organizational reality, and of the structure and meaning of "organizational" knowledge. Besides, in no way it is guaranteed that the chosen metaphor will match the structure and culture of the LGO.

Nevertheless in practice we are condemned to structure and simplify the world around us. Thus we create the opportunity to anticipate future developments in our environment, especially in our workorganization. The LGO, being an organization that is dominantly oriented towards decision making, delivers products and services of which knowledge is a substantial part. So it is certainly not illogical to study LGO's from the viewpoint of knowledge based, or expert systems. This has strong interpretational implications for e.g. the way clients are approached, new products/services are developed, the logistics within the organization are controlled, the marketing function is executed, etc.

8 The expert system metaphor

In LGO's the variety among expert systems (automated or not) can be explained by discriminating between their characteristics (viz. par. 5). Especially the variety in domains is remarkable. Moreover different parts of the LGO use the same knowledge defined for the same domain. It would be natural to think that in these cases organizational combinations are possible, efficient and effective. But reorganizations, triggered by this focus, are not only dependent upon similarities in domain, but also on internal cultural aspects.

To explicate the structure of an expert system, with reference to the LGO as a whole, we can rely on the earlier presented simple version:

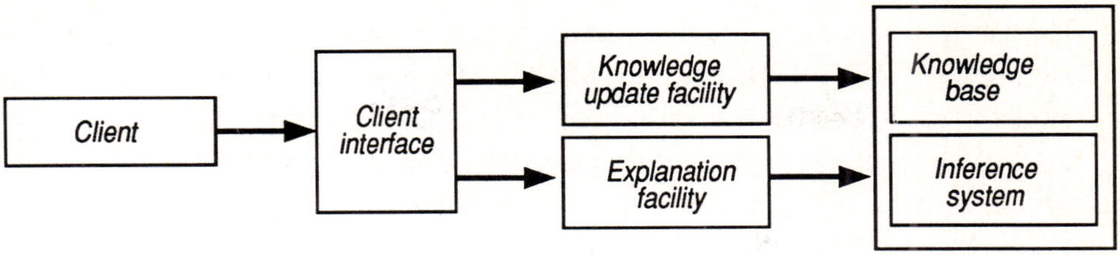

Figure 3: The structure of an expert system with reference to the LGO

The core of a knowledge based system, as sketched, is the knowledge base, and parallel with the knowledge base, the inference system. Knowledge bases are physically introduced in an LGO by experience of the members and by their training. The inference system is mainly constituted by training and in a minor part by experience. The introduction of knowledge based systems may be originated by people internally, the content of a knowledge based system is regularly derived externally from the environment of the LGO. Popularly expressed, the constitution of internal knowledge based systems is dependent upon information that can be extracted from the markets the LGO is operating in. Or, managerial formulated, upon the product-market combinations. With respect to the proper communication with actors in these markets the explanation facility is of interest. While the products of LGO's are heavily relying on information and knowledge it is of interest that the clients are well informed about the features and the characteristics of the products and services. These products and services mostly leave a certain freedom of interpretation. Several examples can be found in reality, concerning decisions that are misinterpreted, cause conflicts, and force government to introduce corrections or alterations. Only by completing products and services with explanations, proper effects can be expected. The explanation facility has to be organized. Often a specialized information service or public relations agency is founded. In several cases it can be shown that this organizational measure alone is not efficacious.

The knowledge update facility is necessary to meet the effects of obsolesence processes. Knowledge is not forever. Especially in the times we are living in knowledge is changing rapidly. Nevertheless it may be recognized that explicit and systemized organizational knowledge update functions are scarce in LGO's.

The client interface at last gives room for interaction between client and LGO-experts. Often in bureaucratic LGO's there seem to be more barriers to interaction than facilities. In many cases LGO's are trying to bureaucratize the clients instead of servicing them.

The LGO at large as well as parts of it can be studied from the perspective of knowledge based systems. This means that the organization of the production function, of the development function and of the acquisition function is seen in the light of the acquisition and transformation of knowledge and of the incorporation of knowledge in products and services. Moreover, human resources are treated from the viewpoint of competence and professionality. The personnel development function is directed to maintain a prestigious level of knowledge and competence.

The different knowledge based systems, sometimes can work in a "stand-alone" mode, without the need of mutual coordination with other systems. In any case it is important to chose the proper system that matches the problem to be tackled. This choice can be supported by the constitution of a proper agenda setting function in the LGO (Van Dalen, 1987) With respect to other problems the interaction of several systems is desirable. Then a proper coordination or integration mechanism has to be designed and implemented. One can analyze these situations by studying knowledge based systems as cells of an overarching system. Coordination plays an important role in the interaction on system level as well as sub-system level, e.g. the inferential sub-system of the expert system.

9 Purposes, uses and benefits of expert systems

When one is researching the development and use of human or artificial expert systems in local government, then several interesting questions arise. One of the very first questions one has to face is: Who are the users of expert systems, and what roles do they fullfill. One of the crucial aspects of the development of expert systems is the identification and specification of user requirements and their functions in a rational efficient decision making process. Especially problems concerning the identification of norms (procedures, etc.) are important. Interesting is the function of economic norms in the construction of expert systems as belonging to -incomplete and biased-images of organizational and decision problems (viz. the earlier mentioned methaphors used by developers as well as -human- experts).

Users with their roles and requirements can be distinguished along a scale that is representing the already mentioned academical/practical contrast. At the "academic" side of the scale one can identify the user who's predominant role is testing and verifying the system by probing its behavior. At the practical end of the scale users are identified who apply an expert system to specific decision making tasks. Between these two extremes one can identify users who manipulate the knowledge in the system by providing additional knowledge or by modifying existing knowledge, and users who have the intention to develop their personal expertise by extracting knowledge from the systems. Or, the scale could also be interpreted in terms of "learning " vs. "using".

A second question to be posed in the process of analysing expert systems is : to what purposes are they fit. The earlier mentioned categories of expert systems (assistent, collegue, expert) indicate such purposes on an abstract level. Within the context of governmental use of expert sytems the following partition may be a proper one:

- expert systems used for policy planning/development tasks,
- expert systems used for production/policy execution tasks,
- expert systems to control the decision making process and its outcomes (monitoring),
- expert systems used for learning within the organization.

People using expert systems in one of these four modes will be focussed on other goals than people using them in another mode. This circumstance will lead to different forms of -economic- evaluation fit to each of the four different situations.

10 Economic norms and expert systems

As mentioned before, expert systems are viewed as the creation of artificial intelligence -partial- models of the real world. It is presumed by many expert systems analysts that there exists an objective reality that can be understood and controlled by individual human expert intelligence, that in its turn can be replaced by machinery. On the other hand it may be supposed that reality is constructed (viz. Van Dalen, 1987; Stamper, 1988) by persons interacting with each other through -shared or conflicting- norms, experiences, cultural traits, etc. This process of constructing reality cannot be managed fully by computers as a replacement of human intelligence. A mix of artificial and human intelligence in organizational decision making will mostly be the adequate form. Expert systems can be viewed as a -partial- representation of the normativity by which the behavior of individuals in an organization is guided. Different norms are guiding the behavior of persons, especially in the context of decision making as we are interested in. These norms form largely the bases of the rationalities-in-use in decision making within the organization. We can distinguish (viz. Van Dalen, 1987) between different rationalities-in-use in relation to decision making:

- representative rationality, referring to the individual's competence with respect to model building of real world problems;
- goal rationality, referring to the coherence of one's normsystem as a basis for his goals;
- methodical rationality, referring to the logical coherence of decision rules one uses to obtain an optimal course of action;
- meta rationality, referring to the ability of persons to make adequate choices with respect to the other rationalities.

To much attention for methodical rationality can e.g. lead to excellent decisions that are made to late. Hence these decisions will turn out to be failures. Meta rationality has much to do with the economic exploitation of expertise. Therefore it is an important factor in the evaluation of expert systems, be it human or artificial. (Especially the artificial systems are of interest here.) The earlier mentioned limitations to the practical development and implementation of expert systems may stress that economic norms play an important role.

When we look more closely to the applications of expert systems as they are implemented in business and government at this time, we can infer that they usually play a role in situations where complex but routine decisions have to be made at an operational level. In a sense decision making of this type is delegated by a human expert to some artificial expert in a bureaucratic manner. This way if formulating suggests that decision making subject to expert systems design -up till now- is strongly based on fixed norms. But reality in governmental decision making practice is mostly not a fixed and objective entity, but a subjective and changing one, founded on human interactions.

Not all the norms, that are underlying human interaction, are economic of nature, most will be social or political. Nevertheless economic norms may be supposed to play an important role. Not only with respect to the process of developing systems, but also in the process of using them (viz. types of users), in the perfomance of the system (efficiency) and with respct to the comparison of different systems or different mode of one system. Economic norms however, are implicit to an expert system as far as they are mentioned by the human experts and recognized by the knowledge engineer (the "translator" of knowledge). An expert system, being a mapping of human knowledge and organizational norms, must contain economic norms. E.g. some subsidy regulations ask for the economic performance of the applicant. Economic norms are of interest too, when it comes to the evaluation of expert systems. The normativity then has to do with economic criteria that are applicated. Practical experiences show that there is no consensus about these types of economic norms. More strongly formulated, in most cases developers as well as users (or principals), meet severe difficulties in explaining what -economic- results may be expected from the use of expert sytems.

11 Economic evaluation of expert systems

Evaluation of expert systems with respect to the economic norms ask for a classification of costs and benefits of such systems, for a methodology of evaluation and for some type of criteria.

The costs and benefits are -in the case of governmental expert systems- not only related to the governmental organization itself, but to a variety of outside users too. A conventional classification of costs, that will help a proper understanding of the cost/benefit problem can be summed up as follows:

- development costs,
- implementation costs,
- operation costs,
- maintenance costs,
- renewal costs,
- termination costs.

Each of these costs can be divided into categories like:

- organizational costs,
- outside user costs,
- societal costs.

Especially this second distinction is necessary in the case of the evaluation of the governmental production process (viz. Bouckaert, 1988):

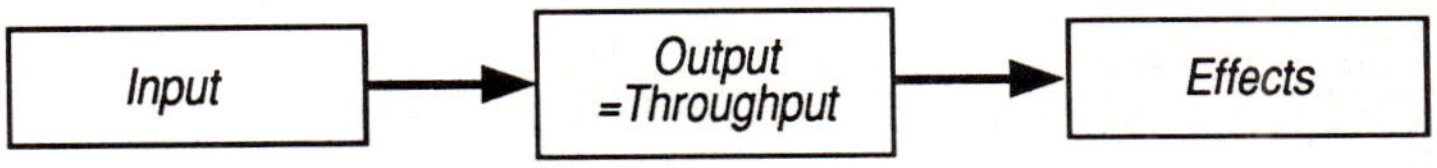

Figure 4:The evaluation of the governmental production process

Not only the output of the process is important, the intended and realized effects too.

It may be stipulated that some costs are stretched over quite a long period, while other costs only count in the short run. This refers to evaluation studies that have a longitudinal character.

With respect to the evaluation of new (production)methods/-measures within organizations it is customary to compare old and new situations on the basis of organizational costs. One of the difficulties connected with evaluation research on governmental organizations is the relative untransparency of the organizational cost structure. Another difficulty is formed by the emergence of costs of the two other types (outside user and societal). These costs are not only difficult to measure, there is no consensus about their existence in specific cases.

The benefits of expert systems in the context of governmental organizations are seldomly explicitly measured. In general the practice in the field of the development and implementation of information systems is to compare the old situation (without information system) with the new situation (with information system) and to atribute the net effect to the implemented information system. Mostly this practice concentrates on cost economy, like decrease of personnel, more efficient procedures, etc.

The validity of this kind of comparisons may be questioned. Mostly validity is threatened by phenomena like quality of services, change in products/services, shift of activities, etc. A special drawback of evaluation studies in governmental organizations is the historical lack of attention -in general- for economic normativity with respect to their own activities and performance.

A proper way to control the complex problems arising from evaluations as mentioned now is introduced by classifying the effectivity of expert systems in concordance to the appropriate levels. We distinguish them as follows (viz. Hufen, 1989):

- individual task procedure, referring to the real micro-level behavioral actions individuals undertake within the context of special case decision making;
- individual task complex, referring to the effectivity of the individual in his dayly work life, mostly described as his function;
- group, referring to the organized group level (task groups, sections, departments, committees, etc.);
- organization, referring to the organization as a whole. A decision has to be made whether only the administrative body is included, or the total organization of administrative and political bodies are at stake;
- political/societal environment, referring to the level at which the effects are of utmost importance.

Now, to these levels the construct "effectivity" can be operationalized by criteria, thus explaining the meaning for the system concerned. Schematically such an operationalization can be given as:

Construct	*Level*	*Criteria*
Effectivity	**Individual task procedure**	Personnel costs Material costs Time, timelags
	Individual task complex	Productivity Motivation Satisfaction Quality
	Group results	Productivity Output quality Goal attainment
	Organisation	Efficiency Flexibility Continuity
	Political/Societal environment	Effectivity Policy violations Reachability

Table 1: Effectivity criteria

The operationalizations can be measured, giving some evidence for an evaluative judgement of the actual performance of the LGO, seen as a knowledge transforming institution.

Eventually, the evaluation of expert systems asks for a controlled experimental approach. Since this is not common practice, it would be advisable to start with a sample of comparable municipal organizations and to design a longitudinal quasi-experiment with one expert system in a limited variety of modes. (A comparable experiment has been carried out with respect to the productivity of municipal organizations (Van Dalen, 1988). An alternative approach would be the structuring of the quasi-experiment as a learning experiment. Such an approach is justified because essentially knowledge engineering is a learning activity that can be properly structured along some learning cycle (viz. Hanken, Van Dalen, 1986).

12 Cases in knowledge based organization design (or change)

a. Shared knowledge in the Social Services Department

Since long in The Netherlands there has been a dispute about the character of the municipal social service departments. The main issue was the question whether such a department is solely producing decisions about payments (like unemployment benefits) or performing social work in a broad sense. Whatever the task may be, members of the departments are engaged in sometimes complex decision problems and are using individual knowledge. An attractive approach to this kind of organizations is to look for opportunities to formalize the knowledge and the decision making process (the inference system) to support the decision making of the individual social worker.

Some municipal social service departments have been studied. Mostly the research assigments started with questioning the management of the department. Often it was emphasized that there was a lack of personnel, leading to a increasing work load. During the research it always was discovered that an important inefficiency was originated by non-shared, extremely uncoordinated and distributed knowledge about the professional tasks. So a first recommendation turned out to be "systemizing the knowledge necessary for individual and organizational performance". This knowledge has to do with formal regulations and acts, local facts about neighbourhoods, but also with methodology of case work, decision procedures within the department and within the LGO at large. So what was done was organizing a most simple kind of (non-automated) knowledge based system, leading to proper diagnosis of cases and the possible solutions. The system was used by individuals for themselves but nevertheless rather uniform on department level. The physical organization was rearranged in that way that groups could be organized based on shared knowledge systems. An advantage of organizing the department this way was the introduction af an agenda-system that functions as a relegation mechanism. Another advantage is the possibility to organize the department in a decentralized, even deconcentrated way.

It will be clear that logically a next step is the development of automated expert systems for departments like this one. Such systems facilitate the decentralized organization, due to the relative simply realizable distributed structure. Experiences with such automated systems, however, are not inviting much optimism in the short run.

Evaluation of the implemented recommendations was executed by checking the redesigned knowledge system, and by controlling for work load.

b. Total Reorganization

Since the sixties another debate in The Netherlands has been devoted to the reorganization of LGO's. A lot of experiments have been undertaken too. With every reorganization project some kind of criterion was chosen. Some of these criteria were ideologically determined (like political control or client friendlyness), others based on ideas about effectivity (like efficient communication or selfmanagement). The result of the reorganization processes is always some alternative structural form. Evaluation of the new structural forms can be undertaken with the help of the expert metaphor. Then, a new structural form can facilitate the constitution of effective knowledge bases to support the problem solving tasks within the LGO. As remarked earlier a LGO is characterized by its transformation process and its product: knowledge processing as a means to produce services or products that are enriched by information (viz. the issue of licenses, the presentation of renovation plans). The "sale" of those services and products is influenced by this characteristic. Clients e.g. will ask for "after sales service" by questioning the whys and wherefores of a governmental decision and its execution. They will ask for explanations and sometimes criticize policy practices. They implicitly question the transformation process, where for instance the interpretation of existing knowledge is at stake.

With one of the municipalities a structural form was chosen that consisted of departments corresponding to the sectors of Town Planning (and Construction), Social Services, Citizen Affairs, Research and Statistics, Personnel and Organization, Finance, Internal Affairs. Especially the first two departments were designed on the basis of shared knowledge. The department of Town Planning covered the activities related to planning, construction and control of land-use, like infrastructure, housing, industry building, etc. All the knowledge covering this field was planned to be concentrated within this department. In the second place the decision procedures had to be coordinated, so that one could speak of one knowledge "centre" in this field, with users (clients) such as the public at large, construction firms, politicians, other authorities, etc. A difficulty in the design phase was the fragmentation in procedures and structures as existed for years. There was no generally accepted way of making inferences on the basis of existing and -in the case of actual problem solving- acquired knowledge. Moreover there existed no procedure to update knowledge nor a procedure to explain to clients decisions that were taken. Traditionally an organization researcher will look for proper archives (knowledge storage) and sound procedures. Working along the lines of an expert system metaphor, however, he will accentuate the characteristics of knowledge structure, will stress the fact that procedures must have a function in the context of decision making as knowledge transformation and will add the requirement that decision making has to be explained to users/clients (if wished) and will add the requirement that a proper updating facility is constructed. Organizational practice confronts the designer with a lot of problems. E.g. the organizational function "public relations", that can be interpreted as an explaining facility, is mostly not close to departments like Town Planning. Another fact often neglected in analysis of daily practice is the negotiability of knowledge to some degree. Not all information (knowledge) can be used by everyone under all circumstances in decision making. To some degree the position of participants in decision making determines the applicability and weight of available knowledge.

The evaluation phase in this project was started as qualitative research into the effects of policies and decisions, on departmental level. Remarkable is the fact that besides the strict departmental focus other factors (e.g. societally determined) were excluded.

c. Handling communication networks

A widespread feature of LGO's is the committee structure. And spread to the same extent are the rumours and complaints about the (dis)functioning of committees. Moreover the knitting of committees is the last two decades enriched by phenomena like project and task groups, consultation meetings, management teams at all levels, etc.

Sometimes even the participants of such fully extended systems of formal and informal meetings are getting irritated. The research concerned was devoted to the question of the efficiency and effectivity of existing committee network. The different committees in the LGO were summed up. In the next step data on the characteristics of the committees were collected. At last a graph of the network was constructed on the basis of shared members of the groups, of the policy field, and of the intensity of the communication flow. It was remarkable that within a policy field several groups existed, with nearly the same members, with slightly different agendas. At first the newly chosen aldermen were a (little) bit upset about this phenomenon, but soon after being socialized to the LGO, they participated whole-hearted. After a certain period it turned out to be very difficult -to a participant- to infer whether some committee is indispensable or not.

The focus on knowledge and expertise then is fruitful to the analysis of this kind of problems. The analysis includes the research into the similarity between the knowledge bases (which were sometimes overlapping), into the similarity of the inference systems (procedures), into the characteristics of the explanation facilities and into the updating facilities. Often it appeared that no updating facility at all existed, so that newly generated knowledge was wasted after some time (at least after termination of a group). It was not incidental that for the some problem a full extended solution procedure was started, although some years ago an adequate solution had been designed for the same type of problem.

Evaluation took place at the organizational level, mainly with respect to efficiency.

13 Discussion and conclusion

Knowledge based systems (mostly labelled as expert systems) are a means to support decision making within industry and government. Several applications are in experimental or in prototype mode in operation. The majority of the applications are purely diagnostic of nature. Since we are interested in organizational applications in local government, the design of knowledge based systems asks for human knowledge (expertise) and for a - maybe small- community where this knowledge is shared. So the construction of a system results in the formalization of norms and normative knowledge in organizations. In this chapter it is proposed that the "idea" of knowledge-based-systems, as characterized before, can be used the other way around. That is: the idea can be helpful as a metaphor for the design of organizations, especially of Local Government Organizations (LGO's). For the sake of convenience the term "Expert System Metaphor" (ESM) is used. In concordance with this metaphorical use of the concept of expert systems it is supposed that a LGO derives its unique place in the market by its product. This product (or service) is generated by smart manipulation of general and domain knowledge and contains itself a large portion of information (or knowledge) as a product specification. The process of producing and delivering services and products must be designed in such a way that knowledge is a dominant aspect. The explanation of the knowledge connected to a product and the way it is derived is essential to the interaction between a LGO and its clients. Empirical cases show that existing LGO's often pass these elements of the metaphor, and thereby cause inefficiencies.

One aspect of the Expert Systems Metaphor is kept out of discussion: the user interface. For organizational design this aspect is important too. Mostly it takes the form of a diagnostic device (e.g. intake). In other situations the interface has more resemblance with a negotiation environment.

The expert systems design process can be interpreted the other way around, and thus leads to a better understanding of LGO's and the decision processes that are so characteristic for this type of organization. Moreover it serves as a pre-design phase of knowledge based systems, destined to support decision making for government.

The effectivity of knowledge-based-systems, human or artificial, can be measured in a proper way when the level dependent variety of effectivity measures is taken into account.

References

Bouckaert, G., *Differences and convergence in concepts and criteria of public productivity,* Valencia, 1987.

Dalen, J.Chr. van, *Agendering in organisaties: afstemming tussen individuele en organisatieplannen in een gemeente-organisatie,* Enschede, 1987.

Dalen, J.Chr. van, *Expert systems in local government,* Leuven ,1988.

Dalen, J.Chr. van & P.G.M. Hufen, *Organisatie-diagnose: Theorie en Praktijk,* Leiden, 1989.

Hubbeling, P., *De gemeente-secretaris als informatie-manager,* Enschede, 1988.

Hufen, P.G.M., Doorlichting van het gebruik van informatiesystemen, in: Van Dalen, J.Chr. & P.G.M. Hufen, *Organisatie-diagnose: Theorie en Praktijk,* Leiden, 1989.

Levitan, K.B., *Government Infostructures,* New York, 1987.

Miles, R.H., *Macro-organizational behavior,* Good Year Publ., 1980.

Morgan, G., *Images of organization,* London, 1986.

Schaik, E. van, *A management system for the information business,* Englewood Cliffs, 1985.

Stamper et al., *Expert systems - Lawyers beware!,* Rome, 1988.

Rolston, D.W., *Principles of artificial intelligence and expert systems development,* New York, 1988.

Part 3

Some policy dimensions

Expert Systems in Public Administration
I. Th.M. Snellen, W.B.H.J. van de Donk, J.-P. Baquiast (Eds.)
© Elsevier Science Publishers B.V. (North-Holland), 1989

Chapter 18

An information systems policy view on expert systems

*Bas K. Brussaard**

Abstract

This chapter examines whether expert systems in public administration differ from information systems in general, and if so in what respects. It concludes that the same information technology and the same information systems metodology is applied in all instances. This is illustrated by experiences with developments in computerised personnel information systems during the last decades. Special attention is given to some basic features of information systems theory as applied to public sector information systems. It is shown that similar normative aspects appear at all levels of system analysis and systems design, and therefore also in evaluation of expert systems. The chapter ends with some policy recommendations on ex ante and ex post evaluation of expert systems, in particular because of their often somewhat opaque and evasive character.

1 Introduction

In principle the use of computers in the public sector is the same as that in the private sector. The same methods and techniques are used, namely those of applied informatics (information systems). The organisational and administrative conditions, too, are more or less the same. Even the objectives

---

* Ministry of Home Affairs,
P/O box 20011, 2500 EA 's Gravenhage, The Netherlands

of the use of computers are less varied than is often thought, and the methods of evaluation do not differ fundamentally. The uses themselves can of course vary, but they do so according to organisational function and area of concern. In the methodology of information systems as a scientific discipline, no a priori distinctions are made according to the nature of the application, such as technical design, financial management, literature search or medical diagnostics. Otherwise every application would require its own methodology and it would be impossible to make general statements about information systems.

However, types of information systems are being sought which differ according to the manner in which they are designed, constructed, implemented and managed and according to the manner in which information systems and services in companies or social sectors are organised.

This chapter examines the types of information systems that occur, especially whithin the public sector, and focusses on the characteristics usually attributed to expert systems. It concludes that the information systems in public administration hitherto designated as expert systems do not have any special features which distinguish them from other information systems. The most obvious explanation is that the field of application of every expert system always lies within a very specific and limited area of knowledge. The evaluation criteria used by the system designer and administrative client are therefore either very general and apply to all types of information systems, or highly specific and therefore relevant to only one individual application.

From a policy standpoint it is particularly important to note that expert systems in public administration have so far been more or less confined to making accessible already formalised information, i.e. information which is not the exclusive preserve of experts. The main result of the more extensive use of expert systems will probably be a further improvement in the availability and accessibility of this information.

2 A preliminary exploration of the problem

It is perhaps instructive to begin by giving a general outline of the development of an information system whose results and financial consequences are constantly seen and felt by everyone. Salary systems are among the oldest applications of computers in all large organisations including the public service. When the first programs were specified in the 1950s, it soon became evident that in the eyes of the system designers the pertinent regulations and their application showed numerous defects. The regulations and the instructions for carrying them out were often incomplete, inconsistent or unacceptable in their effects: incomplete because the rules often covered how one should act in one case but not what should be done in another; inconsistent because sometimes one rule led to one conclusion and another rule to the opposite conclusion in identical cases; and unacceptable because in certain cases the correct application of the given rules led to results which were unacceptable on the basis of common sense or considerations of fairness. The application of the rules, including those laid down in writing, also differed from one salary records department to another and even from one salary clerk to another.

Such flaws in the conventional systems came to light when detailed flow diagrams or decision tables were being drawn up in preparation for computerising salary calculations.

Moreover, only part of the information required for such an analysis could be derived from the formal documents alone. It was constantly necessary to ask experienced personnel officers and wage clerks how they were accustomed to acting in particular cases. It often emerged that the knowledge had been passed on to them by their predecessors and it was no longer possible to ascertain what a particular interpretation was based on. Nobody found or finds it strange that an attempt should be made to establish comprehensive and consistent software for salary systems, to be used in the same manner throughout the field concerned. This field has become increasingly extensive: a growing number of bonuses, deductions and adjustments were included in personnel systems, and an ever increasing number of organisational units with an increasing number of staff began making use of the same information system. Complete harmony has never, however, been achieved and the systems are changing all the time. Regulations have become more and more refined in the course of time, and not only as a result of discoveries in automation, there is significant social and therefore political pressure to continue this process of refinement, which would have been totally impossible to implement by manual methods. Moreover, every alteration or addition revealed or created new inadequacies. Often this did not emerge until later and this in turn led to further additional measures; until then "pragmatic" solutions had to be found since the salaries had to be paid in time. In some subareas, e.g. in the application of overtime regulations and travelling allowances, even permanent differences of interpretation were accepted, despite there being no formal basis for this. The reason was often that within a particular organisation field, one particular course of action was largely followed, albeit a different one from that followed elsewhere.

Alterations would therefore only lead to discontent, because of the customs which had evolved over time and the rights which had been acquired (or which people thought they had acquired). As long as no alarm was raised in other organisational units, e.g. because they felt relatively disadvantaged, there was no problem. The result was of course inefficiency, since different interpretations called for more manual work during data input and more checks. It also led to unequal rights, or at any rate unequal treatment in similar cases.

As already remarked, efforts are being made to ensure that the regulations and their application take increasing account of the particular circumstances of ever smaller groups and even of individual situations. New developments, for example, are the reintroduction of more individualised systems of remuneration and specific performance bonuses.

It is therefore easy to formulate the end result: the payment or otherwise of a specific amount. It is difficult however, to formulate the considerations which lead to it and which must be easy to assess. For the system designer they do not differ in form and complexity from the question of a person's guilt or innocence and the determination of a sentence in criminal law. Only in the former case the number of decisions to be made is much larger. People are therefore compelled at an earlier stage to examine the scope for computer support.

Tentative conclusions

What general lessons can be drawn from the above? After all, the example of salary administration is not a unique case. In terms of organisation and information and from a legal and political point of view (partly determined of course by the concrete situation), it does not differ from other information systems which involve income transfers. All kinds of taxes, premiums and voluntary or compulsory contributions, and all kinds of benefits, allowances and subsidies connected with old age, unemployment, training, living conditions, disability, etc. fall into this category. Moreover, in terms of technical equipment and the complexity of the subject matter, the associated financial interests at macro-level and the personal vulnerability of the individuals concerned, these systems are the largest, most sensitive and politically most important information systems that exist.

On the basis of these experiences the following general observations can be made at this point:

- Efforts are being made to establish comprehensive regulations and equal application, taking into account as many special circumstances as possible.

The former makes the implementation of the regulations more efficient, while the latter satisfies the social and political demands for "fairness".
- Every step in both directions and towards greater scope in terms of organisation and content makes the matter more complex, until the limits of what is technically and organisationally feasible at any particular point are reached and sometimes even crossed. Political counter-moves such as deregulation and privatisation (reduction of government intervention) have little effect (compare also the increasing refinement in private insurance and banking).

To obtain greater insight into the problem of the scope for managing and assessing information systems in general and expert systems in public administration in particular, a more detailed discussion of what information systems really are is required.

3 Fundamental features of the science of information systems

The field of information systems involves the acquisition, storage, transformation, communication and presentation, in short: the processing of information in order to understand and influence, in general control other "real" systems. The object of information systems as a scientific discipline is therefore not computers, for this is the object of computer science; nor is it information, for this is the object of the information sciences and of the sciences dealing with the objects about which information is processed.

Information systems have always existed but it is only with the arrival of computers and the large-scale, integrated use of information technology that the design, construction and management of information systems have become a separate policy field in every organisation. To speak intelligently about the conditions and consequences of the application of information technology (information systems), for example, several basic theoretical and technical systems concepts must be borne in mind.

For instance, all information systems can be placed on a man-machine continuum. At one extreme are information systems in which the functions of the system are performed by machines only. At the other extreme are information systems where the work is carried out exclusively by people. Examples of the former are the automatic control of vehicles, ships, aircraft and tools when computers are directly coupled to other machines without human intervention. The other extreme is found in cultures which do not even use writing.

The vast majority of information systems currently consist of people and machines. Use is nearly always made of telephones and typewriters, and nowadays usually of computers as well (word processors and databanks). There is a marked tendency to transfer as many tasks as possible to computers wherever this is technically and economically feasible and desired, or at least not undesired for other reasons. This works particularly well with mechanical and energy processes. It is also increasingly common, at least to some degree, in personal services and intellectual processes (computer supported systems).

The information paradigm

To put it more accurately, most information systems consist, analytically speaking, of five components: machines and the software which records how the hardware must work, persons and the procedures which prescribe how people are expected to perform their duties, and the information itself (the data banks), whatever the recording medium used. In functional terms, an information system, as already mentioned, always relates to another system, namely the system which one wishes to understand or control, known as the real system. This is expressed in the basic paradigm of applied informatics, the information paradigm. It states that every dynamic open system (and this includes all organisations and all processes within organisations at every level) can be regarded as consisting of a real system (RS) and an information system (IS), with the IS determining the behaviour of the RS. For the purposes of this discussion of expert systems in public administration, the following points concerning systems theory are important for the further elaboration and application of the information paradigm:

a every entity which can be distinguished from and is related to its environment (a dynamic open system) is not essentially an IS or an IS as such, but is considered as such with a particular problem or purpose in mind,
b every information system can, in turn, also be regarded as a real system, usually consisting of the five components mentioned above, and
c all real systems and therefore also all information systems are, in turn, understood and controlled by at least one other information system at a higher level.

These points may become clearer if one remembers that programs (for machines) and procedures (for people) must also be designed, developed, managed and stored in data banks (the fifth component in an information system)[1].

Another fundamental distinction concerns the nature of the information, quite apart from the question of whether it consists of descriptions of an entity to be regarded as a real system or an information system with a particular problem in mind. The distinction in question concerns the difference between structured and unstructured information. Structured information is, by definition, information of which the meaning of the smallest unit (e.g. a word or a number) is determined by its location on the recording medium (e.g. a heading on a form). The computer can derive new information from it (e.g. by calculations or formal logical operations). The meaning of the smallest unit of unstructured information (e.g. words in a text), on the other hand, is determined by the context, i.e. the words and sentences preceding and following it. The computer cannot derive any new information from this at the same level of meaning. Programs for machines have a structured and strictly formal character if they are without error. This is *not* equally true of procedures for people, however carefully formulated in legal texts, job descriptions or other rules of conduct.

Expert systems and information systems

The discussion about knowledge systems or expert systems, which may or may not be distinguished from other information systems, is usually, but not always explicitly, a result of blurring the distinction between structured and unstructured information and decision-making. Here, too, a continuum is involved. One extreme involves strictly formalised but empirically empty manipulations of symbols, which within a defined range are completely consistent and even, in principle, demonstrably correct. The other extreme involves multi-interpretable verbal reports in everyday language with different and changing meanings, this even applying to the rules. The information analyst or the system designer and those for whom he makes the systems, should be fully aware of this problem. Only then is it possible, in collaboration with representatives of the users, to make an evaluation of new information systems or information systems to be altered according to certain criteria. In some cases the users even carry ultimate responsibility for the acceptance of computer results, e.g. political leaders, doctors and judges. This therefore applies if, on the basis of their own responsibility, they are considered to continue giving their own opinion on every individual decision, whatever they are told by the computer supporting them, though taking it into account. As far as the technical and organisational design of the information system is concerned, it is not important whether information presents an earlier, existing, predicted, hoped for or planned situation in the real system, whether it describes empirically established behaviour, or whether it prescribes conduct legally desired or not.

To make an evaluative or normative appraisal possible, a relation must be established between the real system and the information system and this must be done at a preselected level which distinguishes between the IS and RS.

Normative judgements

The taking and presentation of decisions and even the formation of value judgements fit perfectly into this framework. Whether they are made by people or by machines, the final result of what is generally called a decision is an explicit statement of what one's opinion is about something and what ought perhaps to be done. A completely different question is whether such a statement should be seen as a simple communication for information purposes, a non-committal recommendation, a weighty second opinion, an definitive judgement of the best expert available at that moment or of the highest authority competent for the case.

The answer to this question is meta-information of a higher system level. Whether a decision is made by machine or another method does not in itself say anything about the assessment of a decision, whatever the criteria used. A computerised information system can also be used for this assessment. In both cases careful assessment is required in the form of checks within the systems. In public administration appeal procedures or severity clauses are generally incorporated at higher levels.

Some decisions can only be made by machine (e.g. an assessment of the correctness of optimization with help of large mathematical models). At present other decisions can be made only by people, and this will continue to be the case for the foreseeable future and inparticular cases perhaps even for ever. The higher the system level, the more likely this is. It is up to the system designer, together with the expert on the subject in the relevant field, to select the best mix under the conditions prevailing at that time. The final decision is usually taken at a higher level again, since the design and construction of systems also constitutes information processing [2].

4 Information systems in public administration

According to some people the past thirty years have not seen any fundamental breakthroughs in the field of "genuine" machine intelligence. Others share this view but point out that it is impossible to say what real (by which they usually mean human) intelligence is (see, for example, Frøkjær in this volume and Buchanan, whom he quotes). In the last thirty years there has, however, been an incessant stream of mainly commercial slogans, which have repeatedly suggested that something completely new was now available which would replace, or at least surpass, all previous systems: Electronic or Automated Data Processing, Integrated Information Processing, Total Information Systems or Management Information Systems, Decision Support Systems or Knowlege-Based Systems and now Expert Systems, or somewhat more modestly, Expert Support Systems. Scientists have attempted to establish how these fundamentally differ from previous developments[3]. Distinguishing characteristics mentioned include:

- structured versus unstructured or poorly structured problems;
- programmed versus unprogrammed or unprogrammable decisions;
- interactive versus non-interactive computing;
- focus on data structuring instead of on data processing;
- efficiency or effectiveness as an objective (of the IS or RS?);
- use at transaction level or at middle or higher management level as well;
- recurrent routine applications versus policy and other one-off applications.

However, no general historical line of development has been discovered (though it has been postulated). All the characteristics occurred in all the phases, though not always to an equally clear degree, and are always determined by the speed and storage capacity of the available machines and by new aids such as better programming languages and data base management systems.

The only general line of development seems to be that an ever increasing number of subtasks in an ever increasing number of fields of human activity can be carried out by machines[4]. Except in the case of the direct coupling of computers with other machines, this always entails the support of human labour. This also applies to the public sector.

The classification of public fields of application in terms of society-describing object systems (persons, fixed objects, etc.), sector systems (such as public order and security or income distributions) and internal management systems (for personnel, finance, etc.) has proved extremely useful as far as the organisation of public information systems is concerned[5], [6]. The question is whether it also helps to distinguish expert systems as an identifiable category of information systems. It seems that this is true only to a limited degree. As a general model, however, the distinction between operational information and policy information is applicable at a certain level of system analysis. An example will help to make this clear. According to the information paradigm, the real system is composed of real objects such as people. In the public sector this is in principle the whole population: the basic object system as an abstract conception or as a concrete population information system. Subsets include students, patients, delinquents or clients in general such as taxpayers or those entitled to benefits. The same applies to other object sets such as vehicles and ships, fixed objects or legal persons and their establishments. This can be schematically represented as in figure 1.

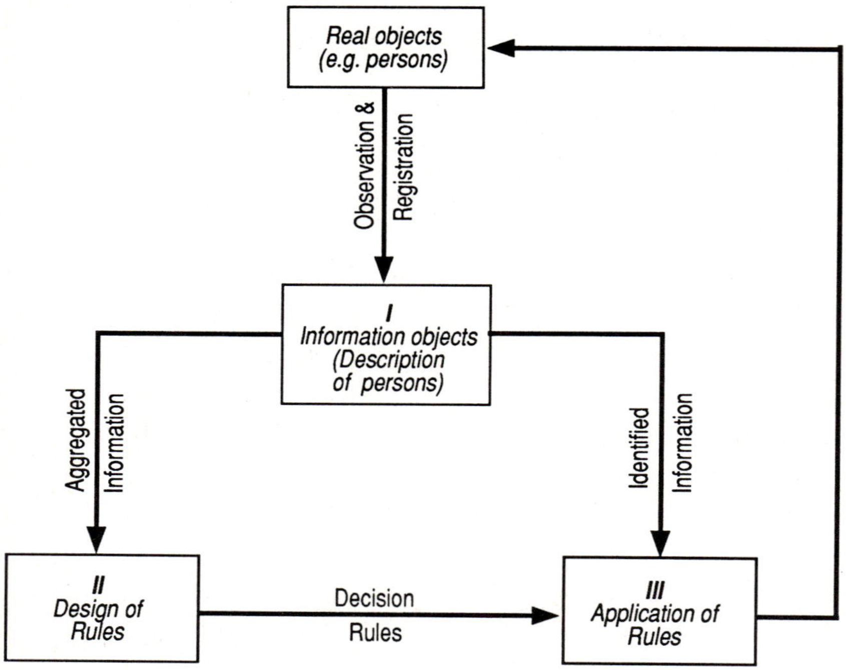

Figure 1: Types of decision making

In principle there are always two informational (computer-supported) processes which are partially routine and partially incidental or even unique. Both make use of basic information systems, and ideally the same basic information system (e.g. a municipal population register, block I). For the support of policy processes (block II, the design and evaluation of rules), the routine part is statistical in nature. For the support of implementation processes (block III), it is registrational in nature. For both processes the internal rules, e.g. legislative procedures in the first case and implementation guidelines in the second, are never complete. It is impossible to predict all future cases and circumstances. The observation and registration process which takes place at least to some extent for various applications in block I is also not 100% determined. Here too, unpredicted or unpredictable exceptions occur or new developments can take place. On the other hand, the parts of information systems which have hitherto been presented or even published as knowledge or expert systems mainly consist of predictable and formally established fields of knowledge (in general regulations and explanations of them). An important way of testing this is to examine where the information analyst or the system engineer has mainly gathered the information required for the system specification. To date this has usually been existing texts, only occasionally supplemented by observations or surveys among experts or the officials regarded as such.

This is also related to the question of whom the final system is intended for. Will it serve to support experts or their successors in the execution of their duties, or does it aim to replace them?

Why use expert systems?

The following arguments are usually given for the development and the application of expert systems:

- shortage or high cost of human experts;
- desired availability of the necessary expertise at times and places where the experts are not available or are available to a lesser degree; reduction of the vulnerability arising from dependence on experts, including in the longer term (staff turnover, retirement, etc.); speeding up and improving the quality of services for which expertise is required;
- reduction of errors or use for more complex situations, e.g. integration of different services (Public Service Centres);
- scope for improving the transparency of and possibilities for monitoring the manner in which experts operate, with a view also to improving regulations (higher system level).

The last point in particular is disputed. Fairly extensive expert systems are not simple but extremely untransparent, both for the experts themselves and for the less experienced users, let alone lay users. However, it is not a question of whether an expert system is transparent in itself but of whether the functioning of an information system improves accessibility and possibilities for monitoring in comparison with those of human expertise. Like all other evaluation criteria, this is a general requirement for information systems. It is also not a question of whether expert systems make errors or require huge investments. The important point is whether they make fewer or more errors and how serious they are, whether they continue to be cheaper than human experts in the long run, and above all whether they are easier to monitor and control than was formerly the case. Against this it is argued that it is not a question of the objective correctness or verifiability of individual decisions or whether there is an improvement in statistical terms. In many cases it is much more important that the person concerned accepts the decision than that the rules have been properly applied[7]. Examples are educators and teachers or doctors and judges. If there is a lower degree of acceptance with expert systems (and opinions do vary on this matter) expert systems ought not to be used. The answer to this objection is that this possible shortcoming of expert systems can easily be remedied by not allowing the final persons involved to consult the expert system directly (at a terminal) but by making "experts" to act as intermediaries. All other advantages (quicker, fewer errors, ease of monitoring) are therefore retained. Ultimately it is therefore human communication and motivation which determine the level of acceptance. The practical experiments so far carried out have had a relatively limited scope and simple structure, for example one hundred or at most several hundred rules in the knowledge base, and there are severe restrictions on the complexity of the conclusions.

Many applications actually do little more than is possible with extensive decision tables or programs with decision trees, especially if the validity of the knowledge elements (facts and rules) is not under discussion. In addition, expert systems are rather difficult to maintain in comparison with structured fields of knowledge and difficult to transfer to other experts or other organisations. In many cases the detailed regulations are considerably more complicated than originally anticipated. In these cases deregulation would probably be a better solution than the development of large expert systems.

Another important factor is whether the expertise concerns real systems which have been entirely designed by people and are dependent only on them, e.g. income transfer systems, or natural real systems such as geological or medical expert systems. Material artefacts constructed by man constitute intermediate examples as in the case of expert systems for diagnosing faults in machines and technical installations.

Perhaps systems for drawing up regulations are the most difficult since then one has to deal with strategic, unpredictable, or at any rate changing, behaviour of people. After all, people, unlike nature or machines, can deliberately play opposite (e.g. tax fraud).

5 Evaluation of expert systems

Finally, if one wanted to try and characterise expert systems on a series of continua applying to all information systems one might well say, on the basis of the literature (not practice), that expert systems are assumed to be able to help solve unstructured problems for which there are no fixed procedures, making use of only partial information and more or less tried and tested assumptions in conjunction with the individual subjective experience of those who are considered to be experts in a particular field.

It is quite right then to ask how and according to what criteria an evaluation can be made. The first question which arises from a policy viewpoint is whether a policy followed to date has been evaluated, whether there are reasons for modifying that policy, and finally how this should be done. Here too, it is first necessary to select the systems level to be considered. Does policy concern information systems (e.g. expert systems if there is such a policy) or real systems, for which an IS (or ES) might be useful?

Three types of justification of new or modified information systems are usually encountered in ex ante and ex post evaluation of information systems in public administration.

First there are efficiency considerations with respect to information systems in terms of the resources applied for the processing of information, given an established specification of the information required. Secondly there are effectivity considerations with respect to the information system in terms of the objectives of the real system which the information systems serves, given fixed or otherwise restricted resources for the information system. Thirdly there is the realisation of political goals by providing public services which were not available hitherto; real system objectives and information system requirements still to be balanced.

More operationally the following variables have to be determined and assessed:

a the economic cost of new or changed information systems in comparison to the existing situation (these costs may be higher than before);
b the economic cost of the objectives of the real system which the new or changed system serves (these ojectives may be cost reductions);
c qualitative individual effects both within the public sector (civil servants) and outside (clients of public services);

d qualitative social or political aspects for instance in terms of equality of rights, protection of privacy of citizens and protection of autonomy of public and private institutions.

In an inquiry into methods for the evaluation of information systems this model of the Netherlands Ministry of Home Affairs was used by the Netherlands Economic Institute in Rotterdam[8]. The principal empirical conclusion was that in practice few well-structured ex ante evaluations take place and virtually no ex post evaluations. The same conclusion emerges from literature searches up till now (a welcome exception is the study by Rae in the St. George's Hospital Medical School, chapter 9). The main policy recommendations which might be made at this point for the evaluation of expert systems can be summarised as follows:

- Develop a general evaluation model and apply it consistently, not because such a model would be fully applicable or adequate in every case but because it at least forces people to justify departures from the model.
- Provide the model with clear, relatively straightforward examples and propagate the methodology in the training and information provided to specialists, policy officials and politicians.
- Incorporate beforehand, not only in experimental pilot projects but also in every information system to be introduced in practice, the way in which the system itself can supply the basic material for periodic or permanent evaluation after it has been put into use or after the period of (experimental) use.
- Continue trying to structure problems, develop formal procedures for them, complete the facts and the relations between the facts as far as possible and use information based on individual experience with expert systems above all as heuristics for further studies in that direction.

Finally, there is the question whether experts will continue to be necessary. The answer is yes, as long as we have nothing better. The best way of making use of their knowledge is to let them help to improve their own work procedures, thereby making themselves superfluous (or more often partially so). This too does not differ from the former situation with other kinds of information systems. Most experts will then undoubtedly formulate new problems for which they will again be required.

Notes

1. Olle, T.W., et al., *Information Systems Methodologies, A framework for understanding*, Addision Wesley Publishing Company, 1988 (ISBN 0-201-41610-7).
2. Sprague R.H., McMurlin B.C., *Information Systems Management in Practice*, Canning Publications, 1986, (ISBN 0-13-464934-6).
3. Langefors, B., et al., *Trends in Information Systems (IFIP-TC8)*, Elseviers Science Publishers, 1986 (ISBN 0-444-87949-8).
4. McLean, E.R., H.G. Sol (eds.), *Decesion Support Systems: A decade in Perspective*, Elseviers Science Publishers, 1986 (ISBN 0-444-70037-4).
5. Brussaard, B.K., *Information Resource Management in the Public Sector, Information and Management*, Elseviers Science Publishers, 15 (1988), pg. 85-92.
6. Brussaard, B.K., Planning of information infrastructures for intergovern mental use, in P. Kovacs and E. Straub (eds.), *Governmental and municipal information systems (IFIP-TC8)*, Elseviers Science Publishers, 1988, pg. 13-22.
7. Stamper, R., The dangers of AI in Information Systems as exposed by the field of Computers and Law, *Journal of Information Technology*, Vol. 3, March 1988, pg. 6-8.
8. "Towards a methodology for the evaluation of information system projects" (1986) and "An attempt on a manual for the evaluation of information systems in public administration" (1988) by The Netherlands Economic Institute, Rotterdam (in Dutch, available with the Netherlands Ministry of Home Affairs, The Hague).

Expert Systems in Public Administration
I. Th.M. Snellen, W.B.H.J. van de Donk, J.-P. Baquiast (Eds.)
© Elsevier Science Publishers B.V. (North-Holland), 1989

Chapter 19

Expert systems in French public administration

*Jean-Paul Baquiast**
*Anne Bedel**

Abstract

Approximately seventy expert systems (excluding those concerning technical areas : agriculture, weapon systems, equipment) are presently being studied, developed or are operational (about ten) in the various ministries. Most of these systems are implemented on PC/XT/AT compatible microcomputers using expert system generators (O+ order motor).

The inventory of expert systems in public administration is carried out by CIIBA (Interministerial Committee for Information and Office Technology in Public Administration), an office which is under the authority of the Prime Minister of France, and which is, notably, responsible for promoting new technologies in the public sector. The widespread success of this tool in public administration has given rise to a certain number of questions, which will be summarized below.

1 State of the art and perspectives

1.1 In which sectors is the use of expert systems expanding at present?

The expert systems used by French public administration are divided between various channels, where they give rise to considerable increases in productivity.

---

* French Interministerial Committee on Informatisation in Public Administration, 56 rue de Varenne, 75007 Paris, France

1.2 Assistance in the drafting of administration texts

The first experiments took place in the field of local authority regulations. BRUITLOG, IMMLOG, SKILOG and LOG-EAU respectively enable local authorities (mayors) to draft by-laws in compliance with the regulations in force, concerning noise levels, derelict buildings, ski-slope warning signs, water quality. The systems are developed by the team led by Miss Bourcier at the CNRS (French National Scientific Research Centre), working under supervision of Conseil d'Etat, see chapter 5 of this volume.

1.3 Assistance in the production of administrative documents

The expert system SEMAPI (soon operational) used by the Ministry of Finance helps in the preparation of contractual documents necessary for the making of public sector computer contracts. Developments are planned in the field of IT standards specifications implementation in public contracts (SEMA-NORM).

An expert system enabling certificates of births, marriages and deaths to be established in accordance with foreign legislation is currently being developed at the Ministry of Foreign Affairs.

1.4 Implementation of a piece of legislation or a regulation

This is the area of greatest potential for expert systems. SYMA (operational), used by the Ministry of Defense to assist the settlement of military pensions, is an example.

The examination and control of candidates' files at the E.N.A (National Administration College) are carried out by the expert system of Mr Levine, Information Technology Manager at the E.N.A., see chapter 13 in this volume.

1.5 Control of the application of a regulation by a subordinate administrative authority

This type of operation comes after the preceding ones. The tool used is different since, in the first stage, the file must be formed (follow-up/refusal letters) and interpreted according to the regulation, and, in the second stage, the completed files are controlled with respect to the law, and even their appropriateness (by different departments, of course).

Numerous applications exist in this area, especially in the Ministry of Social Affairs, where expert systems control the settlement of allowances for handicapped adults, for instance.

1.6 Reception, information and orientation of the public

Many applications are being developed, especially by the Ministry of Education, to assist school leavers and students in choosing a career and finding a job.

The Ministry of Industry has developed expert systems to assist future entrepreneers (operational) or exporters (how to comply with national regulations).

The Ministry of Justice is developing an expert system (soon to be available on Minitel) prividing information on the means of recourse for victims of penal offences.

Finally, the COFI system, available at present in several post offices, will assist the user in choosing a financial investment.

1.7 Financial analysis

The main expert systems in this area concern the Ministry of Finance : fiscal monitoring of companies, analysis of tax files, estimations of the financial risks of loans to foreign countries (operational), and the Ministry of Social Affairs : monitoring of hospital management.

1.8 Personnel Management

This involves matching the profile of a person with the profiles of a job. Using an expert system, the Ministry of fhe Interior aims to assign 130.000 police officers to 457 police stations with maximum efficiency.

1.9 Education, training

Computer Assisted Learning (without artificial intelligence) has been a relative failure, since preparation time is long (approximately 100 teachers hours for one student hour), systems are difficult to update and cannot be matched to the personal level of the student.

Intelligent C.A.L. (C.A.L. assisted by an expert system) solves these problems, since the preparation time is shorter (30 teacher hours for one student hour), updating is simple, and the system adapts to the student automatically.

SERPOLET, used by the Ministry of Defence, is a system for assistance in the writing of administrative teachware. It will in particular create information technology training software.

1.10 Natural Language Questioning

This gives direct "natural" access to information contained in the data bases. The Ministry of Education's "EDUTEL" system aids pupils to obtain information that concerns them by posing questions directly, without passing by menus.

Natural Language questioning of legal data bases in being developed by the Journal Officiel (Official Gazette), one of the Prime Minister's offices.

More generally, all the areas concerning the private sector are being studied by the French public administration. There are projects in the following sectors :

1.11 Optimization

OPTIMO, used by the Ministry of Finance, is a customs system: it will be used to optimize the air-sea monitoring methods (it will be possible to visualize the monitored zones on the screen, in order to locate targets = ships, and ressources = coastguard ships and aircraft).

1.12 Prevention, operational management

SICOSC, used by the Ministry of the Interior, is an expert system for Civil Safety which simulates catastrophes (fire, avalanche, etc).

2 Should the development of expert systems be encouraged?

The important question is whether expert systems are really a means of reforming public administration. The answer would certainly seem to be yes.

Expert systems are available to all civil servants, whether users or developers. The expert system generator will soon become as common a tool as data base management systems, spreadsheets and other software packages. The majority of civil servants will have numerous expert systems at their disposal for consultation on their microcomputer (and on their Minitel). A smaller, but still considerable, number will be equipped (on microcomputer) with an expert system generator for development purposes.

Using the expert systems, administrative regulations and their modifications can be entered much faster and more flexibly than by traditional analysis and programming. They also enable questions asked of the individual or the file under examination to be limited to a minimum, genuinely pertinent to the case in hand.

The expert system should therefore be used whenever the regulations are complex and often amended, and whenever the solutions are to be adapted to suit the individual requirements of the user, by personalizing the dialogue between the user and the administrative body (this occurs most frequently in the area of education and welfare).

This new information technology will not replace the traditional one, since they complement each other. The old method will, due to the mass of data stored, serve as a support for the new one, which will search for data in the large files and process it "intelligently" due to direct dialogue between the user and the expert system via the microcomputer. In the same way, the traditional information system, which is less expensive for simple, non-developing tasks, will centralize and cumulate the results of information processed by the expert system for management and statistical purposes.

Expert systems herald a new aera in the computerization of work : traditional information technology covers simple repetitive tasks (salaries, invoicing, tax or contribution calculations, stock management, accountancy), whereas the expert systems execute complex administrative tasks (orientation of students according to their capacities and preferences towards studies or a career, advice for companies on penetrating foreign markets, assistance in the selection of an information on office technology configuration, application of complex regulations to an individual, inspection of the financial or economic state of an organisation, development of timetables for schools or universities, assistance in drafting administrative documents, assistance in starting a business, police inquiry assitance, matching of individuals and posts, etc).

Knowledge base systems induce the development of new skills and profiles (knowledge-base engineers, developers, consultants, trainers).

3 How can the development of expert systems be encouraged?

In each ministry or department, the initiative to develop expert systems must be taken by senior civil servants, who, if they are suitably informed, will encourage potential users (possibly short-circuiting information technology departments whose representatives may be somewhat reluctant to promote this revolutionary approach!) to implement expert systems. To do this, they will rely on knowledge base engineers or on consultancies specializing in artificial intelligence.

Action is also required at the interministerial level. The CIIBA, in France has been aware of the importance of this technology for the modernization of public administration from the very beginning. CIIBA promotes it in various ways, notably by financing pilot studies : M.FF 19 have been invested since 1986 to develop this promising new technology more rapidly. This money is used to incite ministries to finance action themselves, giving rise to real channels of development.

The CIIBA has furthermore created an expert system users club, with a view to improving the coordination and implementation of projects.

Information and presentation sessions, using audio-visual equipment, have been organized to make as many civil servants as possible aware of expert systems.

Interested readers will find in an appendix to this chapter the major headings used by CIIBA in order to evaluate whether or not the development of an expert system project is appropriate.

Annexe 1: Critical analysis of existing expert systems

Software companies selection

1 Nature and competence of the selected company

2 The contract
- cost/service ratio ;
- clauses concerning the distribution and/or commercialisation of the expert system.

3 Degree of satisfaction of the administration concerned

The development tool

1 Selection criteria
- with regard to the application ;
- O+ or 1 ? Importance of the contribution of external consultants ;
- reason for choosing a certain language (LISP, PROLOG, etc) rather than an expert system generator, and vice versa ;
- possible development (towards videotex, new operating systems, and if so, which).

2 Training
- in using the tool (time, cost, ease, etc) ;
- in transfer of expert knowledge (idem) ;
- profile of persons likely to use the tool. Training time required depending on the profile.

3 Generally
- ability of the administration-customer to recover the know-how ;
- can the expert system generator become a standard computer tool for the customer ? State o+ or 1 ?

Development, updating, tests

1 Who will ensure development, updating?
- the SSO ? Why ? ;
- the administrative body ? Who (profile) ? Problem/satisfaction ?

2 Tests
- duration of test period ;
- when can an expert system be considered fully tested and reliable?;
- who will guarantee the validity of the expert system ?

The expert system and its organizational environment

1 Actual use
- who uses it (outline the users according to several criteria) ;
- frequency of use.

2 Supporting equipment
- microcomputer, minitel, others (advantages, drawbacks, degree of satisfaction) ;
- degree of integration depending on the existing environment, if any.

3 Means of insertion of an expert system in the processing chain.
- direct consultation or via telecommunications ;
- used in single -or multi-station mode, or within a procedure ;
- for what purpose (diagnostic aid, processing, control, etc) ;
- relation with a management system, if any -problems encountered.

4 Degree of satisfaction/opposition of persons involved closely or at a distance(users, experts, information technologists, knowledge engineers, hierarchy).

5 Conformity of the expert system with expectations
- compared with the contract specification ;
- compared with user expectations.

6 User evaluation
- of user-friendliness (time required per consultation, ease of correction, training, etc) ;
- of the analysis of functions compared with work organization ;
- of the number of consultations and their motives- on which types of problems on the pertinence of the replies (are they : contestable? useless ? irreplaceable ?

7 Productivity gains
- in time (average time of an expert system consultation compared with average intervention time of an expert or a manual guide) ;
- in personnel ;
- in training (training of user, or a future expert with or without an expert system) ;
- financial ;
- is the expert still consulted (does he consider his competence to be reinforced ?) or is the expert system itself sufficient ?

8 The legal or statutory validity of an expert system.

Annexe 2: A guide for using expert systems

It has been observed that the "decision makers" are badly informed with regard to the value, but also the limits of utilization, of expert systems.

As a result, the products of models or pilot experiments are under-used and, in particular, there are delays in the distribution of products which have already proved their worth.

Expert systems also remain unused in numerous areas where they could offert gains in effectiveness of various magnitudes.

Generally speaking, the overall impression is that this promising technology is still largely under-used. Action must therefore be taken to "sell" the product, not only to top specialists who are a minority, but also to the "general public", i.o. the decision-makers of all backgrounds in public administration, especially those not involved with information technology.

A widely-distributed methodological guide, aimed at a wide distribution area, is therefore necessary.

In view of the evaluation made and the various written or oral opinions gathered, the methodological guide will explain:

- areas of application (without limiting itself to areas already being examined).
  Why use expert systems ? Various relationships possible between expert systems (traditional informations technology and processes which are still manual.
- critiria to determine whether an application can make use of expert system methodology.
- cost factors to be taken into account (software/equipment), development time (knowledge engineer, expert), training of users (to use the tool and the expert system) and the savings to be expected.
- precautions to be taken or conditions to be provided.
  Particular emphasis should be placed on: prior evaluation, statement of requirements, participation of experts and, more generally, of the personnel (involvement in the "administrative project"), choice of SSO and motors, contract, training, project, execution, follow-up and control, generalization, obtention and redistribution of productivity gains, retrospective evaluation.
- if possible, an expert system type tool capable of formalizing the conditions listed above could be proposed or supplied.

To summarize, the guide should enable the decision-maker not only to implement a rational programme based on the use of an expert system, but also to integrate this programme completely into the *strategic master plan* of the organization.

Expert Systems in Public Administration
I. Th.M. Snellen, W.B.H.J. van de Donk, J.-P. Baquiast (Eds.)
© Elsevier Science Publishers B.V. (North-Holland), 1989

Chapter 20

Informatization in Local Environmental Administration

*Stefan Kuhlmann**

Abstract

This chapter highlights one of the possible application fields of knowledge-based systems in public administrations, knowledge-based systems in the sense of handling systems, advisory systems and expert systems. Referring to experiences from the Federal Republic of Germany the question is asked why the informatization in this field of administrative activity up to now is so little developed, and what can be done to alter this. The chapter is dealing with environmental protection and will focus on the environmental administration, especially on the local level.

1 Environmental administration and informatization

Environmental protection will in the near future belong to the main challenges and tasks of international, national, state and local governments. The regulation of the environmental protection is getting tighter, and international harmonization of the norms lies ahead. But up to now there are drastic defects in the enforcement of laws and rules not only on the international and national level but also, and with considerable negative effects, on the level of local governments (e.g. factory inspectorate division, local environmental

* Fraunhofer Institute for Systemtechnology and Innovation Research, Breslauerstraße 48, 7500 Karlsruhe 1, Germany

administration, civil police). Those deficiencies can be both politically produced and intended and administratively caused and unintended.

The reason for the (more or less) unintended enforcement deficits - besides lack of personnel, problems of staff education and of administrative competence - is above all the deficient availability of data and information of really practical relevance: Partly the local and regional administration misses the chance of fast access to data (e.g. to data on the emission respectively immission of toxic agents measured by other administrative units), partly the data have become obsolete and there are no means to update them systematically, partly the data will not be prepared, connected and evaluated sufficiently, partly the standard frames to be applied are not fully and permanently available or accessible to the administrative staff (e.g. Scholz, 1987). Rarely, current pollution data are made available to the interested, critical public.

Without a doubt, there are many efficient ways to use information and communication technologies in this field: the accumulation, storage, processing, analysis, the transportation and publication of environmentally relevant readings and filed data (e.g. emission and immission registers), the comparison of nominal and actual values, thus the processing of *factual data,* the documentation of technical, legal, and administrative control frames - altogether, thus, the processing of *normative data* - can be optimized using information technology. But even the day-to-day work of local environmental administrations, which is basically also a traditional desk job, can be facilitated through office automation technologies.

But what has actually happened in the local environmental administration? What could be done? In the following, I will advance and shortly outline two theses.

2 Obstacles of informatization

For a number of years in Germany there have been several ambitious approaches with regard to the use of information technology in the field of environmental administrations (c.f. Jaeschke/Page, 1988; Page, 1986). The developed software systems (or the systems that are currently being developed), are most readily demonstrated and discussed among experts. They extend from early warning devices against smog to more or less comprehensive environmental and cartographic information systems up to expert systems for environmental impact assessments (soon a compulsory activity in all EC countries).

When we take a closer look, however, it will become evident that the productive potentials of the information technology have been surprisingly little used by the administration dealing with environmental protection (leaving out of account some special institutions like the Federal Environmental Office and a few more): this applies also to the local environmental administration which is mainly occupied with the important tasks of planning and controlling; this is my first thesis. Document analyses and interviews with experts show that the process of informatization of local environmental administrations is at the time being rather unorganized (it lacks political determination and coordinated planning) and unrealistic (desired systems are often over-proportional, expectations are exagerated). There are at least five reasons for this:

- The establishment of environmental protection as an administrative task with political importance is still in full swing and will not come to a halt soon (there is, for instance, a discussion on environmental protection as a local cross-sectional task vs. the setting up of environment departments and boards; c.f. Fiebig et al.,1986). The institutional background of this development is the relatively high autonomy of the local and state governments in the FRG with respect to their administrative organization. It is still controversial which institutions and which corresponding actors on the political-administrative level will be authorized to what degree in the planning and execution of environmental protection tasks on the local level. The task management has not reached a high degree of routinization yet. Consistent execution is mostly to be carried out crosswise to the traditional, steady departmental structure, thus crossing various spheres of interest and influence. Hence, it is still unclear and disputed who will have what access to data relevant to the planning and execution, and who will receive the capacities for the processing on the information technology level.

- The planning, development, and implementation of computer application in environmental administration was almost exclusively left to computer scientists and technicians for environmental protection. The administration management is still too hesitantly tackling the organization process of informatization. This increases tendencies towards widely designed, technically demanding, and complex computer applications (for illustrations see Jaeschke/Page, 1988; Page, 1986), whose practical use in daily application of local administrative execution will have to be proved yet; we are taking risks that the shortcomings of the automation phase of the sixties and seventies will be repeated (c.f. Brinckmann, 1981; Brinckmann/ Kuhlmann, 1989). There is a trend to repress the idea that successful environmental protection is not in the first place a matter of technical data processing but remains a political problem (c.f. von Weizsäcker, 1988). The daily practical demand of executive civil servants, but also that of citizens and local politicians, for utilization-oriented, technically-based data processing which in the long run might unfold politically changing effectiveness up to now has practically not been made at all the starting point of informatization projects.

- The large and increasing number of environmental norms not inevitably softens the problem of administrative acting under uncertainty (c.f. Wolf, 1987). On the contrary, the uncertainty can increase furthermore because any norm can be and has to be interpreted. Modelling and representation of norms in knowledge-based systems therefore mean selection and determination. But this could be politically undesirable in many cases: It is well known that environment control administrations tend to bargain with the polluters rather than to apply hard sanctions on them (c.f. Mayntz, 1978).
- We can not rule out the possibility that computer applications in the area of environmental protection, in particular comprehensive environment information systems, fulfill rather legitimizing functions than support the task execution (c.f. Kuhlmann, 1986): The input of money for their development and the design of data processing which is finally to be presented, can be taken as a proof of modernization and engagement of municipal administrations; these stand for a high degree of expertise and suggest analogous political-administrative strength. When such legitimizing interests predominate, the consistent realization of the possible practical use for the everyday administration work might lag behind.
- The above mentioned reasons are hindering the development and the introduction of accurate knowledge-based systems in local environmental administrations which would help to improve the bureaucrat's conditions of day-to-day work and which would provide better instruments against the polluters.

The modelling of knowledge-based systems requires a very high degree of consensus between the designers and the users of a system, consensus about the normative understanding and interpretation of the purpose of an administrative task because it consists in determining the user's conditions not only of information processing but also of decision making in the individual case. Without this consensus knowledge-based systems will not fully succeed. In the local arenas of environmental policies indeed such consensus is often lacking.

So the interpretation of an administrative task incorporated in a knowledge-based software system may be desirable in terms of normativity but not compatible with the power equilibrium of a respective local administrative policy. Or, on the contrary, it may be locally acceptable but not adequately normative.

The French example of the BRUITLOG system described in this volume presents a knowledge-based system that will be used by the local authorities all over the country to enforce established law against noise. But one problem remains: If some local bureaucrat's understanding of what noise is deviates clearly from the understanding of the system designer they will not accept the system, that means, they will not use it.

3 Making use of social science research

Searching for a remedy the administrative management should get better opportunities to benefit from the results of social science research on utilization factors of informatization. Such research, which should be conducted by administrative scientists, computer scientists, human factors researchers and ecology experts following an interdisciplinary approach, could give critical and effective feedback to the political-administrative management. Such research will valuate the actual needs for support by information technology in executive offices on the street-level and can investigate factual utilization conditions: Thus, for instance, optimal data processing can at the same time require a reorganization of competence and flow of information; the corresponding requirements of the material and personnel resources have to be valuated objectively. There must not be any expectations regarding short-sighted economizing effects; emerging demands for education and training must be adequately dimensioned in its content and scope. We are talking about the acquisition of profound knowledge in the area of actual administration execution on the spot, in the micro- and meso-sphere, with the aim of adjusting the technical systems to the operational conditions. But up to this day there has scarcely been any differentiation and sociologically profound knowledge about:

- the possibility of compatible and socially assessed, decentralized use of information technologies (e.g. microcomputers) in the executive environmental administration body in order to support the data processing and the decision making (data base software, expert systems; c.f. Wizgall, 1988) and the interrelated daily deskwork (office automation; some short references: Schramm, 1988);

- the prerequisits for a more intensive, socially assessed local use of the complex information supply from huge data bases (f.i. UMPLIS-data bases; e.g. Seggelke, 1988; Bohne, 1988), financed, developed, and made available at the federal state (Federal Ministry of the Environment, Federal Environmental Office).

Therefore, a risk of failure is involved in the effort to economize local environmental administrations through informatization, if we do not succeed in finding socially assessed solutions. In this context, it is worthwhile remembering the almost complete failure of the (also local) "planning information systems", developed in the seventies. The concepts for systems were too comprehensive, over-proportional, and far from practical needs (c.f. Fehl, 1972). Their problems were not in the first place the technical restrictions but rather the vaguely formulated goals and, last but not least, the resistance within the politically-administrative practice which proceeds with a very different logic (c.f. Brinckmann/Kuhlmann, 1989).

The inclusion of the instruments and discoveries of social science research into the informatization of administrative work (c.f. Brinckmann, 1987; Grimmer, 1987; Grimmer,1988) - and this is my second thesis - nowadays can support the process of suggestive, socially assessed, knowledge-based informatization of local environmental administrations. The following research and development tasks belong to this area:

- The sounding of application fields where the use of information and communication technologies can improve and facilitate the administration execution of current environment laws; for this purpose, qualitative empirical investigations must be conducted. That means, above all, inquiring of the executives and staff of municipal and regional environmental administration, inquiring of politicians, of experts from relevant research institutes and interest groups, and not least, of local citizens' committees whose specialized knowledge is often times not to be underestimated.

  With regard to the computerized factual data, there is a need to check on the spot their relevance and adequacy for the administrative execution. If necessary we have to design modified requirement profiles etc. Considering the nominal data, the conditions and possibilities of technology-based connections of technical, legal, and administrative frameworks need to be tested (a topical example is the environment assessment; c.f. Schwabl/ Pietsch, 1988); we also have to examine closer the reasons for factually existing information barriers, within local administration (from department to department), between local and regional and/or central administration, or between local administrations and polluters. Which of them are on constitutional grounds, i.e. binding, and which can be ascribed to bureaucracy, which is to say that they are basically reducible?

Regarding the office automation support of the daily work, knowledge must be gained not only about the quantitative but also about the qualitative dimensions of data processing: Is it feasible to productively carry out data processing and many communication jobs through office automation technologies? Which division of work between officials in charge and assistant employees in the office efficiently supports the settlement of work if new technologies are used (c.f. Kuhlmann, 1988a, 1988b)?

- The definition of skeleton requirements of the control and organization of access rights to technically provided information. We should not underestimate the number of political-administrative obstacles that might turn up. At the same time, technical and organizational over-complexity is to be avoided. Instead we should aim at an easy handling and flexible system design; an important prerequisite for that is the participation of future users in the process of development and design as well as the appropriate training measures (c.f. Brinckmann, 1987). If necessary, the inclusion of interested citizens' groups can also improve the productivity of the desired solution.
- Taking into consideration these frame requirements, to gauge the supply of adequate hardware and software technologies and to illustrate their range of application in scenarios. Such scenarios can comprise the application of microcomputer systems with adapted standard software in stand-alone operation, in network processing with other computer systems, in connection with mobile units, with measuring stations, with centralized large capacity computer systems, with external data basis, or, like in Japan, with publicly accessible terminals of environmental information systems (c.f. Weidner, 1987).

The results of such research will provide plenty of illustrative material and also a basis for discussion to the decision making leaders in the political-administrative arena, which can give an impetus for pilot programs of concepts how to use technology in local government. The time is ripe for that.

References

Brinckmann, H. (1981). *Zweierlei Experten für die gleiche Aufgabe: Das stabile Mißverstehen zwischen DV-Fachleuten und Verwaltungsfachleuten.* In: Reinermann, H./ Fiedler, H./Grimmer, K./Lenk, K. (eds.): Organisation informationstechnikgestützter öffentlicher Verwaltungen (Informatik-Fachberichte, 44), Berlin u.a.: 340-351

Brinckmann, H. (1987). *HdA-Schwerpunkt "Verwaltung und Dienstleistung". Trotz unbestreitbarer Erfolge noch Lücken zwischen Programm und Durchführung - Öffentliche Verwaltung als Vorbild für humane Verwaltungsarbeit.* In: Office Management, 6:22-26

Brinckmann, H./Kuhlmann, S. (1989). *Computerbürokratie. Ergebnisse von 30 Jahren öffentlicher Verwaltung mit Informationstechnik,* Opladen (forthcoming).

Bohne, E. (1988). *Verwaltungsprobleme bei Aufbau und Nutzung von Umweltfaktenbanken.* In: Grimmer, K. (ed.): Informatisierung wenig strukturierter Verwaltungsaufgaben. Ein Symposion, Kassel (Arbeitspapier der Forschungsgruppe Verwaltungsautomation, 46)

Fehl, G. (1972). *Information ist alles ... Anmerkungen zu staatlich-kommunalen Informations-Verbund-Systemen in der BRD.* In: Fehl, G./Fester, M./Kuhnert, N. (eds.): Planung und Information. Materialien zur Planungsforschung, Gütersloh: 264-314

Fiebig, K.H./Krause, U./Martinsen, R. (1986). *Organisation des kommunalen Umweltschutzes.* Berlin, Deutsches Institut für Urbanistik (Umweltverbesserung in den Städten, vol. 4)

Grimmer, K. (1987). *Gestaltungskräfte in der Technisierung öffentlicher Verwaltungen. Probleme und Möglichkeiten zukunftsorientierter Anwendungsforschung.* In: Computer und Recht, 8:523-531

Grimmer, K. (ed.) (1988). *Informatisierung wenig strukturierter Verwaltungsaufgaben. Beiträge zu einem Symposion* (Arbeitspapiere der Forschungsgruppe Verwaltungsautomation, 46), Kassel

Jaeschke, A./Page, B. (eds.) (1988). *Informatikanwendungen im Umweltbereich.* 2. Symposium, Karlsruhe, November 1987, Proceedings, Berlin u.a.

Kuhlmann, S. (1986). *Informationstechnik als Modernisierungs- und Legitimationsmittel.* In: Grimmer, K. (ed.): Informationstechnik in öffentlichen Verwaltungen, Basel/ Boston/Stuttgart: 233-312

Kuhlmann, S. (1988a). *Neue Informationsorganisation: Hat die Schriftgutverwaltung Zukunft?* In: Online/ÖVD, 4:70-72

Kuhlmann, S. (1988b). *Winner or Loser of New Information Organization? The Future Role of Filing and Inhouse Mail Departments in Administrative Organizations.* In: Bullinger et al. (eds.): Information Technology for Organizational Systems, (ECSC/ EAEC/EEC, Brussels/Luxembourg) Amsterdam et al.:282-286

Kuhlmann, S. (1988c). *Informationsanwendungen für Umweltschutzverwaltungen.* In: Städte- und Gemeinderat, 9:287-289

Mayntz, R. (1978). *Vollzugsprobleme der Umweltpolitik.*

Page, B. (ed.) (1986). *Informatik im Umweltschutz. Anwendungen und Perspektiven.* München/Wien

Scholz, B. (1987). *Bessere Umweltinformation - besserer Umweltschutz?* In: Böhret, C./ Klages, H./Reinermann, H./Siedentopf, H. (eds.): Herausforderungen an die Innovationskraft der Verwaltung, Opladen, 253-259

Schramm, H.F.W. (1988). *Die Bürokommunikation hilft beim Arbeits- und Umweltschutz.* In: Office Management, 1:65-66

Schwabl, A./Pietsch, J. (1988). *Ein Expertensystem für die Durchführung einer Umwelt-*

verträglichkeitsprüfung (UVP). In: Jaeschke/Page (eds.), loc.cit.:127-138

Seggelke, J. (1988). *Stand und Perspectiven der Umweltinformationssysteme*. In: Jaeschke/Page (eds.), loc.cit.:8-17

Weidner, H. (1987). *Umweltberichterstattung in Japan. Erhebung, Verarbeitung und Veröffentlichung von Umweltdaten*. Berlin

Weizsäcker, E.U. von (1988). *Ganzheitlicher Umweltschutz - eine Herausforderung für Politik und Informatik*. In: Jaeschke/Page (eds.), loc.cit.:1-7

Wizgall, R. (1988). *Informationstechnik in der Wasserwirtschaftsverwaltung Baden-Württemberg*. In: Jaeschke/Page (eds.), loc.cit.:52-60

Wolf, R. (1987). *Zur Antiquiertheit des Rechts in der Risikogesellschaft*. In: Leviathan, 3:357-391

About the authors

Ignace Th. M. Snellen
is Professor in Public Administration at the Catholic University in Tilburg, the Netherlands. He graduated in Political Science and Law at the University of Amsterdam. As political advisor to the Board of Management of Philips Electronic Industries he wrote a dissertation on "the approaches to strategy formulation"(1975) in the public and private sector. His publications, books and articles, cover a wide range of subjects related to management, policy, planning and control. Since 1985 he is head of a research program on Informatization in Public Administration at the University of Tilburg. He is co-chairman (with Jean-Paul Baquiast) of the permanent study group or EGPA, which organizes regularly conferences on this subject.

Wim B. H. J. van de Donk
is assistant Professor in Public Administration at the Catholic University in Tilburg, the Netherlands. He graduated in Political Science/Administration Science at the Catholic University in Nijmegen. He is member of the research group on Informatization in Public Administration of the University of Tilburg and secretary of the permanent study group on Informatization in Public Administration of the European Group for Public Administration (E.G.P.A.)

Erik Frøkjær
is associate professor of Computer Science at the University of Copenhagen, Denmark. He recieved his MS degree in Mathematical and Electrical Engineering in 1973, and a Bachelor degree in Business Administration in 1972. Areas of research include methods in systems development, programming methodology, programming environments for interactive systems and expert systems. Further he has a special interest in EDP in public administration. After ten years as a systems developer in public administration and as a EDP consultant, he joined the University of Copenhagen in 1985.

Danièlle Bourcier
was born in Segré, France in 1946. She has degrees in linguistics and law, a diploma in political science, and a doctorate in law. From 1968 to 1980 she was a legal analysist and project manager at the Central for Legal Informatics. She is a present Researcher at the National Center of Scientific Research and director of the interdisciplinary research project "Mathematical Linguistics Applied to Legal Informatics". She has published numerous reports and articles on new technologies and law. She manages a Newsletter on Law and Computers (ILIADE).

Roland Traunmüller
is Professor for Applied Informatics with the Department of Informatics at the Johannes Kepler Universität Linz. A graduate from University of Vienna (Chemistry, Physics) he wrote his thesis at the Max-Planck-Institute in Mülheim (Ruhr) and turned

to Administrative Dataprocessing in 1970. After heading various projects for Ministries and OECD (Paris) he became Senior Lecturer in 1977 and Professor in 1983. He is also the Austrian National Representative to IFIP Technical Committee 8 (Information Systems). Besides those activities he is heading the Working Group on Formalization and Expert Systems in Law of the German Computer Society (GI, Bonn) and the Working Group on Administrative Dataprocessing of the Austrian Computer Society (OCG, Vienna).

Jorma A. J. Kuopus

Referendary Counsellor to the Finnish Parliamentary Ombudsman, the Finnish Parliamant(1978-1988). LL.D.(Doctor in Jurisprudence) September 1988, thesis on Legal Informatics(the first of its kind in Finland defended on the 14th of May 1988) on the Rule of Law and Computerized Administration of Taxation.Research Fellow at the Academy of Finland and a doctoral candidate 1985-1988. Special interests: administrative automation/computing including AI, connected with citizen-oriented and computerized public services.

Jon Bing

is currently Professor of Legal Informatics at the Norwegian Research Center for Computers and Law, an independent department of the Faculty of Law of the University of Oslo - an institution of which he is co-founder (1970). Main areas of research are legal informatics and decision systems, but also issues of information law like copyright, data protection and telecommunications. He has published papers and monographs on these subjects and is consultant to several international organizations including the OECD and the Council of Europe. He is serving the latter institution for a term as Chairman of the Committee for Legal Data Processing. Jon Bing has published a number of science fiction novels, short stories, television series, radio and stage plays and is currently completing a libretto for a new, Norwegian opera to open autumn 1989.

John Rae

is a lecturer in Informatics Technology at the Information Technology Institute of the University of Salford, England. His background is economics and he has a strong interest in modelling organisation behaviour and decision making processes.
His doctorate research was conducted in the economics Department of York University and in the Psychology Department of Carnegy-Mellon University, Pittsburgh. The research developed analytical and modelling techniques in the sphere of management decision making based upon Human Information Processing Theory. It utilised Artificial Intelligence(AI) techniques to develop computer based models of both hypothetical and actual decision making, including the construction of a decision support system for use in a CEGB power station. Currently his research is into intelligent managerial support systems via the development of intelligent database interfaces.

Manuel Olave

is presently Senior Adviser at the International Centre for Public Enterprises in Ljubljana, Yugoslavia and Visiting Professor at the Netherlands International Institute for Management Delft. He was Chief of Staff at the Office of the Vice President of Bolivia and Undersecretary of Coordination at the Ministry of Finance in that country. Previously he was Director of the public Management Programme at the Central American Institute of Management (INCAE) in Managua, Nicaragua. He holds a Ph.D. and an M.A. in economics, an M.S. in systems engineering and a B.S. in mathematics/physics.

Vladislav Rajkovic
received a B.S. and an M.S. in electrical engineering and a Ph.D. in computer sciences from University of Ljubljana. In 1970 he joined Department of Computer Science and Informatics at Jozef Stefan Institute in Ljubljana. He is Professor in computing at University of Maribor, School of Organizational Sciences Kranj. He does research and development in the field of decision making using intelligent computer support and consulting in decision making for industry and governmental institutions.

Marko Bohanec
received a B.S. and an M.S. in computer sciences from University of Ljubljana. Since 1981 he works at Jozef Stefan Institute, Ljubljana. His research and development efforts are primarily concerned with artificial intelligence and decision making. He implemented expert system shell DECMAK and collaborated in its applications.

Noël Aucagne
Honorary Controleur d'Etat, France. Former vice-president of the Special Committee on Informatics, Industries and Markets, Former member of the PPSC-IT of the European Committee(DG XIII).

Isabelle de Lamberterie
Director of research at the Institute for Comparative Research on Institutions and Law (National Center for Scientific Research, CNRS), associated with the Special Committee on Informatics, Industries and Markets.

Dominiques Quelenec
Engineer, Graduated in Medical Science, Projectmanager at Framentec Industries.

Michel Rocfort
Head of the Department of Economical Studies, Information and Training of the Special Committee for Informatics, Industries and Markets.

Anne Höhmann
is a lawyer currently working as a researcher with the Research Group on Automation in Public Administration (Forschungsgruppe Verwaltungsautomation) at the University of Kassel. Since 1975, this group has been working at the University of Kassel in the field of implementation conditions and effects of information technology in public administration especially where changes within the internal structure, external relationships, work compliance, and qualifications are concerned.

Jean Luc Minel
is an engineer at the intitute for Text Research of the National Center of Scientific Research, and Technical Consultant at the French National Administration College(E.N.A.) Since several years he participates in the conception and development of Expert Systems in several domains (control of administrative dossiers, management, analysis of historical documents) as well as in projects which are aimed at the integration of expert systems in conventional information systems.

Pierre Levine
holds a doctorate degree and is responsible for informatics at the French Administration College (E.N.A.). He is director of a research team on Expert Systems in Public Administration which was involved in the development of about 10 Expert Systems within the domain of financial analysis, project evaluation, industrial politics and the control of administrative dossiers.

Marcel Aucoin

Graduate in Law and Economics. He studied Mathemetical Economics at the Centre d'Etudes des Programmes Economiques in Paris. He has initiated the program COSIE in 1983, when he was Inspector of the Banque de France and Deputy Director of the Training Institute. Now, he is Director of Organisation of the Banque de France.

Duc Pham-Hi

holds a Doctorate degree with a thesis on the resolution of an integral Hamilton-Belman equation using Operations Research Methods, from the Ecole Centrale engineers schools where he now teaches Decision Aid Systems. He also majored in Finance an Fiscality from the Institute of Political Sciences in Paris where he currently lectures in Economy. He is manager of the Artificial Intelligence group of research engineers at the Banque de France

Kurt Vittrup

is head of the department of research and developement in the danish Directorate of Cistoms and Exice, where he among other things is in charge of the developement of the ESKORT-system. Before this he was working with strategic planning, long term budgetting and overall projectmanagement.

He has a Bachelor of Commerce degree in auditing from the Copenhagen School of Economics and Business Administration and a degree in accounting. Furthermore he has a broad theroretical and practical education in management and informatics.

Jan Chr. van Dalen

is a professor of Management Studies with the Dutch Open University. The speciality of his chair is Strategic Management and Innovation. He studied Econometrics (University of Amsterdam) and Mechanical Engineering. His career includes assistant and associate professorships, as well as management functions in local government. He published several articles and books on Public Management, Decision making, Organization Diagnosis and the Influence of New Technologies on Management. He participated in research in Goverment, Educational Institutions, Hospitals and Industry on Organizational and Managerial problems.

Bas K. Brussaard

is part-time Professor of Information Systems Management at the Delft University of Technology (Department of Technical Mathematics and Informatics), head of the Information Systems Policy Department at the Netherlands Ministry of Home Affairs and secretary of the Dutch Advisory Committee on Government Information Systems. He has previously worked in computing with Royal Dutch Shell in a number of countries and was managing director of the Municipal Data Processing Centre in Rotterdam. He holds bachelor's degrees in electrical and industrial engineering and a master's degree in business economics. His research interest is in information systems policy planning for the public and private sectors.

Jean-Paul Baquiast

Institut d'études politiques et droit (Institute of Political and Legal Studies). E.N.A. (Ecole Nationale d'Administration) (National Administration College) 1962. Administrative officer with the Ministry of Finance, then "chargé de mission" at the Information Technology delegation (1962-1972). Assistant Director for Information Technology, then Deputy Director at the Ministry of Finance (1972-1982). State Inspector 1982. Secretary-General of the CIIBA (Comité Interministériel pour l'Informatique et la Bureautique dans l'Administration) (Interministerial Committee for Information and Office Technology in Public Administration) since 1984.The CIIBA committee is under the authority of the General Secretariat of the Government (Prime Minister). He is co-chairman (with Ignace Snellen) of the permanent study group on Informatisation in Public Administration, European Group for Public Administration

Anne Bedel

Institut Universitaire de Technologie département Gestion des Entreprises, Paris 1970-1972. Institut Régional d'Administration,Lille 1974-1976. Institut d'Etudes Scientifiques des Techniques d'Organisation, Paris 1981-1982. Conseil en bureaucratique au ministère de l'agriculture, 1982-1986. Chargée de Mission au CIIBA(Comité Interministériel de l'Informatique et la Bureautique dans l'Administration) since 1987. The CIIBA committee is under the authority of the General Secretariat of the Government (Prime Minister)

Stefan Kuhlmann

is a social science researcher at the Fraunhofer-Institute for Systems and Innovation Research (FhG-ISI), Karlsruhe, FRG. He is currently investigating national and international technology and innovation policies. Previously he was for a number of years a research fellow at the "Research Group on Automation in Public Administration" at the Gesamthochschule Kassel-University, FRG.

Name index

Subject index